HISTORY

OF

TENNESSEE

FROM THE EARLIEST TIME TO THE PRESENT; TOGETHER WITH AN H[illegible]ORICAL AND A BIOGRAPHICAL SKETCH OF THE COUNTIES OF SUMNER, SMITH, MACON AND TROUSDALE, BESIDES A VALUABLE FUND OF NOTES, ORIGINAL OBSERVATIONS, REMINISCENCES, ETC., ETC.

ILLUSTRATED.

NASHVILLE:
THE GOODSPEED PUBLISHING CO.,
1887.

This volume was reproduced from
an 1887 edition located in the
Memphis Public Library,
Memphis, Tennessee

Please Direct all Correspondence & Orders to:

Southern Historical Press, Inc.
P.O. Box 1267
Greenville, S.C. 29602-1267

Originally published: Nashville, 1882
Reprinted with new material by,
Southern Historical Press, Inc.
Greenville, S.C., 1979, 1995

ISBN # 0-89308-115-9
Printed in the United States of America

PREFACE.

THIS volume has been prepared in response to the prevailing and popular demand for the preservation of local history and biography. The method of preparation followed is the most successful and the most satisfactory yet devised—the most successful in the enormous number of volumes circulated, and the most satisfactory in the general preservation of personal biography and family record conjointly with local history. The number of volumes now being distributed appears fabulous. Within the last four years not less than 20,000 volumes of this class of works have been distributed in Kentucky, and the demand is not half satisfied. Careful estimates place the number circulated in Ohio at 50,000; Pennsylvania, 60,000; New York, 75,000; Indiana, 35,-000; Illinois, 40,000; Iowa, 35,000, and every other Northern State at the same proportionate rate. The Southern States, with the exception of Kentucky, Virginia and Georgia, owing mainly to the disorganization succeeding the civil war, yet retain, ready for the publisher, their stories of history and biography. Within the next five years the vast and valuable fund of perishing event in all the Southern States will be rescued from decay, and be recorded and preserved—to be reviewed, studied and compared by future generations. The design of the present extensive historical and biographical research is more to gather and preserve in attractive form while fresh with the evidences of truth, the enormous fund of perishing occurrence, than to abstract from insufficient contemporaneous data remote, doubtful or incorrect conclusions. The true perspective of the landscape of life can only be seen from the distance that lends enchantment to the view. It is asserted that no person is competent to write a philosophical history of his own time—that, owing to conflicting circumstantial evidence that yet conceals the truth, he can not take that luminous, correct, comprehensive, logical and unprejudiced view of passing events that will enable him to draw accurate and enduring conclusions. The duty, then, of a historian of his own time is to collect, classify and preserve the material for the final historian of the future. The present historian deals in fact, the future historian, in conclusion; the work of the former is statistical, of the latter, philosophical.

To him who has not attempted the collection of historical data, the obstacles to be surmounted are unknown. Doubtful traditions, conflicting statements, imperfect records, inaccurate private correspondence, the bias or untruthfulness of informers, and the general obscurity which envelops all events combine to bewilder and mislead. On the contrary, the preparation of statistical history by experienced, unprejudiced and competent workers in specialties; the accomplishment by a union of labor of a vast result that would cost one person the best years of his life and transfer the collection of perishing event beyond the hope of research; the judicious selection of important matter from the general rubbish; and the careful and intelligent revision of all final manuscript by an editor-in-chief, yield a degree of celerity, system, accuracy, comprehensiveness and value unattainable by any other method. The publishers of this volume, fully aware of their inability to furnish a perfect history, an accomplishment vouchsafed only to the dreamer or the theorist, make no pretension of having prepared a work devoid of blemish. They feel assured that all thoughtful people, at present and in future, will recognize and appreciate the importance of their undertaking and the great public benefit that has been accomplished.

In the preparation of this volume the publishers have met with nothing but courtesy and assistance. They acknowledge their indebtedness for valuable favors to the Governor, the State Librarian, the Secretary of the State Historical Society and to more than a hundred of other prominent citizens of Nashville, Memphis, Knoxville, Chattanooga, Jackson, Clarksville and the smaller cities of the State. It is the design of the publishers to compile and issue, in connection with the State history, a brief yet comprehensive historical account of every county in the State, copies of which will be placed in the State Library. In the prosecution of this work they hope to meet with the same cordial assistance extended to them during the compilation of this volume.

THE PUBLISHERS.

NASHVILLE, May, 1887.

CONTENTS.

SUMNER COUNTY.

SMITH COUNTY.

MACON COUNTY.

TROUSDALE COUNTY.

BIOGRAPHICAL APPENDIX.

SUMNER COUNTY.

THE county of Sumner, named in honor of Col. Jethro Sumner, is bounded on the north by the State of Kentucky, east by Macon and Trousdale Counties, south by the Cumberland River, which separates it from Wilson County; southwest by Mansker Creek, separating it from Davidson County, and west by Robertson County. It has an area of about 500 square miles, one-half of which lies on the Highland Rim, and the other in the Central Basin, and the whole is divided into sixteen civil districts. The dividing ridge at the summit of the escarpment of the Highland Rim, runs nearly east and west through the county and has an elevation of 800 to 900 feet above the level of the sea. South of this ridge the lands are drained by Bledsoe Creek, Station Camp Creek, Drake Creek, and other smaller streams, which flow into the Cumberland River. And north of the ridge the waters flow into Red River which empties into the Cumberland at Clarksville, and through the North Drake Creek, Little Trammell and other creeks, into Barren River in Kentucky. The valleys of these creeks are all separated by ridges extending both ways from the dividing ridge of the Highland Rim. The soil of the southern portion of the county and of all the valleys is exceedingly fertile, while that of the highlands is less productive. The timber on the dividing ridge is principally chestnut and oak, and the other portions of the county grow all varieties of timber common in Middle Tennessee. Through injudicious farming—shallow plowing and constant cropping—some lands have been exhausted and abandoned to grow up with briars, broom sedge, and other rubbish. However, there are many good farmers in the county, and to the skillful husbandman the soil yields a bountiful harvest.

The first permanent settlement in the territory now composing the county, was made in 1779 at Bledsoe Lick, now Castalian Springs, where a few families settled that year. Prior to that time the territory had only been visited by hunters and explorers. The county was then a vast wilderness inhabited only by Indians, and the wild animals, such as buffaloes, bears, panthers, wild cats, deer, etc. Thomas Spencer, a brave and courageous hunter and explorer, who lived in his hollow sycamore tree at Bledsoe Lick in 1779 and prior thereto, seems to have the honor of being the first permanent settler in the county. In the year 1786, Isaac Bledsoe, Robert Desha, John Sawyer, Henry Loving, Wm. Morrison, Jordan Gibson, Jacob Zeigler, Robt. Steele and John Morgan, each entered 640 acres of land. In 1787 Col. Anthony Bledsoe located 6,280 acres, granted to him for his services in the Continental Line of soldiers, and his brother Isaac located 370 acres granted to him for his services as a guard to the commissioners who set apart the lands granted to the aforesaid soldiers; and the same year Henry Ramsey located 960 acres granted to him for the same kind of service. During the next two years Isaac Bledsoe entered 1,836 acres, and all of these lands, thus entered or located, were on Bledsoe Creek and its tributaries; and all of these persons together with William Hall and his son William, the subsequent general and governor of the State, Jesse Bledsoe, Hugh Rogan, George and James Winchester, David Shelby, Robert Peyton, grandfather of Hon. Bailie Peyton, Michael Shafer, Joseph Wilson, George D. Blackmore, Chas. Morgan, James Hays, Robert Brigham, Gabriel Black, Capt. John Carr and other noted men settled in the vicinity of Bledsoe Creek from 1779 to 1786. Also in the year 1786, Edward Douglass, Elmore Douglass, George Mansker, Robert Looney, David Looney, Benj. Kuykendall, Thomas Spencer, John Peyton, Charles Campbell, James McCain, James Franklin, Richard Hogan, John Withers, Benj. Porter, Wm. Crawford, John Hamilton, John Latham and William Snoddy each entered 640 acres of land on Station Camp Creek and its different branches. All of these persons were pioneer settlers. James McCann and James Cartwright settled near the site of Gallatin in 1780, and Joseph and John Burns in 1784. James Trousdale, original owner of the site of Gallatin, John Edwards, Samuel Wilson, Benj. Williams and John Hall were also early settlers in the vicinity of Gallatin. In 1786 William Montgomery, Edward Hogan and Thomas Spencer each entered 640 acres of land on Drake Creek, and the following year Daniel Smith, surveyor of the lands granted to the soldiers of the Continental Line, located 3,780 acres, and William Frazer, guard to the surveying party, located 320 acres, all on the same creek. Benjamin Sheppard entered, by location of land warrants, 10,880 acres in the county north of the ridge, and Redmond D. Barry, father of Judge Thomas Barry, who came to the county in the year 1800, entered, by location of land warrants, thirty-five 640-acre tracts, and four 1,000-acre tracts, in all 26,400 acres, nearly all of which lay within the present limits of Sumner County, and mostly in the northern part thereof. Among the early settlers of that section of the county was Col. Ned Gwin, one of the surviving colonels of the war of the Revolution.

The early settlers were obliged to erect forts or stations to which they could flee for protection when attacked by the Indians. The most noted of these were Bledsoe's Station, at Bledsoe Lick; Mansker's Station, near Mansker Creek; Greenfield Station, about two miles north of Bledsoe Lick; Zeigler's Station, on Zeigler Creek, about five miles southeast of Gallatin, and near Cairo, and White's and Lander's Stations on Desha Creek, and Hamilton's Station on the head waters of Drake Creek. There were other forts erected at various places in the county. These forts consisted mostly of stockades, made of timbers set upright, with port holes between them. They were "bullet proof," and afforded excellent protection from the attacks of the Indians. Around these forts the pioneers settled in groups, and when passing from one settlement to another they generally went as fast as their horses could carry them. But with all their precautions many a brave pioneer lost his life at the hands of the treacherous Indians, who were lying in ambush awaiting their victims. Gen. William Hall and Capt. John Carr, two of the most courageous defenders of the early settlers of Sumner County, have left narratives of their adventures, from which the writer obtains and relates much valuable information pertaining to the struggles of the early settlers with the Indians. The savages commenced their attacks in 1787, and on the 3d of June of that year they killed James Hall, brother of Gen. Hall, at his father's place, near Bledsoe Lick, he being the first white person killed in that locality. In August following they murdered the father of Gen. Hall and another brother, and a Mr. Hickerson near the same place. And in the spring of 1788 they killed John, Robert and Thomas, three boys and sons of Mr. Montgomery on Drake Creek, while they were a short distance from the house, cutting cane-brake. And on the 20th of July following, they made an attack on Bledsoe's Fort with a large force, and though not being able to capture it, succeeded in killing Col. Anthony Bledsoe and his servant, Campbell. And later they killed Col. Bledsoe's son Thomas, and on another occasion they killed two cousins named Anthony, sons of the brothers, Anthony and Isaac Bledsoe, while they (the cousins) were on their way to school. In the winter of 1788 they killed Charles Morgan and Jordan Gibson while on their way to Mrs. Hall's house, and about the same time they killed Mr. Morgan's father at Morgan's Fort. In the summer of 1790, Alexander Neely and his sons, James and Charles, were killed about one mile from Bledsoe's Fort, and the sons of Robert Desha, Benjamin and Robert, Jr., were killed on Desha Creek, about two and a half miles from Bledsoe Lick; and near that time Henry Howdyshall and Samuel Farr were killed near Cumberland River below Cairo; and the same summer or the one following, Henry and William Ramsey were killed in the vicinity of Bledsoe Lick. In 1791 two sons of Col. Sanders were killed at Sander's Station, and two men were killed on Bledsoe Creek, near the house of Gen. Winchester. In June, 1792, they killed Michael Shafer near Zeigler's Station, and the same night attacked and captured the fort, killing Mr. Zeigler, the owner of it, and a young man by the name of Archie Wilson. They wounded Joseph Wilson, who with his son, twelve years old, were all that escaped of his family, his wife and six children being taken and led into captivity. Mrs. Zeigler filled her child's mouth with a handkerchief to prevent its crying, and with it made her escape, while two of her children were captured, the fate of which the narrator, Capt. Carr, failed to give. Mrs. Wilson and her children were finally all returned to her friends. In May of the same year John Purviance was killed on the old Dr. Donnell farm, two miles northeast of the site of Gallatin. In 1793 Maj. George Winchester was killed near the site of Gallatin, and Col. Isaac Bledsoe was killed at Bledsoe Lick, while on the way to his field. And near this date James Steele and his beautiful daughter, Betsey, about seventeen years of age, were killed on their way from Greenfield to Morgan's Station. Soon after this Abraham, a former servant of Col. Anthony Bledsoe, met two Indian chiefs, "Mad Dog" and "John Taylor," a half breed, between Bledsoe's and Greenfield Stations, and shot and killed the former and then made his escape. On one occasion when Thomas Spencer, Robert Jones and Mrs. Parker were riding on horseback, about two miles from Gallatin, they were attacked by the Indians and Jones was killed, and the life of Mrs. Parker was saved by the heroic efforts of the gallant Spencer, who fought the Indians until the lady had safely escaped, and then made safe his own escape. A family by the name of Price was murdered on Station Camp Creek, near the site of Gallatin, and also a young man by the name of John Beard, near the head of that creek. Robert Brigham, Benjamin Kuykendall, James Dickson and a Mr. Bratton were also killed near White's Station on Desha Creek. In 1790 Benjamin Williams settled about two and a half miles from the site of Gallatin, and soon thereafter the Indians killed the whole family, except one boy who ran up the chimney and kept concealed. About the same time John Edwards was killed at the site of the Salem Meeting House, four miles northwest of Gallatin. And later, about 1795, Robert Peyton, grandfather of Hon. Bailie Peyton, was killed at Bledsoe Lick, he being the last man killed in the county by the Indians. This Indian warfare on the early settlers continued from 1787 to 1795, during which time many other persons were killed, whose names have not been preserved to posterity. And many of the savage wretches also were killed by the brave men, who under so many difficulties, founded homes for their posterity in this, then dangerous but now beautiful, country.

In addition to the hardships endured by the early settlers on account of the Indians, they were compelled to suffer many privations while subduing the forest and striving to make comfortable their new homes. Their grain was first reduced to flour or meal by the use of the mortar, and next by small horse mills. The first permanent water mill was erected by George Winchester on Bledsoe Creek, at the crossing of the Nashville and Carthage Turnpike. This was afterward known as Stump's mill. Soon after the year 1800 Hon. Redmond D. Barry erected a mill on Station Camp Creek, about three miles southwest of Gallatin. And another was erected on Drake Creek, near the present site of Hendersonville. Since then grist and saw-mills have been erected as the county developed until it is now well supplied. The raising of cotton and tobacco was introduced in an early day, and for a long period, including the decade of the "twenties," cotton was the staple crop, and since its introduction tobacco has always been the staple crop on the highlands in the northern part of the county, where the soil is especially adapted to the production of that article. The raising of cotton has long since been discontinued except by a very few farmers. In the year 1800 Hon. Redmond D. Barry first introduced the celebrated "Kentucky blue-grass" by sowing some on his farm on the Nashville Turnpike, two miles from Gallatin, it being the farm now owned by James Alexander. Here Mr. Barry erected a fine residence, which is said to be the first brick dwelling-house erected in the county. But little blue-grass was cultivated until 1836, when Gen. Joseph Miller and Maj. Woods Miller settled near Gallatin and introduced it into general cultivation. At the same time they introduced to the farmers the raising of fine breeds of cattle and hogs, for which the county has ever since been noted. Gen. Andrew Jackson, Hon. Redmond D. Barry and Hon. Bailie Peyton were the first men in Middle Tennessee to keep and raise fine blooded horses, and the first horse of that description in this part of the State was "Grey Metley," brought here from North Carolina in the year 1800 by Mr. Barry. Sumner County is noted for its fine stock in general, the raising of which is perhaps the leading industry of its farmers, who vie each with the other to raise the best. The live stock and its productions according to the census of 1880 are as follows: Horses, 6,500; mules and asses, 3,107; cattle, 13,423; sheep, 16,729; hogs, 31,187; wool, 65,504 pounds; butter, 322,222 pounds. In the quality of stock raised Sumner County ranks second to none in the State. According to the same census the principal vegetable productions of the county are as follows: Indian corn, 917,940 bushels; oats, 95,081 bushels; rye, 3,708 bushels; wheat, 140,895 bushels; hay, 5,045 tons; Irish potatoes, 21,094 bushels; sweet potatoes, 29,055 bushels; tobacco, 280,326 pounds.

The county of Sumner was created by an act of the General Assembly of the State of North Carolina, passed in 1786. The act provided that from and after its passage the county of Davidson should be divided by a line "beginning where the county line crosses the West Fork of Stone River; thence down the same to the junction with the main Stone River; thence in a direct line to the mouth of Drake Lick Creek; thence down Cumberland River to the mouth of Caspers Creek; thence up the said creek to the head of the War Trace Fork; thence a northwesterly course to the Virginia line, at a point that will leave Red River Old Station one mile to the east; and all that part of Davidson County that lies to the west of said line, shall continue and remain the county of Davidson, and all east of said line shall thenceforth be erected into a new county by the name of Sumner." Prior to the passage of this act the county of Davidson extended eastward to the Cumberland Mountains; hence the county of Sumner was created to embrace all the territory lying between the line above described and the Cumberland Mountains, and south of the Kentucky line, then known as the Virginia line. The act also provided that the court for the said county of Sumner should be held by the justices thereof on the second Mondays of January, April, July and October of each year, and that the first court should be held at the house of John Hamilton, and subsequent terms at such places as said justices should from time to time adjourn, until a courthouse should be erected. In accordance with the foregoing the following justices of the peace—viz.: Daniel Smith, Isaac Bledsoe, Isaac Lindsey, David Wilson, John Hardin, Joseph Kuykendall, William Hall and George Winchester, holding commissions as such from the governor of North Carolina—met on the second Monday of April, 1787, at the house of John Hamilton, and organized the court of pleas and quarter sessions, it being the first court ever held in Sumner County. David Shelby was then appointed clerk of said court, and John Hardin was appointed sheriff, and Isaac Lindsey, ranger. The court, after being thus organized, ordered "that Richard Searcey, a minor orphan, be bound to James McKain until he arrives at the age of twenty-one years, and that John and Reuben Searcey, orphans, be bound unto Thomas Masten until they arrive at the age of twenty-one years; and that William Price, a minor orphan, be bound to John Hardin until he arrives at the age of twenty-one years." Letters of administration were then ordered to be issued to John Hardin on the estate of Wm. Price, Sr., deceased. On the following day Simon Kuykendall, Ephraim Peyton, John Norris, John Hardin, Edward Hogan, Elmore Douglass, George Mansker, John Brigance, Thomas Masten, John Hamilton and others came into court and had their stock marks, consisting of peculiar "crops" and "slits" of the ears of their domestic animals, recorded. The following constables were then appointed, viz.: Philip Trammell, Thomas Peal, Joshua Campbell, David Brigance and Obadiah Tonnell. George Mansker, James Wilson, Wm. Montgomery and Simon Kuykendall were appointed overseers of certain proposed highways. This ended the business of the first term of the court, the record of which was signed by Isaac Bledsoe as chairman.

At the following July term Capt. Charles Morgan was appointed "to take a list of the inhabitants in Capt. James Lynn's company, James Douglass for Capt. Elmore Douglass' company, and Ezekiel Norris for Capt. Kuykendall's company." The following militia officers then produced their commissions and took the oath prescribed by law, for the faithful performance of their duties: Anthony Bledsoe, lieutenant-colonel commandant; Isaac Bledsoe, first major; Rasper Mansker, second major; James Lynn, Elmore Douglass and Joseph Kuykendall, captains; Abner Bush, George Mansker and James Frazer, lieutenants; John Hickerson, Joseph McElwrath and Zachariah Green, ensigns. Col. Smith was then appointed "to list the taxable property in Capt. Simon Kuykendall's district, Joseph Kuykendall in his own district, Capt. Hardin in Capt. Douglass' district, and George Winchester in Capt. Lynn's district." The Indians being then very hostile, the militia companies were ordered to clear and make certain roads in the county.

At the following October term of said court, the will of Abner Bush, deceased, was probated. By the will Elender Bush, relict of the deceased, was appointed executrix, and John Hamilton became her surety in the sum of £200 of English money. This was the first will probated in Sumner County and Mrs. Bush was the first executrix. The court then levied taxes for the year 1787 as follows: "One shilling on every poll and four pence on every 100 acres of land, to defray the contingent charges of the county; also one shilling on every poll and four pence on every 100 acres of land for the purpose of building the court-house, prison and stocks; and that corn be received in taxes at 2s. 6p. per bushel, beef at 3 pence per pound, pork 4 pence per pound, 4 pence per pound for good fat bear meat, if delivered at the place where the troops are stationed; 3 pence per pound for prime buffalo beef; 1 pence per pound for good venison, if delivered as aforesaid; 9 pence per pound for bacon; 6 pence per pound for dried beef; 2s. 4p. per pound for salt; each person to pay in proportion, as follows, to-wit: One-fourth in corn, one-half in meat, one-eighth in salt and the eighth part in money." Captains of companies were appointed to recover these specific taxes, and

Thomas Maston to superintend the removal of the same from the different places at which they were collected to the places where the troops were stationed. In the records of the proceedings of said court at the October term, 1788, the following entry appears: "The court regulates and rates taverns and ordinaries in the following manner, to-wit: One-half pint of whiskey, such as will sink tallow, 2 shillings; ditto of taffia, 2 shillings; ditto West India rum, 2s. 6 pence; ditto, Jamaica spirits, 3 shillings; one bowl of toddy made of loaf sugar and whisky, per quart, 3s. 6 pence; ditto of taffia, 3s. 6 pence; ditto West India rum, 3s. 6 pence; ditto Jamaica spirits, 4s.; dinner and grog at dinner, 4s.; dinner and toddy, 4s. 6 pence; dinner, 3s.; breakfast, 2s.; supper, 2s.; one horse-feed of corn, 3 pence; lodging, 6 pence; pasture for horse twenty-four hours, 9 pence; stablage with hay and fodder, 2s.; horse-feed of oats per quart, 3 pence; one-half pint of brandy, 2s.; one quart bowl of punch made with fruit, 10s.; one bottle of wine called port, 10s.; ditto Madaria, 15s.; ditto Burgundy, 15s.; ditto champaign, 20s.; ditto claret, 8s.; ditto any other species, 5s."

Prior to July 1796, the court of pleas and quarter sessions was held at the following places, to-wit: John Hamilton's from April, 1787, to the close of that year; Elmore Douglass, 1788; Simon Kuykendall's first half of 1789; then at Elmore Douglass' until July, 1790, when it was held in the first courthouse which was a small log building erected on West Station Camp Creek at the place formerly known as Mrs. Clark's. The sessions were held at this courthouse until January, 1793, when the court met at the plantation of John Dawson. The April term 1793 was held at the house of Pearce Wall, and from July, 1793, to January, 1796, the sessions were held at the house of Ezekiel Douglass. And from that date to January, 1800, the sessions were held at the house of William Gillespie, and from April, 1800, to July, 1802, at the town of Cairo, and from October, 1802, to January, 1803, at the house of James Trousdale in Gallatin, and then at the house of James Cryer in Gallatin until October, 1803, when the first term of the court was held in the first courthouse at the permanent seat of justice. The first term of this court held under the organization of the State of Tennessee, was in July, 1796, when it was composed of the following justices commissioned by John Sevier, the first governor of the State, viz.: David Wilson, Thomas Donald, James Winchester, James Pearce, Edward Douglass, Wm. Cage, Stephen Cantrell, Isaac Walton, Thomas Masten, James Gwynn, Witheral Latimer and James Douglass. The first grand jury under the State organization was composed of the following named gentlemen: Archibald

Martin, foreman; Edward Williams, James Farr, Joshua Wilson, Robert Hamilton, Lazarus Cullum, James Snowden, Wm. Crabtree, Thomas Walten, Jeremiah Doney, Peter Looney, Ormund Alton and Wm. Edwards. By an act of the General Assembly of the State of Tennessee, passed October 26, 1799, Sumner County was reduced to its constitutional limit, 625 square miles. And by subsequent acts creating new counties, it has since been reduced to its present limits. The General Assembly of the State, by an act passed November 6, 1801, appointed Samuel Donelson, Shadrick Nye, James Wilson, Charles Donoho and Maj. Thomas Murray commissioners to purchase forty acres of land and lay out a town for the seat of justice to be called Gallatin, to superintend the sale of lots, the erection of public buildings, etc. The act also provided that all general elections and musters should be held at the house of Capt. James Trousdale until the courthouse should be erected and accepted, then at said courthouse. Accordingly the aforesaid commissioners on the 25th of February, 1802, purchased of James Trousdale, for $490, the original site of the town of Gallatin containing forty-two and a half acres including one acre reserved by the grantor, and one and a half acres in the public square. The town was surveyed and platted, and the sale of lots made in the spring of 1802. Andrew Jackson, John C. Hamilton, James Cage, Wm. Montgomery, David Shelby, Robert Trousdale, Wm. Sample, Peter Looney, John Brigance and G. D. Blackmore were among the purchasers of lots.

The first courthouse in Gallatin was finished to the acceptance of the commissioners in 1803. The court-room occupied the whole of the first story, and the county offices the second. This building stood until about 1837, when it was taken down and the present one erected in its stead. The latter, which is a commodious two-story brick structure, was repaired and remodeled in 1867. It contains the county court-room and four offices on the first floor, and the circuit and chancery court-room and two offices on the second floor. The first jail, built about the same time the first courthouse was erected, stood about 100 yards north of the female academy, and between Main and Franklin Streets. It had dungeons underneath where some prisoners were incarcerated in total darkness. In an early day Mr. John Tomkins was the keeper of this jail. It stood until some time in the forties, when it was abandoned, and a second one was built near where the present workhouse stands. This latter jail was abandoned in 1867, when the present one was built near the public square. All the public buildings in Gallatin thus far described were made of brick.

In an early day the county purchased a farm north of the ridge and west of the tunnel on the Louisville & Nashville Railroad, for the support of the poor. Being of little value and not sufficient for its intended purpose, it was discontinued as a home for the poor in 1867, when the present poorhouse farm was purchased. The latter is situated on the Red River Turnpike, about eight miles northwest of Gallatin. This is an excellent farm, with ample buildings for the accommodation of the unfortunate inmates, and all is under first-class management. A number of poor persons outside of the asylum are provided for by appropriations made by the county court.

The aggregate of taxes charged in Sumner County for the following years was: 1820, $4,032.70; 1830, no record; 1840, $9,394.48; 1850, $9,478.70; 1860, $9,429.88; 1870, $26,190.90; 1880, $36,055.55; 1886, $59,511.64. Population in 1860, white, 14,227; colored, 7,803; total, 22,030. Population in 1880, white, 16,294; colored, 7,331; total, 23,625. The population of 1860 included the territory which has since been cut off to compose part of Trousdale County. These figures are here given to enable the intelligent reader to make comparisons and draw conclusions therefrom.

The Louisville & Nashville Railroad was completed through the county in 1858, and it has stations within the county at Mitchellville, Richland, Fountain Head, Buck Lodge, Gallatin, Pilot Knob, Saundersville and Hendersonville. For the construction of this road, the county subscribed $300,000, and sold bonds to raise the money. These bonds have all been redeemed and canceled, the profits received by the county from the investment being nearly equal to the amount invested. In 1867 the county sold bonds to the amount of $30,000, to raise money with which to build the new jail, to purchase and improve the poorhouse farm, and remodel and repair the courthouse. These bonds have all been redeemed. In 1873 the county subscribed $300,000 for the construction of the Cumberland & Ohio Railroad, and issued bonds to run twenty years, with 6 per cent interest payable semi-annually, to raise the amount. To provide for the redemption of said bonds, an annual tax of 40 cents on each $100 of taxable property, also a sinking fund tax, and a tax on privileges equal to one-half of the State tax on same, has since been levied. These bonds to the amount of $25,000 have since been taken up and canceled. The county sold its interest in the Cumberland & Ohio Railroad to the Chesapeake & Nashville Railroad Company, for $75,000 in stock. Consequently it owes $275,000 on the bonds and has $75,000 in stock as assets. The floating debt of the county is merely nominal. The Chesapeake & Nashville Railroad was completed from Gallatin to the Kentucky State line in December, 1886. It has stations in Sumner

County at Gallatin, Cairo, Trousdale, Elmwood, Cumberland, Rogana, Bethpage, Bransford and Westmoreland.* The Middle & East Tennessee Central Railroad is now under construction from its intersection with the Chesapeake & Nashville Railroad at Bledsoe Creek via the east fork of said creek to Hartsville.

The following is a list of county and other officers with dates of service. County court clerks: David Shelby, 1787–1822; A. H. Douglass, 1822–35; Wm. Cothran, 1835–36; Thomas Donoho, 1836–40; A. McGlothlin, 1840–42; Wm. S. Munday, 1842–50; John L. Bugg, 1850–68: Lee H. Alley, 1868–70; Jesse Cage, 1870–78; O. H. Foster, 1878–86; Harris Brown, 1886. Registers: Capt. George Winchester, 1787–94; David Wilson, 1794–1804; James Douglass, 1804–36; John L. Bugg, 1836–46; John Bruce, 1846–54; R. D. Moore, 1854–66; Robt. Hallum, 1866–81; T. C. Mulligan, 1881–82; J. F. Gray, 1882–86 and re-elected. Sheriffs: John Hardin, 1787, a few months only; Thomas Masten, 1787–88; James Douglass, 1788–89; Edward Douglass, 1789–90; Wm. Cage, 1790–96; Reuben Cage, 1796–1800; James Cage, 1800–02; Edmund Crutcher, 1802–04; Thomas Masten, 1804–08; Wm. Hall, 1808–14; John W. Byrn, 1814–18; * * * Moses H. Henry, 1836–40; Wm. Rice, 1840–42; * * D. P. Hart, 1846–52; John A. Littleton, 1852–56; George Love, 1856–62; R. T. Warner, 1865–66; Wm. A. Lovall, 1866–68; Joseph B. Hobdy, 1868–72; W. H. Joyner, 1872–74; J. K. Dodd, 1874–80; John M. Cantrell, 1880–86; J. H. Terry, 1886. Circuit court clerks: * * * J. W. Baldridge, 1836–39; Geo. F. Crocket, 1839–48; Pascal Head, 1848–56; Dr. P. Hart, 1856–60; Jesse F. Joyner, 1865–70; T. E. S. Russwurm, 1870–72; L. W. Barry, 1872–74; Thomas H. King, 1874–86; Wm. Hall, 1886. Clerks and masters of chancery court: J. W. Baldridge, 1830–36; W. M. Blackmore, 1836–53; N. D. Smith, 1853–55; W. M. Blackmore, 1855–61; G. B. Guild, 1861–62; C. W. Parker, 1865–66; J. R. Barry, 1866–82; J. Y. Robb, 1882, present incumbent. Trustees: A full list cannot be obtained from the records. James Winchester, James Reese and Zaccheus Wilson were first trustees in the order named. J. H. McLaren is the present incumbent. State senators: James Winchester, 1796, first speaker of the Senate. * * * Edward Douglass, 1805 and 1807; John Dow, 1809; John K. Wynne, 1811; * * Wm. Montgomery, 1817; Edward Douglass, 1819; Gen. Wm. Hall, 1822–26; David Burford, 1829 and 1833; Wm. Trousdale, 1835; Josephus C. Guild, 1837; Timothy Walton, 1839; Joseph H. Peyton, 1841; Wm. Cullum, 1843 and 1845; James L. McKoin, 1847; * * Wm. McClain,

*Names given by the civil engineer.

1851; J. G. Frazer, 1853; W. S. Munday, 1857; James L. Thompson, 1859; John W. Bowen, 1865; H. S. Patterson, 1867; Bailie Peyton, 1869; J. Howard Young, 1871; N. W. McConnell, 1873; Thomas H. Butler, 1875; J. A. Trousdale, 1877; S. F. Wilson, 1879; George H. Morgan, 1881; J. W. Blackmore, 1883–85; Lewis I. Cobb, senator elect for 1887. Representatives: William Montgomery, 1796; * * * John K. Wynne, William Moore and Elijah Chisholm, 1803 and 1805; * * John Hawkins, 1809; William Montgomery and Peter Looney, 1811 and 1813; James Cryer, 1815; Peter Looney, 1817; J. H. Conn, 1819; Charles Watkins, 1821 and 1823; Robert Desha, 1825; * * Josephus C. Guild, 1833; O. F. Bledsoe and Thomas Gilmore, 1837; Thomas Barry and Z. G. Goodall, 1839; Thomas Barry and Moses Henry, 1841; J. C. Guild and M. C. Duffy, 1845; W. M. Blackmore and King Kerley, 1847; Robt. Bate and James Butler, 1849; D. S. Donaldson, 1855 and 1857; R. A. Bennett, 1859; * * * Wm. Wright, 1865; T. McKinley, 1867; J. T. Baber, 1869; J. A. Trousdale, 1871 and 1873; W. G. Pond, 1875; S. F. Wilson, 1877; J. A. Dinning, 1879; J. M. Head, 1881 and 1883; J. A. Trousdale, 1885; D. A. Montgomery, representative elect for 1887. Representatives in Congress: Andrew Jackson, 1796–97; Wm. C. C. Claiborne, 1797–1801; Wm. Dickson, 1801–03; * * * Robert Weakley, 1809–11; Felix Grundy, 1811–13; John H. Bowen, 1813–15; Bennett H. Henderson, 1815–17; Samuel Hogg, 1817–19; Robert Allen, 1819–27; Robert Desha, 1827–31; Gen. William Hall, 1831–33; Bailie Peyton, 1833–37; Wm. B. Campbell, 1837–43; Joseph H. Peyton, 1843–45; Edwin H. Ewing, 1845–47; Gen. Washington Barrow, 1847–49; Andrew Ewing, 1849–51; Wm. Cullum, 1851–55; Charles Ready, 1855–59; Robert Hatton, 1859–61; vacant from 1861–65; Wm. B. Campbell, 1865–67; John Trimble, 1867–69; Wm. F. Prosser, 1869–71; Edward I. Golladay, 1871–73; Horace H. Harrison, 1873–75; Haywood T. Riddle, 1875–79; Benton McMillen 1879–87.

The court of pleas and quarter sessions continued in existence under that name until the year 1836. It had always been presided over by one of its members chosen annually as chairman, and during the first years of its existence Isaac and Anthony Bledsoe, Daniel Smith, David Wilson, Edward Douglass and James Winchester, pioneer settlers of the county, presided as chairmen in the order here named. The first term of the county court as provided for by act of the General Assembly, under the constitution of 1834, met in May, 1836, and organized by electing Elijah Boddie as chairman. This court consisted then of thirty-eight justices of the peace, elected by the people, to all of whom the oath of office was administered by Thomas Anderson, the last chairman of the court of pleas and quarter sessions. The county court was first presided over by a chairman and subsequently by a chairman and two associate justices until 1860, when, under a new law, judges of the court were elected by the people, the first one being Judge G. W. Allen, who presided from 1860 to April, 1862, when business was suspended on account of the civil war. The court was reorganized in March, 1865, and subsequently was presided over by the following judges, to wit: S. Heerman, 1865–66; Thomas C. Douglass, 1866–67; William Dodd, 1867–69; S. Heerman, 1869–70; H. M. Austin, 1870–78. The law providing for a judge of the county court was then repealed, and since September, 1878, Hon. Lee Head has presided as chairman of said court. The circuit court of Sumner County was established in 1810, under an act of the General Assembly passed November 16, 1809, which created the Third Judicial District, to comprise the counties of Smith, Warren, Franklin, Sumner, Overton, White and Jackson. Subsequent changes of the judicial districts of the State have been made, so that Sumner County now belongs to the Tenth District, composed of Stewart, Houston, Humphreys, Dickson, Montgomery, Robertson and Sumner Counties. The minute books of this court prior to 1815 have not been preserved. The following is a list of the judges of the circuit court: Hon. Nathaniel W. Williams, 1810–13; Bennett Searcey, 1813–17; Thomas Stewart, 1817–36; William T. Brown, 1836–38; James Rucks, 1838–39; Thomas Manny, 1839–52; Nathaniel Baxter, 1852–56; William K. Turner, 1856–60; Josephus C. Guild, 1860 to October, 1861, when the business was suspended on account of the civil war; James O. Shackelford, part of 1865; Thomas Barry, 1865–68; Charles G. Smith, 1868–70; J. E. Rice, 1870–72; J. C. Guild, 1872–77; J. E. Rice, 1877–78; J. C. Stark, 1878–86; A. H. Munford, 1886, judge elect. The first term of the chancery court, established under the constitution of 1834, was held in April, 1836. The presiding chancellors have been as follows: L. M. Bramlett, 1836–44; Terry H. Cahal, 1844–45; Bloomfield L. Ridlay, 1845–60; Josephus C. Guild, 1860 to March, 1862; J. O. Shackelford, 1865–66; Thomas Barry, 1866–69; Charles G. Smith, 1869–75; Horace H. Lurton, 1875–78; B. J. Tarver, 1878—one year, and since that time George E. Seay, the present chancellor.

Among those executed for crime in the county was a colored man who was hung about the year 1810, for the crime of rape. And about the year 1819 a colored woman killed her mistress, and by sentence of court was hanged and beheaded, and her head extended on a pole at the forks of the Nashville Turnpike, one-half mile west of Gallatin. And a few years prior to the civil war a colored man killed his master, a Mr. Lewis, by mistake in an attempt to injure or kill a negro trader to whom he had just been sold. He was tried and suffered the penalty of his crime on the gallows.

The bar of Gallatin has always been distinguished for its many eminent practitioners. Among its early members was the Hon. Thomas Stewart, who began the practice in 1796, in the court of pleas and quarter sessions, and soon acquired eminence in the profession, and served with distinction as judge of the circuit court from 1817 to 1836. Along with him was the Hon. Redmond Dillon Barry, a native of Ireland, and a classmate of the British Gen. Packenham in the schools of the city of Dublin, where he (Barry) was educated as a physician and surgeon. After coming to this country and obtaining a fortune at his profession in North Carolina, he studied law under the father of John C. Breckenridge in Kentucky, and in the year 1809 came to Gallatin where he practiced law with great distinction until his death, which occurred in 1821. Of him it is said that his great hospitality and excellent manners were never excelled. He was one of the few who mastered two professions, and rose to eminence in both. No man ever stood higher in the estimation of the people of Sumner County than Judge Josephus C. Guild, who rendered "eminent services as a lawyer, a circuit judge and chancellor, a legislator, a political leader, and an officer in the army." Hon. Bailie Peyton was also a member of the Gallatin bar. (For further mention of these gentlemen see elsewhere in this work.) John C. Hamilton began his professional life at Gallatin, and practiced along with Stewart & Barry, and afterward became a prominent judge in West Tennessee. Anthony B. Shelby, John H. Bowen early representative in Congress; Gov. Wm. Trousdale, former attorney-general of this judicial district; John H. Turner, Wm. Hadley, John J. White and others were prominent among the early members of the bar. Judge Thomas Barry, son of Redmond D. Barry, began the practice in 1828, and has served with distinction as a lawyer, legislator, judge and chancellor, and still resides at Gallatin retired from the practice. Gov. Wm. B. Bate began the practice, and was for many years a member of the Gallatin bar. Prominent among its members was Judge George W. Allen, who died in May, 1881, after an active practice of forty-one years, during which time he served a full term as attorney-general; Hon. John W. Head was also a prominent member of the bar from 1843 until his death which occurred in November, 1874. He served as reporter of the supreme court, and edited *Head's Reports*. Also prominent and highly esteemed was Hon. M. S. Elkin, a member of the bar from 1866 to his death, which occurred

December 27, 1884. He was elector for the Fourth Congressional District in the presidential election of 1884. Geo. W. Winchester was for many years an able member of the bar. The present members are Maj. Wm. S. Munday, Col. J. J. Turner, Hon. B. F. Allen, Judge George E. Seay, S. F. Wilson, C. R. Head; T. C. Mulligan, who was attorney-general from 1870 to 1878; B. D. Bell, attorney-general from 1878 to 1886; M. R. Elliott, attorney-general elect in 1886; J. W. Blackmore, Lee Head, W. B. Swaney, R. G. Gillespie, S. A. Wilson, J. W. Wickware, G. W. O. Griffin and F. C. Allen. Felix Grundy, Judge John Haywood, Jenkin Whitesides and others of State and National reputation have practiced law at the Gallatin bar.

The pioneer settlers of Sumner County were among those who volunteered to make the first settlements in Middle Tennessee, then inhabited by a savage foe, the encounters with whom have already been given; and in all of the wars of the country the citizens of Sumner County have been among the first to offer their gallant services in its defense. It may, therefore, appropriately be called the Volunteer County of the "Volunteer State." In the war of 1812–15 it furnished a full company of soldiers, commanded by Capt. Hamilton, of which James Stratton was first lieutenant, and Gov. Wm. Trousdale, Dr. Elmore Douglass, LaFayette Sanders and Porterfield Graham were members. The four last named persons, at the time of their enlistment, were pupils and classmates in the male academy at Gallatin, then taught by Prof. John Hall. This company served under Gen. Jackson, and participated in the battle of New Orleans; and in 1818 the county contributed a number of soldiers to assist Jackson in the trouble with the Seminole and Creek Indians in Georgia and Florida, and in 1836 a full company and three of the principal officers of the regiment in which it served—viz.: Col. William Trousdale, Lieut.-Col. Josephus C. Guild and Maj. Joseph G. Meadow—went from Sumner County and served in the Florida war until March, 1837, when, its services being no longer needed, it returned home. In 1846, when war was declared with Mexico, the Polk Guards, commanded by Capt. Robert A. Bennett, and Lieuts. J. M. Shaver and Patrick Duffey, and the Tenth Legion, commanded by Capt. S. R. Anderson and Lieuts. Wm. M. Blackmore and P. L. Solomon, and Legion Second, commanded by Capt. Wm. S. Hatton, were volunteer companies from Sumner County, which served through that war. The first two of these commands served in the First Regiment Tennessee Volunteers, and the other in the Third Regiment, and the names of the soldiers of these commands, who lost their lives in battle and by disease during that war, are all inscribed on a large monument standing in the cemetery at Gallatin, on one face of which is the following inscription: "This monument was erected by the liberality of the citizens of the county of Sumner to the memory of her patriotic sons, who sacrificed their lives in defense of the flag of their country in the war with Mexico in 1846–1848." On the occasion of the erection of this monument, which took place soon after the close of the war, the people of Sumner County assembled at the Presbyterian Church in Gallatin, where appropriate services were held, and an oration delivered by Col. Thomas Boyers, whose biography appears elsewhere in this work.

At the first approach of the late civil war, the citizens of Sumner County were generally opposed to separation from the Federal Union, but when the time came for them to take sides either for or against the Union, they were found to be almost unanimously in sympathy with the Southern Confederacy. (See vote on the question of "separation" elsewhere in this work.) The raising of companies of soldiers for the Confederate Army commenced in April, 1861, when three companies, commanded respectively by Capts. L. Charlton, Humphrey Bate and D. L. Goodall, were raised and mustered into the Second Confederate (Tennessee) Regiment, commanded by Col. William B. Bate, who is principally entitled to the credit for raising the first company, the one commanded by Capt. Charlton. Immediately following, two companies, commanded respectively by Capts. James Baber and D. C. Douglass, were raised and mustered into the Seventh Tennessee (Confederate) Regiment. Capt. Baber died the following December at Millsboro, Va., and then First Lieutenant John D. Fry was elected captain, and O. H. Foster first lieutenant. In consequence of severe wounds received at the battle of Seven Pines, Capt. Fry was compelled to resign, and then Lieut. O. H. Foster was elected captain, and as such served till the close of the war. At the reorganization of the regiment in April, 1862, James Franklin, present proprietor of the celebrated Kenesaw stock farm near Gallatin, was elected captain in place of D. C. Douglass, and at the battle of Cedar Run, August 9, 1862, he received a wound which compelled him to retire from the service, and then Robert G. Miller became captain and served to the close of the war. Capt. W. H. Joyner raised a company from Sumner and Davidson Counties, a majority being from the latter county. Early in June, 1861, this company was mustered into the Eighteenth Tennessee (Confederate) Regiment at Camp Trousdale. In the same month, two other companies, commanded respectively by Capts. Patrick Duffey and James A. Nimmo, were raised and mustered into the Twentieth Tennessee (Confederate) Regiment at Camp Trousdale. Also in the same month, June, 1861, Capt. Alexander Baskerville's company was mustered into the Twenty-fourth Tennessee (Confederate) Regiment at Camp Anderson, near Murfreesboro, and in the summer of 1861, four other companies, commanded respectively by Capts. J. L. Carson, John H. Turner, William A. Lovell and William T. Sample, were raised and mustered into the Thirtieth Tennessee (Confederate) Regiment, and in the latter part of 1861, two companies, commanded respectively by Capts. James L. McKoin and J. H. Joyner, were mustered into the Forty-fourth Tennessee (Confederate) Regiment. Other commands, including five cavalry companies, commanded respectively by Capts. — Minnis, C. L. Bennett, M. Griffin, H. B. Boude and J. T. E. Odom, in all twenty-seven or twenty-eight companies were raised in Sumner County for the Confederate Army. Camp Trousdale, located in Sumner County, near Richland Station on the Louisville & Nashville Railroad, was established in May, 1861, and continued until the Confederate troops fell back after the battle of Fort Donelson. This camp was used for the organization and military instruction of the Confederate troops.

The town of Gallatin, established in the year 1802, as heretofore stated, is situated on a branch of Station Camp Creek, about three miles north of the Cumberland River, and on the line of the Louisville & Nashville Railroad, and in latitude 36° 16′ north, and longitude 9° 18′ west from Washington. In accordance with an act of the General Assembly of the State, passed September 11, 1806, five commissioners were elected by the people to levy taxes, make laws and govern the town, and in 1809 the original site of the town was increased by the purchase of twenty-nine acres of land adjoining it on the east. The town continued to be governed by commissioners until it was first incorporated under an act of the Legislature, passed November 7, 1815. Two years later it was re-incorporated by an act passed November 17, 1817, under the name of "Mayor and Aldermen of the town of Gallatin," and under this charter seven aldermen were elected annually by the people, and the mayor was chosen by the board of aldermen thus elected. The town was again re-incorporated by an act passed February 29, 1856, which required the people to elect both the mayor and aldermen annually; and that the board thus elected should, at its first meeting each year, elect a recorder, treasurer and high constable. This charter was amended by an act passed March 27, 1869, defining the new boundary of the corporate limits of the town. The charter was again amended by an act passed March 29, 1883, which provided that the election of mayor and aldermen should be held biennially, and that certain changes should be made in the boundary line. The early growth of Gallatin was so gradual that in the year 1830, nearly three decades after its origin, it contained, according to the "Tennessee Gazetteer," "a good courthouse, jail and public offices, a large brick church (free for all denominations of Christians), a Cumberland Presbyterian Church, a Masonic hall, a printing office, twelve stores, two taverns, eleven lawyers, four physicians, one cabinet shop, one chair factory, three tailor shops, two shoemaker shops, two saddler shops, one wagon-maker, one tanyard, one tinner and coppersmith, three blacksmith shops, one hatter, one male and two female academies, 666 inhabitants, of which 234 were blacks; thirty-five log, thirty-eight frame and twenty-seven brick houses." The mail stages between Lexington, Ky., and Nashville, Tenn., then passed and repassed Gallatin three times a week, and the eastern stage to Carthage arrived and departed semi-weekly. The steamboat landing was then at the mouth of Elliott Branch, Boyers' Warehouse, on the Cumberland River. The Union Church, above referred to, stood on the north side of Bledsoe Creek, at its intersection with the street fronting the cemetery. It was torn down during the civil war. The Cumberland Presbyterian Church, above mentioned, was the same building now occupied by the Christians. The Masonic Hall referred to was the building now occupied for a residence by John Clark, near the Presbyterian Church, and in which Hon. Bailie Peyton, Hon. John H. Turner and Judge Thomas Barry studied law. Among the merchants of that period were R. M. Boyers, Stanfield and Montgomery, Mr. Edwards, Mr. Prince, James Robb, Desha, Reese and Franklin, and Minnick and Bullus. One of the taverns was kept by George Crockett in a building on Main Street, on the lot where Maj. Munday's office now stands, and the other by John Mitchell, in the building now standing on the corner of Main and Boyers Streets, opposite the Baptist Church. The eleven lawyers were John J. White, William Trousdale, John H. Turner, David M. Saunders, William M. Blackmore, Josephus C. Guild, George A. Baskerville, Bailie Peyton, Thomas Barry, George W. Parker, J. W. Baldridge; and among the physicians of that period were Dr. Elmore Douglass, Dr. William T. Hodge and Dr. Ned. Rollins. At a later period Howard and Safferen, James McCally, Banks Vaughan and S. R. Anderson were among the merchants of the town. And the hotel near the Baptist Church was afterward kept by Bowler Brizendine, and the one on lower Main Street by John Stuart.

The town continued its gradual and substantial growth until the beginning of the civil war when nearly all business was suspended and remained so during the whole of the war period. Somemercantile business was carried on by parties who obtained permits from the military authorities to sell goods. Most of these temporary merchants were foreigners. The first occupation of the town by Federal troops took place in February, 1862, after the Confederate troops retreated south from Fort Donelson. The Federal troops continued to occupy the town until July of that year, when Col. Boone, who then occupied it with a regiment of soldiers, was captured with his command by Gen. John Morgan of the Confederate Army. Boone and his men were paroled and allowed to retire into the Federal lines. Soon after this Gen. Johnson with a force of Federal cavalry crossed the Cumberland at Hartsville and advanced upon Gallatin with the intention of capturing it. He was met by Gen. Morgan's command at the forks of the turnpike east of the town, where a battle ensued, which resulted in the killing and wounding of many of his men and his final capture with most of his command. A portion of his men made their escape and recrossed the river. Johnson and those captured with him were paroled and conducted by way of Hartsville to the south side of the river. The Confederate authorities continued to hold Gallatin until Gen. Bragg's army fell back from Kentucky, and the Federal Army, under Gen. Rosecrans, returned to Tennessee in November of that year, when Gen. Payne with his command took possession of Gallatin. From that time to the close of the war, the town, remained in possession of Federal forces. As soon as peace was restored the citizens of Gallatin, as well as those of the county, accepted the results of the war without complaint, and with commendable energy and cheerfulness, began the work of retrieving their lost fortunes. The following is a list of the merchants and other business men of the town at this writing (January 1, 1887): Dry goods, B. O'Shinskey, Myers & Johns, W. H. Joyner, R. Beebe, C. Levi & Bro., R. Cohen; general store, H. Kamien; groceries, W. H. Brown, M. L. Bass, W. G. Schambery, J. Wile, W. Witherspoon, Wm. Killebrew, J. E. Sweeney, Love Brothers, A. D. Peyton, J. C. Rodemer & Co., J. B. Gainer, Wm. Hallorn, J. H. Guthrie, S. W. Love, Bruce & Enloe, Jack Pyles, colored; drugs, J. W. Knight, A. R. Schell & Co., R. M. Foster; millinery, Mrs. S. Levi; banks, Bank of Gallatin, Farmers' & Traders' Bank; stoves and tinware, James House, D. K. S. Pillars; saddles and harnesses, John Fry & Co., C. H. Cocke; livery stables, Buchanan & Sindle, Pearce, Burford & Howerson, J. B. Malone, T. R. Love, Day & Allen; hotels, Sindle House, Buckingham's Hotel, Day's Hotel; undertakers, W. C. Blue, T. H. King; furniture, W. C. Blue & Son; bakery and confectionery, J. Iss; books, J. A. Dilliard; saloons, A. D. Chrisman, P. T. Buckingham, John Glasgow, J. R. Bruce, M. L. Bass, Wm. A. Robinson, C. H. Moseley, Wm. Killebrew, S. W. Love, Bruce & Enloe; boot and shoemakers, Joseph Natcher; sewing machine agents, J. F. White, J. C. Lucas; insurance, G. R. Dismukes; barbers, H. Bugg, Arch Miller; butcher shops,

John Fry, S. H. Moseley; tailors, R. G. Merrill; manufactories, merchant mills and general wood work combined, by Walton & Son; the Gallatin Flouring Mills by Samuel Lyon; chair factory; tannery, by John Fry; machine shop, by G. D. Reed; planing-mill by S. R. Simpson; carriage factory, by Sindle & Buchanan; Nickelson Woolen Mills, established during the civil war; Nickelson Foundry established about 1850, also an extensive cotton factory established in 1850, and destroyed by fire in 1873, and afterward rebuilt to contain 4,096 spindles and 80 looms. This did an extensive business until 1885, when it was closed on account of depression of business, and has since stood idle. There are also many mechanics' shops, and some other establishments of business not here enumerated. The physicians of Gallatin are T. M. Woodson, A. J. Swaney, W. T. Allen, X. B. Haynie, R. M. Foster, W. R. Tomkins, and E. N. Franklin; Dr. T. J. Holder is the dentist. Gallatin contains the following religious denominations, viz.: Methodist, Presbyterian, Baptist, Christian, Cumberland Presbyterian, Episcopal and Catholic. All have fine church edifices except the Cumberland Presbyterian and the Episcopal. Among the colored people there are the Methodist, African Methodist, Christian and Baptist Churches. The town also contains the Howard Female College, and the public schools.

The first secret society in the town of Gallatin was King Solomon Lodge of F. & A. M., No. 6, in the State of Tennessee, and No. 52 in the archives of the Grand Lodge of North Carolina, whence the charter was issued December 9, 1808. The charter members and first officers were John Johnston, W. M.; Andrew Buckham, S. W., and John Mitchell, J. W. This lodge erected and owned the Masonic Hall to which reference has already been made. The last representation this body had in the Grand Lodge of the State was in 1836, and soon thereafter its charter was surrendered. King Solomon Lodge, No. 94, F. & A. M. was chartered October 9, 1840, by the Grand Lodge of Tennessee, the charter being signed by Moses Stevens, who was then the Grand Secretary. The charter members were John Bell, W. M.; George W. Parker, S. W., and Gen. Samuel R. Anderson, J. W. This lodge continues to labor and has a membership of about fifty. There is also a lodge of the Royal Arch Chapter of the Masonic fraternity in Gallatin. Howard Lodge, No. 13, I. O. O. F., was instituted December 5, 1845, with the following charter members: Wm. M. Blackmore, Geo. T. Crockett, John W. Franklin, Jas. M. Owen and Thomas G. Moss. The charter was granted December 2, 1845, by H. W. Calhoun, G. M., and W. S. McNairy, G. S. The first officers were Wm. M. Blackmore, N. G.; George F. Crockett, V. G., Thos. G. Moss, Sec., and J. M. Owen, Treas. With the exception of the period covered by the civil war, the lodge has met regularly. The present membership is twenty-four tried and true. An Encampment of Patriarchs of this order was chartered in August, 1848, but it has not met for several years. A charter was granted October 8, 1877, to George E. Seay, Wm. H. Brown and others, for a lodge of K. of H., which was instituted and continues to work with a fair membership. Local Branch, No. 53, of the Iron Hall, was chartered May 6, 1882, with John W. Walton, J. B. Donelson, E. O. Buchanan and others, as charter members. There is also a lodge of the K. of P., and other societies.

As early as 1815 a paper was published in Gallatin by Wm. L. Barry, the name of which, from the best information at hand, was *The Tennessean.* Its further history seems to be unknown. *The Union* was established at Gallatin in 1832, by H. S. Watlington, and its seventeenth issue (a copy of which is in possession of Col. Boyers) contained President Jackson's message dated December 10, 1832. The motto of this paper was "The Union—it must be preserved." It was established when the "Union," to which its motto referred, was only fifty-six years old. Happily the Union has been preserved, though with great loss of blood and treasure, until it has nearly doubled that age, and is now moving sublimely forward in its second century. *The Union* changed into the hands of D. C. Gaskill who published it as late as 1844 or perhaps later, when it was purchased by Gov. Wm. B. Bate, and the name changed to *Tenth Legion.* When Gov. Bate went to the Mexican war the paper was taken charge of by Col. Boyers, who continued with it until 1849. The *Courier and Enquirer* was established during the fifties by Baber and Tabb and afterward passed into the hands of Lewis and Duncan, who published it about one year on the eve of the civil war, and then it was suspended. A monthly magazine called the *Southron* was published a few years in the forties by D. C. Gaskill. In 1840 a Whig paper was established and edited by Mr. Sharpe. It continued only a year or two. *The Gallatin Examiner* was established in 1855 by Col. Thomas Boyers, who is still connected with its publication. It is a first-class, fifty-six column weekly newspaper, well sustained with a large circulation. *The Tennessean* was established in 1872, and is published by A. A. Lewis & Sons. It is also a first-class, thirty-two column weekly newspaper, well-sustained and has a large circulation. Gallatin was visited in 1849, 1852, and 1873, with the scourge of cholera. The first visitation was very severe, and the last probably more severe than the first. In 1873 the highest daily rate of mortality was about eighteen. The town is located in a rich agricultural district, and there are nine excellent turnpikes converging into it. Its population, according to the census of 1880, was

1,938. Its municipal government consists of a mayor, seven aldermen, a recorder, treasurer and marshal. The present officers are mayor, George R. Dismukes; aldermen—Dr. W. R. Tomkins, John Fry, Carroll Cocke, Samuel Lyon, James I. Walton, Dr. X. B. Haynie and H. H. Dewitt; recorder, J. W. Knight; treasurer, F. D. Blakemore; marshal, J. C. Clark.

Bledsoe Lick, now called Castalian Springs, is situated eight miles east of Gallatin, on the Carthage Turnpike. It is noted as being one of the most beautiful and picturesque places in the State, and also for its mineral waters of high medicinal qualities. It contains a postoffice, general store, blacksmith and wagon shop, a Methodist Church and a few dwelling-houses. Col. Wynne, a resident of the place, who was born there in 1800, showed the writer certain trees which he transplanted when a youth, that are now fully three feet in diameter. (For full mention of this historic place see elsewhere in this work.) Cairo, on the Cumberland River, about three-fourths of a mile below the mouth of Bledsoe Creek, was establishment with the early settlement of the county. It was incorporated in 1815, and in 1834 it contained thirty families, two physicians, a church and an academy, one tavern, one cabinet-maker and several other mechanic's shops, and a cotton factory, which was established about the year 1810. The factory closed when the farmers ceased to raise cotton, and the town has ceased to be a place of any considerable business. Hendersonville, located on the Louisville & Nashville Railroad, at the crossing of Drake Creek, contained in 1830, a store and stage office. It now contains four stores, two schools, two churches (Methodist and Presbyterian), and a few mechanic's shops. Saundersville, on the Louisville & Nashville Railroad, eight miles below Gallatin, contains four stores and other things in proportion. Mitchellville, an old town on the same railroad, near the Kentucky State line, contains a postoffice, two stores, etc. Fountain Head, also on the same railroad, thirteen miles above Gallatin, has four stores and a tobacco factory, and is noted for the large amount of tobacco annually shipped therefrom. South Tunnel, Buck Lodge and Richland Station, are points on the same line of road above Gallatin, each containing a postoffice and store. Cotton Town, on the Red River Turnpike, seven miles from Gallatin, contains two stores, saw and grist-mill, etc. Bethpage, on the Scottsville Turnpike, ten miles northeast of Gallatin, contains a postoffice, store and church. There are several other hamlets throughout the county, each containing a postoffice and store, and some of them also contain a grist-mill or other mills.

The first school in Sumner County was undoubtedly taught at Bledsoe Lick, mention being incidentally made of it by Gen. Hall, in his narrative concerning the early settlers and their encounters with the Indians, as early as 1787, 100 years ago, when "a little schoolmaster named George Hamilton" was shot, and severely (but not fatally) wounded by the Indians at Bledsoe Fort. The first schools were those known as "subscription schools," and not of a high grade, but as soon as there were enough families congregated in a neighborhood, an academy was established, and thus the education of the children was not neglected for a great period of time in the settlement of the county. The first school of much note was the Transmontania Academy, at Gallatin, which was chartered by an act of the Legislature passed September 13, 1806. This act provided that James Winchester, David Shelby, Edward Douglass, Henry Bradford and William Montgomery, should be the first trustees of said academy. The building in which this school was taught for many years is now the Nickelson Foundry. The trustees of the academy sold this building before the civil war, and erected a new one on Main Street, where Capt. Gloster now lives. The new building was destroyed by fire during the war, and since that time the male school has been merged into the public school. The Transmontania was a very popular school, well sustained, and among its earliest teachers, probably the first one, was Prof. John Hall, a brother of Gen. Hall. It was in this school, while taught by Prof. Hall, that Hon. Bailie Peyton, Judge Thomas Barry and their compeers, were educated. The first female academy in Gallatin, established in a very early day, soon after the Transmontania, was taught by Dr. Berry. The Sumner County Female Academy was incorporated by an act of the General Assembly, passed November 3, 1837, and the trustees appointed by the act were Thomas A. Baber, James A. Blackmore, Joel Parrish, R. H. May, Elijah Boddie, J. W. Baldridge and William Edwards. After this the trustees were elected annually on the first Monday of January by the stockholders. The authorized capital was $75,000. The building now occupied by the Howard Female College, was erected by the trustees of the Sumner County Female Academy, about the year 1837. This was a good school, and was well sustained until it was succeeded by the Howard Female Institute, which was established by an act of the General Assembly passed February 18, 1856. This act provided that Howard Lodge, No. 13, I. O. O. F., should constitute the board of trustees of said institute. Hence this school has always been under the supervision of this lodge of the I. O. O. F. Prof. Joseph S. Fowler was the first principal, and continued as such until 1862, when the school was closed on account of the civil war. After the close of the war Prof. Fowler was elected United States

Senator, from Tennessee, and was one of the Republican senators who voted against the impeachment of President Johnson. The principal teachers since the war have been Prof. H. B. Todd, Prof. W. J. Wood, Rev. W. A. Haynes and Alfred M. Burney, A. M., the present president of the faculty. He is ably assisted by Pattie Malone, Miss Bessie Bell, Miss Mollie Heerman, Miss Allie V. M. Luse, Mrs. Lizzie M. Hicks, Miss Mary C. McMillan, Miss Marion M. Luse and Miss M. Adelene Moffat. Prof. Burney has been president of the faculty for the last three years. For the school year of 1885-86 there were 139 students matriculated in this institution of learning. The college building is large and commodious, and very pleasantly located on Main Street. The faculty is able and popular, and is doing excellent work in the educational line. The Rural Academy, located about two miles north of Castalian Springs, was founded about the year 1812, and for many years was taught by Prof. Robert Minton, who was an able educator. It is still sustained, and continues to be one of the leading schools of the county. John Williams taught in that neighborhood before the academy was established. The Bledsoe Female Academy was founded about the year 1840, and was well sustained until about the year 1860, when the school building was consumed by fire.

To show what is being done in Sumner County in the way of education under the public school system, the following statistics are taken from the latest published report of the State superintendent, it being for 1885—Scholastic population: White—male, 3,182; female, 3,104; total, 6,286. Colored—male, 1,259; female, 1,195; total, 2,446; grand total, 8,732. Number of pupils enrolled during the year: White—male, 1,564; female, 1,419. Colored—male, 458; female, 488. Number of schools: white, 73; colored, 23; total, 96. Number of consolidated schools, 5. Number of schools controlled by city boards, 3. Number of teachers employed: White—male, 46; female, 28. Colored—male, 10; female, 14; total, 98. Amount of school money received during year from all sources, $25,295.75. By a study of these figures it is plain that of the scholastic population of the county, less than one-half, both white and colored, were enrolled in the public schools. This, in consideration of the further fact, that the average daily attendance of those enrolled equaled only about three-fourths of their number, leads to the inevitable conclusion that the public schools of Sumner County are not as well sustained as they ought to be.

Christianity accompanied the brave pioneers of Sumner County, and before it was possible to erect church edifices, religious services were held in the primitive dwellings of individuals. Soon, however, rude log meeting-houses were erected and regular preaching maintained in every sufficiently settled neighborhood. And before the beginning of the present century, camp-meeting grounds were established at different points throughout the county, the most noted of which was Beach Camp-ground, ten miles west of Gallatin. Among the first divines of note in Sumner County were the Rev. Wm. McGee, of the Presbyterian Church, and Revs. John Gwynn, John McGee, John Page and Bishop McKendree, of the Methodist Church, and John Wiseman of the Baptist Church. The Presbyterian, Methodist and Baptist were the pioneer churches of the county and have always continued to be the most prominent. Other early ministers were Revs. Hardy M. Cryer, John Henry and John Maffit, of the Methodist Church, and John W. Hall and Gideon Blackburn, of the Presbyterian Church. While all of these were eminent revivalists, Rev. Blackburn is said to have been one of the most powerful. He preached at times to the Indians and also to Gen. Jackson's troops before they departed for New Orleans, in the war of 1812–15. In the vicinity of Bledsoe Lick and Cairo, the Presbyterians are said to have been the most numerous among the early Christians of the county. A great religious revival occurred in the county at the close of the last and beginning of the present century, concerning which the reader is referred to the religious history of the State. In addition to the above named church societies are the Cumberland Presbyterian, Christian, Catholic and other denominations, which have been established in the county. Numerous church edifices exist in the towns and throughout the county sufficient for the public worship of the people.

SMITH COUNTY.

THE county of Smith is bounded north by Trousdale and Macon Counties, east by Jackson and Putnam, south by DeKalb, and west by Wilson. It lies mostly in the central basin, and is drained by the Cumberland River, which flows through it from east to west, and so divides it as to leave about three-fourths of its area on the south side, and the other fourth on the north side. The tributaries flowing into the Cumberland from the north are Peyton Creek and Defeated Creek, and other smaller streams. The principal one flowing into it from the south is Caney Fork, which is navigable for small vessels about forty miles from its mouth, which is just above the town of Carthage. The spurs of the Highland Rim extend far into the county from the north and east, thus making that part lying north of the Cumberland and east of Caney Fork extremely hilly and uneven. The balance of the county has a more even surface. The streams have broad valleys, and "the soil of the county, with the exception of the caps of the ridges, rests everywhere on limestone belonging to the Nashville and Lebanon formations, but principally the former. The tops of the ridges present the siliceous rocks of the highlands, being the sub-carboniferous. Immediately below these siliceous rocks, and separating them from the limestone, is the black shale formation."* The lands having a limestone soil are rich and productive, and those on the highlands produce an excellent quality of tobacco, but the yield is light. The timber is similar to that of Trousdale County.

William Walton, original proprietor of the site of Carthage, settled, according to best information, on the north side of the Cumberland, opsite the mouth of Caney Fork in 1787. He is said to have been the first settler in the territory now composing Smith County. Daniel Burford, Richard Alexander, Tilman Dixon, William Saunders and Peter Turney were among the first settlers in the vicinity of Dixon Springs. Peter Turney was the father of the noted lawyer, Hopkins L. Turney, and grandfather of Judge Peter Turney, now of the supreme bench of the State. The best agricultural lands being in the vicinity of Dixon Springs, that locality soon became the most thickly settled one in the county. Micajah Duke was an early settler in what is now the Second District; David Apple in the Eighth; William McDonald in the Eleventh; Armstead Flippen in the Thirteenth; William Goodall, and James Hodges, with his son Richard, and Arthur S. Hogan in the Fourteenth; and Zachariah Ford in the Fifteenth. Other early settlers were David Cochrane, John Baker, Thomas Dies, George T. Wright and also all persons hereinafter mentioned in connection with the organization of the county. "The grandfather of S. M. Fite, with his family, and two other men, with their families, made the first settlement on Smith Fork, fifteen miles south of the Cumberland River. The first night after camping Mr. Fite had family worship, no doubt the first Christian worship ever made in that vast region."* When the first settlers appeared in Smith County, they found the territory inhabited with Indians, and many kinds of wild animals, such as bears, wolves, panthers, wild-cats, deer, etc. Wild game was also abundant, and those hardy pioneers, during their struggles to subdue the forest and establish civilization in a vast wildnerness, often supplied their families with meat secured by

*"Resources of Tennessee."

means of their trusty rifles. Bear meat, venison and wild fowl were then common articles of food. The Indians were here about ten years after the first settlers located, and during this time the pioneers, no doubt, had many encounters with them; the history of which, unfortunately, has not been preserved. One incident which occurred in this county before it was settled, between citizens of Sumner County and the Indians, may be related here. "In February, 1786, John Peyton (father of the late Hon. Bailie Peyton); Ephraim Peyton, his twin brother; Thomas Peyton, another brother; Squire Grant and John Frazer were out hunting and surveying. They encamped on an island in Defeated Creek, near where Capt. C. N. West now resides. On Sunday night they sat up late playing cards, when they were attacked by the Indians. Four out of the five were wounded—all except Ephraim Peyton. They separated and fled, leaving their horses and instruments. The Indian party was commanded by Hanging Maw. All made their escape and survived, and the next year John Peyton sent word to Hanging Maw to return the stolen horses, to which the chief replied, 'that the horses were his, that he (Peyton) had run away like a coward and left them, and as for his 'land-stealer,' the compass, he had broken that against a tree."* Robert Smith and Lucy Gordon were the first couple married in Smith County, and Richard Hodges and Delilah Risen the second. The latter were married by Arthur S. Hogan, Esq., in 1803.

Large tracts of the best land in the country were entered by surviving soldiers of the war of the Revolution, or by their assignees, by locating the land warrants granted to said soldiers by the State of North Carolina. These tracts ranged from 640 to several thousand acres. The early settlers of Smith County were mostly from North Carolina, Virginia, and East Tennessee, and after erecting their rude log cabins, they began the clearing of their lands, and the raising of the cereals. Subsequently, and for many years, including the decade of the twenties, they raised cotton to a considerable extent, and afterward abandoned its cultivation. The cultivation of tobacco was early introduced and this crop has always been, and still continues to be, a staple production of the county, which ranks as the sixth county in the State in the amount of that article produced. The cultivation of blue-grass, and the raising of fine breeds of cattle were introduced into the county in 1836, by Dr. F. H. Gordon, who was then a teacher in Clinton College. He went to Kentucky and on his return, brought to the farm on which the college is located, a herd of Durham cattle, and began to sow blue-grass for pasture. Since that time considerable attention has been given to the raising of fine

*Reminiscences of Gen. William Hall.

breeds of stock of all kinds, and to the cultivation of the grasses. The cereal, and other productions of Smith County, according to the census of 1880, were as follows: Indian corn, 1,071,050 bushels; oats, 47,240 bushels; rye, 3,228 bushels; wheat, 104,945 bushels; orchard products, $11,927; hay, 2,730 tons; Irish potatoes, 13,817 bushels; sweet potatoes, 29,335 bushels; tobacco, 1,799,981 pounds; live stock and its productions—horses, 5,112; mules and asses, 1,973; cattle, 8,623; sheep, 10,234; hogs, 31,871; wool 40,393 pounds; butter, 221,381 pounds. The population of Smith County in 1860, including that part which has since been attached to Trousdale County, was as follows: White, 12,015; colored, 4,342; nearly all of the latter were then slaves, and in 1880 it was—white, 14,215; colored, 3,578. Notwithstanding the reduction of the territory, and the ravages of civil war, the white population of the county increased 2,200 in the twenty years following 1860, while the colored population decreased 764 during the same period. The transportation of produce and merchandise to and from Smith County has always been by way of the Cumberland River. But the citizens are now anticipating the early completion of the Middle & East Tennessee Central Railroad, and also the Nashville & Knoxville Railroad through the county by way of Carthage. These railroads when completed will be of great advantage to the county, in hastening its future development.

Smith County was organized in accordance with an act of the General Assembly of the State, passed October 26, 1799, providing "That a new county be established by the name of Smith, to be contained within the following described bounds: Beginning on the south bank of Cumberland River, at the south end of the eastern boundary of Sumner County; thence north with the said eastern boundary to the northern boundary of the State, and with the said boundary east to where it is intersected by the Cherokee boundary, run and marked agreeably to the treaty of Holston; thence with that boundary to the Caney Fork of Cumberland River; thence with said fork, according to its meanders, to the mouth thereof; thence down the south bank of Cumberland River, according to its meanders, to the beginning." According to this description Smith County originally contained a portion of what is now Trousdale, DeKalb, Putnam, Jackson, Clay and the greater part of Macon Counties. By an act passed November 6, 1801, the county was changed in size by attaching to it a large portion of Wilson County, lying south of the Cumberland River and west of Caney Fork, and by cutting off a portion on the east side to constitute the county of Jackson. And by a subsequent act of the same session of the Legislature Smith County was extended southward to the line between Tennessee and Alabama—thus causing the county to embrace a strip of territory extending from the northern to the southern boundary of the State. In 1805 an act was passed to reduce the county to its constitutional limits of 625 square miles, still allowing its northern boundary to reach the Kentucky line. And by an act passed January 18, 1842, the northern portion of Smith County became a part of Macon County in its formation. And in 1870 a tract in the northwestern part of the county was cut off to form a part of Trousdale County. And thus by these and other acts of the Legislature Smith County has been reduced to its present limits, embracing about 360 square miles. In accordance with the act of creation the first bench of justices of the peace for Smith County, consisting of Garrett Fitzgerald, Wm. Alexander, James Gwinn, Tilman Dixon, Thomas Harrison, James Hibbetts, Peter Turney and Wm. Walton, met at the house of Tilman Dixon, near Dixon Springs, on the 16th of December, 1799, and organized the court of pleas and quarter sessions by electing Garrett Fitzgerald, chairman thereof, and Moses Fisk clerk *pro tempore.* The next day the following county officers were permanently elected by said court, to wit: Sampson Williams, clerk; John Martin, sheriff; Chas. F. Mobias, coroner; James Gwinn, trustee; Daniel Burford, register; Bazel Shaw, ranger, and Benj. Sewell, State's attorney. Amos Lacy, Silas Jonokin, Robt. Cotton, James Strain, James Wright, Wm. Levington and Henry Huddleston were then appointed constables, and thus the organization of the county was completed. Then on motion of Tilman Dixon it was "ordered that all tavern-keepers be allowed to sell spirituous liquors at the following rates: Good whisky and brandy, 12½ cents by the half-pint; for breakfast, dinner and supper, 25 cents; for corn and oats by the gallon, 12½ cents; for two bundles of fodder, 2 pence; for pasturage twenty-four hours, 12½ cents; for lodging, 6¼ cents." The next action of the court was to grant to Tilman Dixon, the mover of the aforesaid motion, a license to keep a tavern at his house. License was then granted to Edmond Jennings to keep a ferry near the mouth of Jennings Creek, at the following rates: "For man and horse, 18⅓ cents; single man and single horse, each 9 cents; wagon and team, $1.25; cattle, hogs and sheep, 6¼ cents each." For many years after the organization of the county no person was allowed to keep a tavern, or a ferry, or to build a mill-dam without license from the court, which also established the rates to be charged by the persons obtaining such privileges. Henry McKinsey, Wm. Saunders, Samuel Caruthers, Elisha Oglesby, Wm. Gillespie, Wm. Gilbreath and others were then appointed overseers of certain public roads.

The first grand jury in Smith County, consisting of Grant Allen, Willis Haynie, John Barkley, James Draper, William Pate, Anthony Samuel, James Ballow, William Kelton, Daniel Mungle, John Crosswhite, Thomas Jemison and Nat Ridley were impaneled by the court of pleas and quarter sessions at its March term, 1800. The county not being then divided into civil districts, assessors were appointed to list the taxable property in each captain's company of the militia. The following persons were then appointed assessors for the year 1800, to wit: Garrett Fitzgerald, for the Flinn Creek company; Charles Hudgspath, for the Obed and Roaring River company or settlement; William Walton, for Capt. Vance's company; Thomas Harmand, for Capt. Pate's company; Peter Turney, for the Peyton Creek company; Tilman Dixon, for Capt. Bradley's company; James Hibbetts, for Capt. Shaw's company, and James Gwinn, for Capt. Gwinn's company. Several persons then appeared in court and had their stock marks recorded, it being the custom then to allow the stock to run at large on the unoccupied lands, and each man had his own peculiar stock mark. The bounty on wolf scalps was then established at $1. And David Venters was allowed to build a mill on Goose Creek near the Big Spring. The same year, 1800, William Saunders was permitted to build a saw and grist-mill on Dixon Creek, about 200 yards below the Blue Spring. The dam was not to be over twelve feet high, and the water was to be drawn off, if requested by Mr. Dixon, by the 15th of June each year. At the June term, 1801, of said court the sheriff returned a long list of delinquent tax lands belonging to non-resident owners. Many of their tracts contained several thousand acres, and all were ordered to be sold to satisfy the taxes and costs charged thereon. The court of pleas and quarter sessions continued to be held at the house of Tilman Dixon until June, 1802, when it was held at the house of William Saunders. And from that time till 1806 it was held alternately at the houses of the said Dixon, Saunders, William Walton and Peter Turney. At the December term, 1804, Willis Jones, Benjamin John and Wilson Cage were appointed commissioners to select and purchase a site for the seat of justice, and to lay out a town thereon, and to sell the lots and appropriate the proceeds to the payment of the land, and the erection of the public buildings. These commissioners selected the site of the present town of Carthage, then owned by William Walton and from him purchased the same, consisting of fifty acres, for the consideration of 1 cent, and secured title thereto by deed dated December 28, 1804. And during that winter they laid out the town of Carthage and sold the lots thereof and erected the first courthouse for the county, on the public square, in 1805. This courthouse was constructed of brick and was about fifty feet square, with four offices and a hall on the first floor, and two offices and the court room on the second. All the rooms had large wood fireplaces. The first term of the court of pleas and quarter sessions held in the courthouse was in March, 1806. This courthouse stood until 1877, when it was taken down and the present one erected in its stead at a cost of about $18,000. This is a substantial two-story brick building of considerable architectural beauty, with the county offices and hall on the first floor and the court room and some small rooms on the second. Col. Fite was the general superintendent of the erection of this building, and Henry C. Jackson, of Murfreesboro, was the contractor and builder. The first jail in the county was built about the year 1812 by James Walton. It was made of logs and contained two rooms, one above the other, and cost about $700. It stood on the site of the present jail and was replaced by the latter about the year 1835. The old poor-farm on Peyton Creek, consisting of seventy-five acres, was purchased and fitted up in an early day. It was sold in 1871 to Henry, William, and Thomas Hacket for $761, and at the same time another farm containing 211 acres was purchased in the horse-shoe bend of the Cumberland River, in District No. 20, for $1,200. Buildings were erected thereon and other improvements made, costing about $3,500. The location of this farm being considered unhealthy, as well as very inconvenient, it was afterward sold and the present one purchased. The latter is situated two and a half miles west of Carthage and contains forty-five acres of good tillable land. The poor asylum, which is a substantial and safe brick building of modern architecture and heated with two furnaces, was erected in 1885 at a cost of $9,000. At present writing there are fourteen paupers in the asylum.

During the early history of the county, the revenues were not assessed and collected according to the value of the property. To illustrate the method, the rates for the year 1811, which are similar to other years of that period, are here given as established by the then authorities. They are as follows: For county purposes—on each 100 acres of land, 12½ cents; each white poll, 12½ cents; each black poll, 25 cents; each town lot, 25 cents; each stallion, $1; each retail store, $5. For jurors—on each 100 acres, 6¼ cents; each white poll, 6¼ cents; each black poll, 6¼ cents; each town lot, 6¼ cents; each stallion, 25 cents; each retail store, $1. Thus it will be seen that the taxes were levied on specific property, without any regard to its value. The taxable property of the county at present writing consists of 202 town lots valued at $84,835, and 197,279 acres of land valued at $2,335,195, and personal property valued at $347,125, and other property valued at $25,755, making a grand total of taxable property of $2,792,910. There are also 2,709 taxable polls. The total taxes levied on the foregoing property and polls for the year 1886 amounts to $32,788.51. The finances of Smith County have always been so well managed that her warrants have seldom if ever been below par. The county is well supplied with public buildings, all of which have been erected without the issuing of bonds. And at present the county has no outstanding bonds or warrants, and is entirely out of debt. The following is a list of the county officers with dates of service: County court clerks—Sampson Williams, 1799–1804; Robert Allen, 1804–12; Joseph W. Allen, 1812, a few months and died; Robert Allen, 1812–19; Jonathan Pickett, 1819–35; John I. Burnett, 1835–48; W. V. R. Hallum, 1848–56; David C. Sanders, 1856–64; E. W. Turner, 1864–68; John P. Yelton, 1868–70; B. F. C. Smith, 1870–74; Samuel Allison, 1874–82; John B. Jordan, 1882–86 and re-elected. Sheriffs—John Martin, 1799–1802; Lee Sullivan, 1802–04; George Matlock, 1804–12; John Gordon, 1812–16; Wm. Goodall, 1816–27; David Burford, 1827–29; S. B. Hughes, 1829–34; Samuel P. Howard, 1834–38; Wyatt W. Bailey, 1838–44; John Bailey, 1844–48; John Bridges, 1848–52; Samuel Allison, 1852–58; John W. Hughes, 1858–60; B. B. Uhles, 1860–62; Larkin Cornwell, 1862–64; H. S. Patterson, 1864–66; J. H. Smith, 1866–68; J. E. Clark, 1868–70; Wm. Arrington, 1870–72; J. H. Corder, 1872–76; John B. Wilson, 1876–80; Wm. T. Barrett, 1880–84; A. J. Dawson, 1884–86, and re-elected. Registers—Daniel Burford, 1819–25; Alex Allison, 1825–32; Harvey Hogg, 1832–42; A. S. Watkins, 1842–46; David C. Sanders, 1846–54; Quaintance C. Sanders, 1854–58; S. R. Thompson, 1858–62; J. P. McKee, 1864–70; W. P. Pettie, 1870–74; A. N. Williams, 1874–78; Joseph P. King, 1878–80; W. W. Ford, 1880–82; E. B. Price, 1882–86; D. C. Sanders, 1886. Trustees since 1840—David K. Timberlake, 1840–52; A. W. Allen, 1852-54; John P. Haynie, 1854–56; Ira W. King, 1856–62; J. H. Newbell, 1862–66; Joseph A. Pendarris, 1866–70; E. H. Knight, 1870–72; D. J. Lynch, 1872–74; D. A. West, 1874–76; S. R. Johnson, 1876–78; N. J. Kemp, 1878–80; W. V. Harrell, 1880–82; W. J. Johnson, 1882–84; J. B. Duke, 1884–86; W. M. Johnson, 1886. Circuit court clerks—Robert Allen, 1810–13; John W. Overton, 1813–20; Charles Sherwood, 1820–23; Wm. Hart, 1823–48; Henry Wm. Hart, 1848–52; N. B. Burdine, 1852–56; Thomas Fisher, 1856–64; Ira W. King, 1864–65; John L. Arendall 1865, March to August; W. J. Cleveland, 1865–66; Thomas Waters, 1866–68; W. B. Pickering, 1868–70; Thomas Fisher, 1870–74; W. B. Pettie, 1874–82; T. B. Read, 1882–86; W. W. Ford, 1886. Clerks and Masters of chancery courts—Robert L. Caruthers, 1825–27; John G. Park, 1827–37; Wm. C. Hubbard, 1837, one term; John G. Park, 1837–38; A. Moore, Jr., 1838, to the civil war; D. H. Campbell, 1865–71; John A. Fite, 1871–77; Wm. D. Gold, present incumbent ever since 1877. For list of congressmen see history of Sumner County.

The court of pleas and quarter sessions, for many years after its organization, had jurisdiction over all kinds of business, both civil and criminal. One of its early criminal cases was that of the State *vs.* Dr. Charles F. Mabias. The defendant was indicted for stealing a cow bell, of the value of 6 cents, from one Joseph Cannon. He was tried and found "not guilty," whereupon the costs of the prosecution were all taxed against Mr. Cannon, the prosecutor. This occurred when the court was held at the house of Wm. Saunders. The following novel resignation was discovered in the records of the May term, 1814, of said court:

A justice of the peace, you see,
No longer now I mean to be;
I therefore now resign to you,
As by these lines you see it true.
You therefore now your order may
Give to the clerk without delay,
That he may your right transmit
To the next session when they sit.

—*Henry Mc Whorter.*

The last term of the court of pleas and quarter sessions was held in February, 1836; and the first term of the county court, which was established instead of and to succeed the court of pleas and quarter sessions, was held in May, 1836. The county court was then composed of forty-two justices of the peace, all of whom were present and to whom the oath of office was administered by Judge Abraham Caruthers. Exum Whitley was elected chairman of the court. This court is now composed of forty-five justices of the peace, and its present chairman is Irenus Beckwith. The Third Judicial District of the State, including the counties of Smith, Warren, Franklin, Sumner, Overton, White and Jackson, was formed by an act of the Legislature passed November 16, 1809. The circuit court, according to this act, was to be held in Smith County, beginning on the fourth Monday of March and September of each year. The first term of this court was probably held in March, 1810, but the records thereof not being found among the records of the clerk the exact date cannot be given. Hon. Nathan W. Williams was the first judge of the district, and he continued to preside alternately for many years with Judges Archibald Roane, P. W. Humphreys, Thomas Stewart, Bennett Searcy, J. C. Isaacks, Charles F. Keith and others until 1834, since which time the court has been presided over by the following judges, to wit: Abraham Caruthers, 1834–47; Wm. B. Campbell, 1847–51; Alvan Cullom, 1851–52; James T. Quarles, one term in 1852; John L. Goodall, 1852–58; S. M. Fite, 1858–64; Andrew McClain, 1864–69; S. M. Fite, 1869–75; N. W. McConnell, 1875–86; John A. Fite, 1886. The chancery court of Smith County was established by an act of the Legislature passed October 29, 1824, and its first term was begun and held on the third Monday of May, 1825, with Hon. John Catron presiding as chancellor, and Hon. Robert C. Caruthers clerk and master. Prior to 1840 this court was presided over by Chancellors John Catron, Robert White, Nathan Green, Will A. Cook, Wm. B. Reese and Thomas L. Williams, in the order here named. From 1840 to 1860 Hon. Bloomfield L. Ridley was chancellor and presided for forty terms, and then Smith County was changed by act of the Legislature from Ridley's district. Since 1860 the chancery court has been presided over as follows: Josephus C. Guild, 1860–61; Jas. O. Shackelford, 1865–66; Thomas Barry, 1866–67; B. C. Tillman, 1867–69; Charles G. Smith, 1869–70; W. W. Goodpaster, 1870–72; W. G. Cowley, 1872–86; W. W. Wade, 1886—elected. The bar of Carthage has contained many resident members whose reputation for ability was widely extended. Among those who rose to eminent distinction may be mentioned the Hon. Robert L. Caruthers, Judge Abraham Caruthers, Gen. Wm. Cullom, Wm. B. Campbell, the noted jurist, soldier, and subsequent governor of the State; Judge Samuel M. Fite, Hon. James B. Moore, Col. W. H. DeWitt, Capt. W. W. Ward, Capt. J. W. McHenry, Col. Jordon Stokes, Judge John D. Goodall and Hon. Andrew McClain; all too well known to need further mention here. The present bar of Carthage consists of the following honorable gentlemen: E. L. Gardenhire, A. A. Swope, John A. Fite, judge of the circuit court; H. M. Hale, T. J. Fisher, Sr., J. B. Jordon, W. D. Gold, Col. A. E. Garrett, C. W. Garrett, E. W. Turner, B. F. C. Smith, J. B. Luster, W. W. Fergusson, J. M. Fisher, W. V. Lee, L. A. Ligon, the present representative in the State Legislature, and D. A. Witt.

Smith County was represented in the war with Great Britain in 1812–15 by two companies of soldiers commanded respectively by Capts. — Roberson and James Walton. These companies went to New Orleans and participated in that famous battle under the heroic Gen. Jackson. There were four companies of soldiers raised in this county, which served through the Mexican war; two of them, commanded respectively by Capts. Wm. Walton and L. P. McMurry, served in the First Regiment of Tennessee Volunteers, commanded by Col. (since governor) William B. Campbell. Capt. Don Allison's company served in a Tennessee regiment of cavalry, commanded by Col. Thomas. And soon after entering the service Capt. Allison was promoted to the office of lieutenant-colonel of his regiment. Capt. John D. Goodall's company served in the Fourth Regiment of Tennessee Volunteers, commanded by Col. Waterhouse. The first three companies entered the service in 1846, and the latter in 1847, and all served to the close of the war. At the approach of the late civil war there was a strong Union sentiment in Smith County, but being inside the Confederate lines when the war began, no companies of soldiers were organized for the Union Army. Several Union men subsequently joined Federal commands. There were twelve companies raised in Smith County for the Confederate Armies. The first one was raised in April, 1861, and was commanded by Capt. (now judge) John A. Fite. It joined the Seventh Tennessee Regiment. Two other companies, commanded respectively by Capts. W. W. Ward and — Cossett, served in Col. Bennett's regiment. Three companies, commanded respectively by Capts. — James, H. W. Hart and Alex Dillaha, served in the Twenty-fourth Tennessee Regiment. One company, commanded by Capt. W. H. McDonald, served in the Twenty-fifth Tennessee Regiment. Capt. Q. C. Sanders' company served in Col. Baxter Smith's regiment of cavalry. Two companies, commanded respectively by Capts. Tom King and A. B. Cates, served in Col. Bartow's regiment of cavalry, and two companies commanded respectively by Capts. H. B. Haynie and William B. Burford, served in other regiments. Including with the companies raised in the county, the individuals who joined companies raised in adjoining counties, it is estimated that fully 1,200 men served in the Confederate Army from Smith County. Being outside of the direct line of march of the contending armies, Smith County did not suffer as much as many other counties from the ravages of war. The first occupation of Carthage by Federal troops took place in February, 1863, when Gen. George Crooks with his command took possession of the town. He was relieved in June following by Gen. Spears, who commanded a brigade of East Tennesseans, and subsequently the town was occupied by Col. Jordon Stokes and his command. From the time Gen. Crooks first occupied it until the close of the war, it was in possession of Federal troops.

Carthage was laid out as heretofore stated in the year 1805, on lands purchased from William Walton, and being the oldest town in a large scope of country, the trade of which it commanded, it soon became a place of considerable business importance. In 1830 it contained, according to the "Tennessee Gazetteer," "about 700 inhabitants, eight lawyers, three doctors, one divine, thirteen stores, four taverns, one grocery, two tailors, two blacksmith shops, one printing office, one tanyard, one male and female academy, one church and a steam grist and saw-mill." As the country became settled other towns were established, which took the trade away from Carthage, so that its business has declined to that of a small village. It now contains, aside from the county buildings, the general store of Joseph Myer & Son, the drug, hardware and furniture store of Capt. T. P. Bridges, two groceries kept by E. B. Price and T. B. Read & Son, the wagon and blacksmith shop of W. I. Chandler, a few other mechanics' shops, two printing presses, three hotels—the Carthage Hotel, the McDonald Hotel and Fisher's Hotel—two schools (one white and one colored), four physicians, five churches (four white and one colored), two livery stables and a lodge each of Free Masons and Good Templars. The names of the physicians are J. S. Cornwell, Frank Swope, H. M. Blair and H. C. McDonald. The population of the town is about 400. *The Carthage Mirror* and *The Record* are weekly newspapers, both having a good circulation and both being well sustained. The former was established in May, 1883, by J. B. Luster, who continues its publication, and the latter was established in the fall of 1883, by W. D. Gold, who continues its publication. Dixon Springs contains three general stores, one drug store, one grocery, one saddler's shop, one livery stable, one grist and saw-mill, two hotels, one union church, an academy and a colored school. Gordonsville was established in 1804, and named after John Gordon, its first merchant. It now contains two stores, a livery stable, one school, two churches, a tobacco factory, some mechanics' shops, and about 175 inhabitants. Chestnut Mound, in District No. 8, contains three stores, a cabinet shop, livery stable and a school. Elmwood, located east of Caney Fork, contains two stores, one church and the Elmwood Institute. Rome, situated on the Cumberland, at the mouth of Round Lick Creek, contains several business houses. Monoville, Riddleton, Stonewall, Grant, Lancaster and Middleton are post villages each containing from one to four stores, etc.

According to the custom in all newly settled countries, the children of the first settlers of Smith County were deprived of many educational advantages. As soon, however, as a neighborhood became sufficiently settled, a private school or academy was established therein. There being no free schools, the children of the poor who were not able to pay "rate bills," continued to remain without school privileges. Among the first schools of note in the county was the Geneva Academy established at Carthage in the first decade of the century. This was a county school entitled to the public school fund, meager though it was, of the county. The Carthage Female Academy was established in 1842, and subsequently made a branch of Geneva Academy in order to enable it to draw a portion of the aforesaid public fund. The building of the original Geneva Academy was sold a few years ago, and the Female Academy, which is still sustained, was then opened to both sexes. The most noted school the county has ever had was Clinton College, founded by Dr. Francis H. Gordon, James B. Moores and Willie B. Gordon, and established in October, 1833, on the Lebanon and Trousdale Ferry Turnpike. Dr. F. H. Gordon and Prof. James B. Moores (the latter of whom became an eminent lawyer) were for many years the principal teachers in the college, the doors of which were permanently closed some time during the decade of the fifties. There are several high schools distributed throughout the county, prominent among which are the Elmwood Institute and Dixon Springs Academy. To show how the county is progressing under the free school system, the following statistics are taken from the last published report of the State superintendent of public instruction: Scholastic population—White: male, 2,775; female, 2,440; total, 5,215. Colored: male, 629; female, 626; total, 1,255. Number of pupils enrolled during the year—White: male, 1,461; female, 1,338; total, 2,799. Colored: male, 398; female, 358; total, 756. Number of teachers employed—White: male, 44; female, 12. Colored: male, 14; female, 4; total, 73. Number of schools, white, 56; colored, 17; total, 73. Amount of money expended during the year, $11,916.79. By comparing the above figures it will be seen that only a little over one-half of the white children attended the free schools while a larger percentage of the colored children were in attendance.

It is thought that the Baptist organized the first religious society in the county, at the house of Grant Allen near Dixon Springs in the year 1799. It is now known as the Dixon Creek Baptist Church. Rev. John McGee, a noted pioneer minister of the Methodist Church, settled near Dixon Springs in 1798, and a meeting-house was built on his land, called the McGee's Meeting-house. And this was no doubt the first Methodist Church in the county.* Rev. McGee was noted for the active part he took in the great religious revival at the beginning of this century. Other noted pioneer ministers of the county were Revs. John Page, John Maffit, David K. Timberlake, John Mann, David Halliburton, Sr., Jesse Moreland, Stephen B. Lysle, Wm. Cherry, Wm. H. Johnson, Ira W. King and Robt. Trawick. The first church in Carthage was built by the Methodists at the upper end of Main Street soon after the town was established. The next was the present Methodist Church built jointly by the Methodists and Cumberland Presbyterians about the year

*Reminiscences by Dr. J. W. Bowen.

1830. The Cumberland Presbyterians built their church a few years later. The Baptist and Christian Churches in Carthage are both of recent construction. The first camp-meeting ground, known as the Hodge's camp-ground was established one and a fourth miles west of Carthage. The site of it is now in possession of Horace Oliver. A meeting-house was erected at that point soon after it was settled. The noted evangelist, Lorenzo Dow, preached in Carthage to the soldiers raised for Jackson's army, just before their departure for New Orleans. This was about the year 1813. The Methodists, Baptists and Presbyterians were the pioneer Christian denominations of the county, and they have always been, and still continue to be the leading religious sects. The establishment of the Christian Church in the county has been of a more recent date. The people of Smith County are primitive in their habits and customs—generous and hospitable, and sustain a high standard of morality.

MACON COUNTY.

THE county of Macon, in Middle Tennessee, is bounded, north by the State of Kentucky; east by Clay and Jackson Counties; south by Smith and Trousdale, and west by Sumner. It contains about 300 square miles, nearly all of which is on the Highland Rim. The ridge of the Rim passes nearly east and west through the center of the county, south of which the lands are drained by Goose Creek, Dixon Creek, Peyton Creek and other streams which flow into the Cumberland River. North of the ridge the lands are drained by Long Fork, Salt Lick, White Oak and Long Creeks, which flow into the Big Barren River in Kentucky. The surface of the county is very uneven and hilly. The soil of the valleys is rich and productive, while that of the uplands is mostly thin and less productive. The timber of the highlands consists of poplar, oak, hickory and chestnut, and on the hillsides are found beech, sugar, walnut, poplar, hickory, oak and sweet gum. There are many mineral springs in the county, the most noted of which are the Red Boiling Springs, situated about twelve miles east of La Fayette, and the Red Sulphur Spring at La Fayette, and Epperson Springs in the western part of the county. These springs are all noted for the medicinal qualities of their waters, and all are visited during the hot season by invalids and pleasure seekers. The Red Boiling Springs, and the farm of nearly 200 acres on which they are located, have recently been purchased by Mr.

James F. O. Shaughnessy for $15,000 cash. This gentleman intends to erect suitable buildings and fit the place for a great summer resort.

The settlement of the territory composing the county began about the year 1787, one hundred years ago, when the country was a wilderness inhabited only by Indians and wild animals. No traditions of the early settlers have been handed down to posterity; their names only remain, prominent among which are Patrick and Alexander Ferguson; William, Robert and Thomas Bratton; Vincent and Sherwood Willis, Moses Rhoads, Wm. Holland, Joseph Cartwright, John Sitton, Wm. Chamberlain, Eason Howell, W. K. Carr, Wm. Hunter, Wm. Claiborne, Joseph Jenkins, Joel Blankenship, Jackson Crowder, Bennett Wright and Samuel Morrison. Most of the early settlers came from Virginia and the Carolinas. Grains, vegetables and tobacco have been the products of the soil ever since the first settlement. But the great staple crop for the market has always been tobacco, the other products having only been raised for home consumption. In an early day the tobacco was hauled to the Cumberland River and then shipped on floats to New Orleans, where it was sold. Since the building of the Louisville & Nashville Railroad the farmers of Macon County have hauled their tobacco to markets on its line, and much has been sold to home dealers who have had to market it in the same manner. Live stock has also been raised extensively for the market. And until recently the loom and spinning wheel has been found in almost every house, and nearly all the clothing used by the citizens was of domestic manufacture. But the loom and spinning wheel are disappearing and more foreign cloth is being used. According to the United States census for 1880 the productions of the county were as follows: Indian corn, 436,804 bushels; oats, 34,581 bushels; rye, 1,338 bushels; wheat, 31,495 bushels; hay, 768 tons; Irish potatoes, 10,098 bushels; sweet potatoes, 18,295 bushels; tobacco, 893,592 pounds. Live stock and its productions: horses, 2,356; mules and asses, 891; cattle, 4,843; sheep, 6,031; hogs, 15,866; wool, 13,716 pounds; butter, 110,906 pounds. The population of Macon County in 1860 was white, 6,244; colored, 1,046. In 1880 it was white, 8,429; colored, 890; thus showing an increase of the white population and a decrease of the colored. Macon is truly an inland county, having had no means of transportation other than by wagons, nearer than the Cumberland River and the Louisville & Nashville Railroad.

The county of Macon was organized in accordance with an act of the General Assembly of the State passed January 18, 1842, which provided that a new county should be established, to be known and distinguished by the name of Macon, to be composed of parts of the counties of Smith and Sumner: "Beginning at a white oak, the northeast corner of Smith County and northwest corner of Jackson County, on the Kentucky line; running thence south with said line, fourteen miles and 260 perches to a stake in Neal Carver's field, on Wartrace Creek; thence west crossing the head of Defeated Creek, near John Carter's and Peyton Creek, below Joseph Cocker's. and the east fork of Goose Creek, north of Brevard's, and the middle fork of Goose Creek, north of Mungle's, and the west fork below Sloans', thence to a mulberry tree, near Richard Hickerson's farm, making twenty-tree miles and three-quarters; thence north running east of said Hickerson's farm, fourteen miles and 260 perches to a large white oak west of Big Tramell Creek on the Kentucky line; thence east with said line to the beginning." The act also provided that the courts should be held at the house of William Dunn, and at other points to which they might adjourn, until the seat of justice should be located and a suitable house erected for that purpose, and that the county court at its first term should appoint some suitable person to open and hold elections in each civil district in said county on the first Saturday of March, 1842, to elect county officers, and that the justices of the peace of the old districts should constitute the county court until others were elected; that the citizens of the county should vote for governor and congressmen with the old counties until a reapportionment of congressional districts should be made. And by further provision of the act, Britton Holland, Wm. Dunn, Samuel Sullivan, Eason Howell and Jefferson Short were appointed commissioners to hold elections on the last Saturday of March, 1842, at four of the most public places in the county, for the purpose of selecting a suitable site for the county seat. Said commissioners were empowered to purchase a sufficient quantity of land upon which to lay off a town and name it, and to sell the lots and apply the proceeds to the payment of the land, and to defray the expense of erecting public buildings. The act also provided that Bennett Wright, Alex. Ferguson, Edward Glover and Jefferson Bratton should subdivide the county into seven civil districts, in each of which a justice of the peace and constable should be elected, and that the county should form one regiment of militia to be attached to the Ninth Brigade.

In accordance with the foregoing act, the first bench of justices of the peace for Macon County, consisting of Edward Bradley, John Henderson, Patrick Ferguson, Thomas Dodson, L. D. Hargass, James Patterson, John Claiborne and Taylor G. Gillum, met on the 7th of February, 1842, at the house of William Dunn, and organized the first county court by electing Patrick Ferguson, chairman, and Eason Howell, sheriff, *pro tempore.* Jacob S. Johnson was then appointed to open and hold elections in each civil district in the county on the first Saturday of March following to elect county officers. Before this election took place the county was subdivided into seven civil districts by the commissioners appointed for that purpose, and the election precincts established respectively at the houses of John B. Johnson, Moses Meador, John Vance, Meadowville, William Weaver, Henry Davis and John Wakefield. The elections were held at the time and places aforesaid, and the following officers were elected, to wit: Anderson Bratton, William Roberson, Charles Simmons, Haylum Pursley, Taylor G. Gillum, Jefferson B. Short, Ichabod Young, Jacob S. Johnson, Lewis Meador, William Roarke, James J. York, James Patterson and John Henderson as justices of the peace; Thomas A. Williams, clerk; King Kerley, sheriff; William Weaver, register, and Daniel O. Pursley, trustee; Thomas A. Meador, George White, Edward Barbee, Ensley Wilmore, B. Y. Turner, Bennett Wright and James G. Slone, constables. These officers all qualified and assumed the duties of their respective offices at the April term, 1842, of the county court, which was then composed of the new justices of the peace. At this term Willard Blackmore was appointed county surveyor, and Daniel Claiborne coroner. Overseers of public highways were then appointed. The commissioners appointed to hold elections on the last Saturday of March, 1842, to enable the people to decide upon the site for the seat of justice, put in nomination for such site the places of John B. Johnson and William Holland. A majority of the votes cast at said election were in favor of the former place. Accordingly the commissioners purchased of John B. Johnson, for the sum of $500, a tract of land containing twenty-eight acres, more or less, on the dividing ridge between the Cumberland and Big Barren Rivers, and on the waters of White Creek, and procured a deed for the same, dated May 26, 1842. The town was immediately laid out, containing the public square, the streets, and seventy-five lots, and named La Fayette. The job of clearing the timber from the public square and streets was let to Gilbra Seegraves for $98, and at the June term, 1843, of the county court, the work was reported completed. Prior to July, 1842, the courts were held at the house of William Dunn, and from that date until February, 1843, they were held at La Fayette, in a small log house furnished by Britton Holland, and after that date at the house of Thomas A. Williams until the courthouse was completed.

The first courthouse was a two-story brick building torty feet square, with the court room on the first floor, and a large jury room and two offices on the second. It was erected on the public square in the year 1844 at a cost of about $4,000, and stood until March 10, 1860, when it was consumed by fire. The contract for the brick work of the present courthouse was let to Robert Allen, and the wood work to Charles Carter. The walls of the building were erected in 1861, and the work was then suspended on account of the civil war until 1866, when it was completed, the total cost being about $10,000. It is a plain, substantial two-story brick building, 40x52 feet, with hall and stairs, and four offices on the first floor, and the court room and two jury rooms on the second. The first jail was a hewed log house, fifteen feet square, and was erected in 1843, in the northeast part of the town. In 1876 the county purchased from J. W. Johnson for $200, a new jail site containing one acre in the south part of the town. The same year the present jail was erected thereon by Charles Carter & Brother at a cost of $2,800. The building consists of the jail and jailer's residence combined. The jail is made of hewed logs, and the residence is a frame structure. In 1845 the county purchased from Joel Driver, for $510, a farm containing about forty acres on White Oak Creek, and six miles from La Fayette. This was fitted up as a home for the poor, and used as such until 1858, when the present county poor-farm was purchased from W. D. Coley for the sum of $760. This farm contains 100 acres, and is located one and a half miles east of La Fayette. The poor asylum consists of good and ample buildings, where the paupers, averaging from six to eight in number, find a comfortable home. The wants of a number of poor persons outside of the asylum are supplied by appropriations made by the county court.

The following is a list of county officers with date of their services: County court clerks—Thomas A. Williams, 1842–46; Jefferson B. Short, 1846–58; George L. Walton, 1858–74; T. J. Gregory, the present incumbent, continuously since 1874. Sheriffs—King Kerley, 1842–46; Bennett Wright, 1846–50; William K. Carr, 1850–54; Charles J. Bratton, 1854–58; Nathaniel M. Claiborne, 1858–64; William T. Gregory, 1864–70; John R. Holland, 1870–72; John P. Tuck, 1872–76; James W. McDonald, 1876–80; W. T. Gray, 1880–84; W. L. Tuck, 1884–86 and re-elected. Registers—William Weaver, 1842–46; Andrew Simmons, 1846–50; George L. Walton, 1850–58; James H. Brockett, 1858–66; E. G. Cartwright, 1866–70; John B. Carver, 1870–74; E. G. Cartwright, 1874–86 and re-elected. Trustees—Daniel O. Pursley, 1842–48; Moses Burnly, 1848–50; C. J. Street, 1850–54; Daniel O. Pursley, 1854–56; M. B. Johnson, 1856–60; Wash. M. White, 1860–64; Eason Howell, 1864–66; William L. Buie, 1866–70; J. W. Stinson, 1870–72; James M. Chamberlain, 1872–76; George L. Walton, 1876–80; Jesse West, 1880–86; M. B. Freeman, 1886. Circuit court clerks—Silas Pinkney, 1842–46; Elijah Gillenwaters, 1846-50; P. A. Wilkinson, 1850–68; James A. Rhoads, 1868–70; M. N. Alexander, 1870–74; James M. Marshall, 1874–82; V. M. Whitley, 1882–86; W. J. Gray, 1886. Clerks and Masters of chancery court—A. J. Wade, 1845–47; Daniel D. Claiborne, 1847–55; John Claiborne, 1855–61; E. G. Price, 1861–62; * * * James H. Brockett, 1865–67; H. S. Young, 1867–82; J. W. Eaton, 1882–86; H. C. Claiborne, 1886.

The taxable property of Macon County, as shown by the tax duplicate for 1886, consists of sixty town lots valued at $11,640, and 181,452 acres of land valued at $792,750, and personal property valued at $63,745, making a total of $868,135; and the number of taxable polls is 1,391. The total amount of taxes charged thereon is $13,670.10. The county is entirely out of debt and her warrants are redeemed at par upon presentation.

At the completion of the organization of the county the county court was composed of thirteen magistrates, but since then the county has been redistricted, and changed from seven to twelve districts, and the number of magistrates increased to twenty-six. J. C. Marshall is the present chairman of the court. The first term of the circuit court was begun and held at the house of William Dunn, on the first Monday of May, 1842, with Judge Abraham Caruthers presiding. He continued as judge of the court until 1847, and his successors in that office have been as follows, to wit: William B. Campbell, 1847–51; Alvan Cullom, 1851–52; John L. Goodall, 1852–58; S. M. Fite, 1858–61; * * * Andrew McClain, 1865–69; S. M. Fite, 1869–75; N. W. McConnell, 1875–86; John A. Fite, 1886, elected. During the war period no business was transacted in this court from November, 1861, to March, 1865. The first term of the chancery court of Macon County was begun and held in La Fayette on the fourth Monday of March, 1844, with the Hon. Bloomfield L. Ridley as chancellor, presiding. He continued to preside until 1860, and his successors in that office have been as follows, to wit: Josephus C. Guild, 1860–61; * * * James O. Shackelford, 1865–66; Thomas Barry, 1866–67; James F. Lauck, 1867–69; Charles G. Smith, 1869–70; W. W. Goodpaster, 1870–73; W. G. Crowley, 1873–86; W. W. Wade, 1886, elected. On account of the civil war this court suspended business from August, 1861, to August, 1865. The resident members and attorneys of the bar of La Fayette are I. L. Roark, M. N. Alexander, John S. Wootten, Avery Harlin and V. M. Whitley.

In regard to the participation of the citizens of Macon County in the wars of the country, it is claimed that nearly one-half of the company known as the "Polk Guards," commanded by Capt. Robert A. Bennett, and which served through the Mexican war, was enlisted in this county.

At the approach of the civil war the people of the county were about equally divided politically, and the dividing ridge through the center of the county seemed to divide them geographically—those on the north being in favor of the "stars and stripes" and those on the south being in favor of the "stars and bars." Owing to the early occupancy of the territory by the Federal Armies, only one company was raised in the county for the Confederate Army, and that was Capt. John M. Uhle's Company C, of the Twenty-fourth Regiment Tennessee Confederate Infantry. Over 200 men belonged to this company from first to last during the war. Many individuals went out of the county and joined other Confederate commands. It is estimated that about 500 men of the county served in the Confederate Armies and a like number in the Federal—there being four companies raised in the county for the latter. They were commanded respectively by Capts. Bonham, M. B. Freeman, Green Meador and Bennett Cooper. Being outside the line of the passing armies, the citizens of the county did not suffer much from the depredations of the soldiers.

The town of LaFayette, the origin of which has already been given, is situated on the dividing ridge near the center of the county, and owing to its location in a rural district, far from lines of transportation, it has only attained the size of a small village, with about 400 inhabitants. Marshall & Mansfield and Samuel Sullivan were its first merchants. During the civil war the business of the town was mostly suspended. It now contains the following business houses: Walton & Haley, general store; W. L. Chamberlain, same; M. L. Kirby & Co., drugs; Freeman & Wakefield, groceries and hardware; two hotels, the Foust House and Johnson's Hotel; two livery stables; two manufacturing establishments, known as the LaFayette Ax Handle Company, and the Turner, Day & Woolworth Manufacturing Company. The latter manufactures ax handles and other handles in general. There is also W. L. Chamberlain's combined steam saw and grist-mill and wool-carding machine. The town also contains six church societies—four white and two colored, and three church edifices, two belonging to the white and one to the colored people. The Baptist Church edifice was erected soon after the town was laid out, and the societies of the Methodist Episcopal Church, and the Methodist Church South hold their services in the Baptist Church. The society of the Church of Christ was organized in LaFayette June 19, 1869, by the labor of Isaac T. Reneau, evangelist, and the church edifice was erected in 1873. The colored people have two religious societies in the town—Methodist and Baptist—and they worship in the same house. The town also contains the Macon Male Academy, a school which is well sustained, and is open to both sexes, and a colored free school. Also LaFayette Lodge, No. 149, F. & A. M., which was chartered in 1848, and now has about sixty members. Also LaFayette Chapter, No. 96, R. A. M., with about twenty-five members. Stores, postoffices, churches and schoolhouses are scattered throughout the county to suit the convenience of the people.

The following statistics taken from the last published report of the State superintendent of public instruction will serve to show the condition of the public free schools. Scholastic population: White—male, 1,743; female, 1,845; total, 3,388. Colored—male, 164; female, 154; total, 318. Number of teachers employed: White—male, 43; female, 8. Colored—male, 3; female, 1; total, 55, the number of schools being the same. Total amount of money expended during the year, $5,835.85.

The Baptists and Methodists were the pioneer religious denominations of the county, and the churches of the county at present, named in order of their numerical strength, are Missionary Baptist, Methodist, Christian, Primitive Baptist, and general Baptist. LaFayette is connected by telephone with Hartsville, Carthage and Gallatin, and has daily communication with these towns by way of the stage line of Messrs. Day & Allen.

TROUSDALE COUNTY.

THE county of Trousdale is bounded north by Sumner and Macon Counties, east by Smith, south by Smith and Wilson, and west by Sumner. It lies in the valley of the Cumberland River, which runs through its southern portion, and in that division of the State known as the Central Basin, and contains about 110 square miles. The surface of the county is greatly diversified. The ridges extending out from the Highland Rim run into the county, and widen and flatten as they approach toward the Cumberland River, and break into numerous hills. The soil of the county is generally productive, being similar to that of most other counties in the Central Basin. The timber is poplar, oak, walnut, maple, and other varieties. The lands are drained by the Cumberland River and tributaries flowing into it from the county, of which the principal one is Goose Creek and its three forks. The geology of the county, according to the report of the commissioners of agriculture for the State is as follows: "The Nashville group of limestones is the prevailing formation, though near the river the country is cut down to the Lebanon rocks. The ridges, especially in the more northern portion, are often capped with the siliceous rocks of the Highlands. Immediately below these the black shale is always met with cropping out on the hillsides. A short distance from Hartsville, near the top of a ridge, is a bed of mill-stone grit, which has supplied Middle Tennessee with many pairs of stones. The bed is six to eight feet thick in its heaviest part. The rock is the top layer of the Nashville group, and is principally a mass of silicified shells mixed with more or less limestone matter." The settlement of Trousdale County was made with the settlement of the old counties from which it was composed, beginning about the year 1780. In an early day cotton was raised to a considerable extent, but has long since been abandoned. The principal products are now corn, wheat and tobacco. The cereal productions in 1880, as given in the tenth United States census, were as follows: Indian corn, 396,384 bushels; oats, 26,197 bushels; rye, 878 bushels; wheat, 37,284 bushels, and the number of live stock as follows: Horses and mules, 2,845; cattle, 3,397; sheep, 3,799; hogs, 10,825; and the population of the county was 6,646. For transportation the people of Trousdale County have always had to rely upon the river, the navigation of which is closed for several months during the year, or upon the Louisville & Nashville Railroad, the nearest station of which is at Gallatin, sixteen miles from Hartsville. But there is a fair prospect that the Middle and East Tennessee Central Railroad, which is now under construction, will be completed from Hartsville to its junction with the Chesapeake & Nashville Railroad, at Bledsoe Creek in Sumner County, during the year 1887, and thus give the people an outlet by rail.

The county of Trousdale was organized in accordance with an act of the General Assembly of the State, approved June 21, 1870. The act provided that a new county be established out of fractions of the territory composing the counties of Sumner, Macon, Smith and Wilson, around the town of Hartsville, to be called "Trousdale" in honor of Gov. Wm. Trousdale, and that the boundary of said county should be as follows, to-wit: "Beginning on the north bank of Cumberland River, near the house of Dr. James Alexander, in Smith County; running thence in a northeasterly direction on an arc of ten miles from Carthage to a stake on the Hartsville & Carthage Turnpike, near the house of Mrs. Bradley; thence north 45° east to Mou's Hill; thence with the meanderings of said hill to a stake in the Macon County line, near Raglan's; thence with said line some ten miles to where said line crosses the middle fork of Goose Creek, near Ephraim Parsley's; thence with the meanderings of said creek to the mouth of the west branch of the middle fork; thence up said branch with its meanders to James Barnley's, at the mouth of Love Hollow; thence due west to the Macon County line; thence with said west boundary line southward to a mulberry tree, the southwest corner of Macon County; thence on a continuation of the south boundary line of Macon County, due west to where said line intersects the east fork of Bledsoe Creek, near George Brown's; thence south to the Cumberland River, crossing the Gallatin & Hartsville Turnpike, ten miles from Gallatin, between Hallum's shop and the old toll-gate; thence up said river with its meanders to David Jackson's, in Wilson County; thence eastward on an arc of eleven miles from Lebanon to Cumberland River at the mouth of Everett branch; thence up the river with its meanders to McDonald's warehouse; thence eastwardly on an arc of eleven miles from Lebanon, near Fred Terry's and Whitson's to a point in the Smith County line between James Calhoun's house and Henry Ward's; thence on an arc of ten miles from Carthage to the beginning." By further provision of said act, E. T. Seay, S. W. Lesueur, J. S. Dyer, Howard Young, Col. Jas. H. Vaughn, Robert Burford, Cyrus H. Lauderdale, John Carr and E. P. Lowe were appointed commissioners to perfect the organization of the county by designating three voting places in the Sumner fraction, one in the Macon fraction, four in the Smith fraction and two in the Wilson fraction, where elections should be held, and each voter desiring to vote for the establishment of the new county should have on his ticket the words "new county," and those desiring to vote against the new county should have on their tickets "old county." And if upon the counting of the votes cast at said election, it should appear that two-thirds of the qualified voters in each of the aforesaid fractions of counties were in favor of the new county, then it should be established. The act also provided that said commissioners should cause the boundary lines of the county to be surveyed and marked, and they should appoint suitable persons to open and hold elections, for the election of county officers, on the first Thursday in August, 1870; and that the different courts of said county of Trousdale should be held in the town of Hartsville, and that the permanent location of the county seat should be submitted to the qualified voters of the county, at an election to be held for that purpose.

Accordingly, on the 25th of June, only three days after the passage of the aforesaid act, the commissioners appointed thereby, met at Hartsville and organized by electing E. T. Seay as chairman and S. W. Lesueur as treasurer. Suitable persons were then appointed to hold elections on the 9th of July following, at designated places in each of the fractions of the old counties, when the qualified voters thereof shall vote, according to their preferences, for or against the organization of the new county. The said elections were held and the returns thereof counted by the commissioners July 12, and the following results announced:

	New County.	Old County.
Smith County fraction	351	51
Sumner " "	359	42
Wilson " "	46	7
Macon " "	97	..
Totals	853	100

After announcing the result of the election and declaring the county of Trousdale established, the commissioners subdivided the same into ten civil districts, and defined the boundaries of each. An election was then ordered to be held in each civil district on the 4th of August, 1870, for the purpose of electing county officers. The elections were held accordingly, and the returns thereof made to the said commissioners on the following day, when it was found that the following officers were duly elected, to wit: C. H. L. Bennett, clerk of county court; B. S. Martin, register; W. A. Pursley, trustee; Archibald Allen, sheriff; Benj. W. Petway, tax collector; Thomas Patterson, clerk circuit court, and Thomas T. Stovall, John Reese, Chas. Goad, Benj. Payne, Chas. McMurry, J. S. Johnson, Hiram Warren, Geo. L. Hughes, George T. Brown, Thos. W. Browning, Wm. Locket, Edward Lewis, Joseph A. Jones, James Puyear, James R. Debow, Wm. King, E. P. Lowe, Richard Belcher, Thomas Petty and James B. Jeffreys were elected justices of the peace. The commissioners ran and marked the boundary line of the county as required by the act of creation, but slight changes of portions of it have since been made. The first term of the county court, consisting of the aforesaid justices of the peace, was held in the Methodist Church at Hartsville, beginning on the first Monday of September, 1870. James R. Debow was elected chairman, and James R. Jeffreys and Charles McMurry associate justices. An election was held on the last Saturday of November, 1870, to submit to the voters of the county the selection of the permanent location of the county seat. This election resulted in favor of Hartsville. The county purchased of H. C. Ellis, for the sum of $800, the lot on which the courthouse now stands, and received a deed for the same, dated May 12, 1876. The contract for the erection of the courthouse was awarded to Joe B. Patton for the sum of $8,945. Subsequent changes in the plan of the building, furniture for the same and fences of the lot, etc., increased the cost of the premises so that the whole amounted, according to the building committee's report, to $10,082.15. Lot 18 in the town of Hartsville was purchased for $60, as a site for the county jail, and a deed dated April 24, 1875, was procured for the same from Mary G. Reed. The contract for the jail built on said lot, was let to Bennett & Crump, and the building was erected in 1875, at a cost of about $6,000. The "poor farm," consisting of sixty-eight and one-half acres, and situate in District No. 5, was purchased from John D. Harris for the sum of $1,000, and a deed procured for the same, dated April 7, 1875. This farm is under a good state of cultivation, and has good and comfortable buildings for the accommodation of the paupers. The average number of the inmates, from year to year, is about eight, and about twice that number of poor persons are partially supported at home with their friends by appropriations made by the county court.

The following is a list of the county officers with term of service: County court clerks—C. H. L. Bennett, 1870–78; D. L. Goodall, 1878–86 and re-elected. Circuit court clerks: Thomas Patterson, 1870–72; R. M. Potts, 1872–86 and re-elected. Trustees: W. A. Pursley, 1870–72; A. M. Tinsley, 1872–76; Archibald Allen, 1876–78; Chas. Hughes, 1878–80; J. F. Wood, 1880–86 and re-elected. Registers: Benj. Martin, 1870–74; John D. Stalker, 1874–82; M. A. Wise, 1882–86; Wm. Dickens, 1886 elected. Sheriffs: Archibald Allen, 1870–76; J. M. Gleaves, 1876–82; Archibald Allen, 1882–84; D. W. Carson, 1884–86; Pleasant Sanders, 1886 elected. John D. Harris, the present surveyor of the county, has held that office ever since the organization of the same.

The tax duplicate of the county for the year 1886 shows the number of acres assessed to be 67,117, valued at $776,149, and the number of town lots, 123, valued at $71,385, and other taxable property valued at $124,898, making the total taxable property amount to $972,432. The total amount of tax charged thereon for the year is $10,210.53. The county has no outstanding bonds—is entirely free from debt, and has several hundred dollars in the treasury, with which to commence the year 1887.

The county court, the origin and organization of which has already been given, consists of twenty magistrates, presided over by one of their number chosen as chairman. The first term of the circuit court was held at the place for holding courts in the town of Hartsville, in September, 1870, with Judge W. H. Williamson presiding. He continued to preside until 1873, when he was succeeded by Judge Samuel M. Fite, who held the office until 1875. He was succeeded by Judge N. W. McConnell, who served until 1886, when Hon. J. A. Fite was elected to that office. The first term of the chancery court was begun and held February 6, 1871, with Hon. Edward H. East presiding as chancellor by interchange with Chancellor Charles G. Smith. The office of chancellor for Trousdale County has been filled as follows: Hon. Chas. G. Smith, 1871–75; Hon. Horace H. Lurton, 1875–78; Hon. B. J. Tarver, 1878–79; Hon.

Geo. E. Seay, the present chancellor, from 1879 to the present. Clerks and Masters: J. W. Johnson, 1871–74; R. S. Smith, 1874–85; J. D. Stalker, present incumbent since 1885. The bar of Hartsville consists of the following gentlemen of whom mention is made: Judge N. W. McConnell began the practice of his profession before the county was organized, and developed such ability, that he was elected judge of the circuit court in 1875, and served as such until 1886; Hon. John S. McMurry has been a safe counselor, and successful practitioner at the bar ever since it was organized at Hartsville; A. F. Burnley, John D. Andrews and W. M. Hammock are young lawyers of fine ability, and members of the bar.

Hartsville is situated on the west fork of Goose Creek, about one mile north of the Cumberland River. It was established in 1817 on the lands of James Hart, and in 1830 it contained twenty to thirty families, four stores, two taverns, and sundry mechanics' shops. The town consists of three parts, viz.: Hartsville, East Hartsville, and North Hartsville. The former, which contains all the business, lies on the southwest side of the creek, the second lies east of the creek on the Carthage Turnpike, and the latter lies north of the creek. As a whole the town has a romantic and beautiful location, and is surrounded with the most magnificent natural scenery. The original town commenced at East Hartsville, and was first called Damascus. Prior to 1830 a postoffice was established on the west side, and the business moved to Hartsville proper, and since then the combined village has been called by that name. Maj Alex Allison was the first merchant of the town, and James Dunn, and Duffey & Phelps were merchants of the place as early as 1830. James A. Andrews, H. C. Ellis, James D. Bennett, E. T. Seay, J. W. Locke, M. & P. Duffey, Frank Duffey, and J. & A. Towson were merchants in the forties, Mr. Andrews having commenced the business in 1836. In 1860 those who sold dry goods and general merchandise were James A. Andrews & Co., F. G. Harris & Co., C. L. Bennett & Co., J. & A. Towson, H. C. Ellis and S. T. Harris. There were also four or five family groceries at that time. During the civil war nearly all business was suspended, and the town was occupied from September, 1862, until the war closed, by Federal troops. Before daylight on the morning of December 7, 1862, Gen. John Morgan with a force of 1,400 men surprised and attacked Col. Moore, who occupied the town with 2,500 Federal troops, and after a sharp engagement in which the Federals lost about twenty-five killed and the Confederates ten, Col. Moore surrendered with 2,200 men—the balance of his command being cavalry escaped. Morgan had barely crossed the river with his prisoners, when the town was reoccupied with another

Federal force. The business of the town at present writing, January, 1887, is as follows: Hartsville Bank, chartered April, 1874, H. C. Ellis, president, and W. M. Wright, cashier; dry goods, Jas. A. Andrews & Co., F. G. Harris, Richard Love, B. P. Reese, John Oglesby, Herod Bros.; groceries, Hicks & Co., S. T. Harris, Jr., John Harris; drugs, P. W. Hager; saddles and harness, John Dishman, and G. W. Miller; hardware, Payne & Dayton; undertaker, Francis Throp; also a hotel, livery stable, several mechanics' shops, and a grist and saw-mill.

Newton Lodge, No. 113, F. & A. M., was chartered in October, 1845, with Humphrey Bate, W. M.; Thomas Stalker, S. W.; and Paschal Head, J. W. This lodge continues to labor with success. Hartsville Lodge, No. 378, of K. of H., was chartered October 9, 1877. The charter was granted to H. G. Donoho, John D. Stalker, R. M. Potts and others. The membership of this lodge is about sixty. On August 12, 1886, a charter was granted to Prudis Henry, Jennie King, Prussia Wise, John Henry and others, for the organization of Redemption Lodge, No. 147, of the Independent Order of Good Templars. This lodge is doing effective work in the cause of temperance.

In an early day a Union Church was erected in Hartsville, in which all the religious denominations worshiped, and about the year 1850, the Methodists erected the first denominational church in the town, and about eight years later the Cumberland Presbyterians erected their church. The Christians erected a church in 1871, and the Baptists in 1884. The Presbyterians worship in the Cumberland Presbyterian Church. At this writing these churches are supplied as follows: Methodist, Rev. Jos. Webster, pastor; Cumberland Presbyterian, Rev. W. W. Suddorth, pastor; Presbyterian, Rev. Arbuthnot; Christian, Dr. J. R. Crenshaw, elder; Baptist, Dr. Anderson, pastor. These are the prevailing religious denominations throughout the county, where church edifices have been erected at convenient distances for the accommodation of the people. In Hartsville the colored people have three churches: Methodist, Cumberland Presbyterian and Baptist, all of which have been erected since 1880. The business portion of Hartsville is sometimes damaged by reason of the "back water" from the river. The highest the water has ever been in the town was in December, 1847, when it rose until it was eighteen inches deep on the first floor of the hotel, which is still standing on the corner of Main and Church Streets. In 1883 the water was so high that a steamboat of ordinary size came up from the river, and moved on the first street north of the courthouse as far west as Church Street. The *Sentinel*, a twenty-eight column weekly newspaper, was established in Hartsville in

December, 1869, by A. C. Welch, who continued its publication about twelve years. It was then published by H. S. Kennedy until June, 1885, when it was purchased by J. M. Price, the present editor and proprietor.

The "Hartsville Female Institute," was chartered by act of the Legislature in 1856, and the charter was amended by an act passed April 1, 1879, so as to change the name to that of "The Hartsville Masonic Institute," and to admit both male and female students. Rev. James C. Bowden was the first principal of this school, and was succeeded in 1859 by Prof. (since judge) N. W. McConnell, who taught until February, 1862, when he entered the Confederate Army. And after the war closed he taught again from September, 1865, until June, 1867. His successors have been Profs. T. M. Patterson, J. M. Phillips, James E. Nowlen, H. S. Kennedy, ——— Weeden, and F. W. McConnell. The latter, who is a son of Judge McConnell, and the present principal, has taught since September, 1885. The faculty of the school, consisting of the principal and four lady assistant teachers, is able and popular. For the school year of 1885–86, there were 207 students in attendance. The buildings of the institute, which are of brick, were erected in 1879, and are located on an eminence overlooking the town, and about 100 feet above it. The Hartsville Male Academy was founded in an early day in North Hartsville, where a school was maintained until male students were admitted into the Hartsville Masonic Institute. The condition of the public schools in Trousdale County can be learned from the following statistics, taken from the last published report of the State superintendent of public instruction: Scholastic population, white—male, 806; female, 740; total, 1,546. Colored—male, 380; female, 395; total, 775. Number of pupils enrolled: white—males, 535; females, 493. Colored—males, 253; females, 263. Number of teachers employed, white—males, 12; females, 6. Colored—males, 5; females, 4; total, 27. Number of schools—white, 16; colored, 10; total, 26. Total amount expended during the year, $4,063.21. In behalf of the people it can be truthfully said that the county is well supplied with schools and churches, and there is not a drinking saloon in it.

SUMNER COUNTY.

James Alexander, a retired banker and agriculturist of Gallatin, was born in Sumner County September 27, 1813. He is the only surviving child of a family of seven children born to David and Rebecca Alexander. The father was of Scotch descent, born in 1790 in Mecklenburg County, N. C. His father and Mr. Race came to Sumner County in 1796, and purchased 640 acres of land, erecting a fort to protect themselves from the Indians. They were among the first settlers of the county. David married in 1811, and afterward located on the homestead, where he died in 1826. His wife was of Scotch-Irish origin. She died in 1831. The subject of this sketch had but limited educational advantages, as the country was new and the schools few. When quite young he became a carpenter's apprentice. Three years later he began working on his own responsibility, and for twenty years devoted himself to his trade, assisting in the erection of many of the buildings now to be seen in Gallatin. In 1850 he entered upon his career as a farmer, two miles from Gallatin, Tenn., in which occupation he has been more or less engaged ever since. Previous to the war, in connection with farming, he was an extensive stock-raiser, and very successful. In April, 1837, he married Miss Jane, daughter of John Stewart. Mrs. Alexander was born in 1809 in Sumner County, and became the mother of five children. Charles S. is the only surviving one. After Mrs. Alexander's death, our subject married Nancy J., the only daughter of Gen. Joseph Miller, who was a native of Madison County, Ky. She died in 1870, leaving Susan K. (wife of S. E. Lackey) and Jennie L. (wife of Branch Donelson). In 1871 our subject was united in marriage to Mrs. C. E. Mentloe, *nee* Norman, a native of Virginia. Both are consistent members of the Missionary Baptist Church. In 1869 Mr. Alexander was appointed claim agent of the Louisville & Nashville Railroad by the superintendent, and has held the position since that date. In 1871, at the establishing of the Sumner Deposit Bank, he was elected president, remaining such until 1884, when it was reorganized as the Farmers' & Traders' Bank, and Mr. Alexander declined to retain the position of president. He is a director and stockholder in the concern. In 1884 he deeded to his children 326 acres of land, still retaining 350 acres. He is a Democrat, was a Whig before the war, and cast his first presidential vote for Hugh L. White, in 1836. He is a Master Mason, a member of the State Historical Society, has taken all the degrees of the I. O. O. F., and is one of the oldest native born citizens of Gallatin, where he has the highest regard of the entire community.

Hon. B. F. Allen, attorney at law, of Gallatin, was born in Sumner County in 1826, a son of John and Latitia (Saunders) Allen. The father was of Irish descent, born in 1776, in Pennsylvania. In his youth he went to Virginia; soon after immigrated to Smith County, Tenn., and spent several years. He came to Sumner County about 1807, locating in Gallatin, when the following eighteen or twenty years he was engaged in merchandising. He then purchased about 800 acres of land on the Cumberland River and began farming, so continuing until his death in 1833. His wife was of Scotch origin, a native of North Carolina, born in 1792, and died in 1832. His parents came to Sumner County about 1796 and settled on the Cumberland River. Her father was an extensive land holder of that day. Our subject was bereft of his parents when a mere lad, and made his home with his brother. His education was acquired in the academy at Gallatin, and the University of Nashville where he graduated in 1844, receiving the degree of A. B. The following year he began the study of law, under tuition of his brother, Judge George W. Allen, and two years later was admitted to the State bar. After the war he formed a partnership with the above mentioned brother, which continued until the death of Geo. W. in 1881. Judge G. W. Allen was attorney-general of Sumner, Davidson and Williamson Counties for eight years, and judge of the Sumner County Court the same length of time. He was one of the most brilliant and able members of his profession. January 31, 1850, our subject married Miss Laura, eldest child of Gen. Wm. and Mary (Bugg) Trousdale. Mrs. Allen was born in Gallatin in 1828; is a member of the Presbyterian Church, and mother of Alice, wife of W. W. Berry, a druggist of Nashville; Wm. T. and M. D. of Gallatin; Valeria, Frank C. and Louise. Our subject is a life-long Democrat; cast his first presidential vote for Lewis Cass in 1848. He belongs to the I. O. O. F.; has taken all the degrees. He is a competent and successful lawyer, efficient business man, and honored citizen. He has devoted himself to the practice of his profession, and has never sought public office.

Capt. L. C. Armistead, farmer in Hendersonville, Tenn., was born near Florence, Ala., in 1842. He is one of nine children of G. G. and Alice V. (Fountain) Armistead. The father, of English origin, was born in Loudon County, Va., in 1812. A farmer and planter, he purchased of Chief Colbert a portion of the land reserved by Andrew Jackson for the Creek Nation, in Lauderdale County, Ala., where he farmed until his death in 1866. The mother, of French origin, born in the same county as her husband, in 1815, died in 1842; educated at Florence Western University and at the United States Naval School, appointed through Hon. G. S. Houston, he went to Memphis on the secession of Tennessee, and assisted in raising Company D, of which he was elected first lieutenant. He then joined the Fourth Tennessee Infantry, under Col. Nealy, and after Shiloh was made captain. He was in the battles of Belmont (Mo.), Island No. 10, Shiloh, Munfordsville, Perryville (Ky.), Murfreesboro, Chickamauga, Missionary Ridge, and in all the retreat to Atlanta, Franklin and Nashville. He was captured twice, but escaped. After his parole he began farming. At Louisville, Ky., in 1867, he married Rosalie, daughter of Hamilton R. and Jane M. (McFarland) Dobbin, born in Louisville in 1845. Their eight children are Jennie D., Harry G., Lewis H., Mary M., Carter B., George M., Charles H. and Rosalie. His wife died in 1885. She was a Presbyterian, of which church Capt. A. is an elder. Four of his children, Jennie, Hattie, Hamilton and Mary, are also members. Capt. A. is a free trade Democrat. He has lived in his present home since 1883.

Henry J. Barker (deceased) was a native of Chester, Conn., born in 1816, and a mechanic by trade. He was educated in Essex, Conn., and at the age of eighteen began selling clocks for a Connecticut firm and traveled over most of the State. He was very successful and worked at this business for fifteen years, having his headquarters at Nashville, Tenn. About 1836 he established a merchant tailor store in Nashville, where he remained for several years. September 10, 1845, he married Julia A. Farnsworth, a native of Oxford, N. Y., born in 1827, and to them were born two children: Mary (deceased, wife of William Schell) and Julia B. (wife of Capt. Samuel Lyon). In 1846 Mr. Barker came to Gallatin and began merchandising, selling cast plows, being the first man to introduce them in Middle Tennessee. In 1851 he erected a foundry and machine shop and began the manufacture of said plows. In 1854 he sold out to Jonas Nickelson, who has since been manager. In 1853 or 1854 he, Col. Munday and Moore Bros. erected a flour-mill called Spencer's Mills, but afterward Gallatin Mills. The last few years of Mr. Barker's life he and Charles Hitchcock were partners. Mr. Barker died in December, 1862, and since his death Mrs. Barker has been possessor of the mill, but it is managed by her son-in-law, Capt. S. Lyon. Mr. Barker was an excellent man, was universally respected and was a natural mechanic. During the war he was a consistent Unionist. He was a member of the I. O. O. F. and was buried by that order. He was a member of the Universalist Church and Mrs. Barker believes in the same faith. His parents were Brader and Mary (Jones) Barker.

J. R. Barry, a farmer of the Tenth District, was born three miles west of Gallatin, in 1836. He is one of six children born to the union of Thomas and Sarah H. (Peyton) Barry. The father is of Irish descent, born in 1806, two miles west of Gallatin, on the Nashville Turnpike. He began the practice of law when thirty years of age. In 1865 he was appointed chancellor and circuit judge of the Sixth District. The latter position he retained six years. He has since been a pension and claim agent a portion of the time. He now resides in Gallatin, at the advanced age of eighty-one. His wife was of English origin, born in 1812 or 1814, three miles west of Gallatin, on the Station Camp farm. She died in 1877. The subject of this sketch was educated at Gallatin. He was engaged in farming until 1866, when he was appointed clerk of the county court, retaining the position until 1882, when he resumed his agricultural pursuits. His farm is at Elmwood, six miles northeast of Gallatin, on the Scottsville pike, and contains 565 acres. In 1865 he married Martha Douglass, a native of Lebanon, Tenn. Their union resulted in the birth of Mary Elizabeth and Young Blythe; the latter died July, 1873. Mrs. Barry departed this life in 1877. In 1879 our subject married Mrs. Mary L. (Alexander) Barr, who bore him three children: John A., Sally Peyton, and Laura. Mr. Barry entered the Confederate Army in the spring of 1861, Company A, Twentieth Tennessee Regiment, under the command of Col. Joel Battle. He took part in the battles of Millsprings, Murfreesboro, and the seven days' fight before Richmond. He was discharged in the fall of 1862. He is a Democrat, and cast his first presidential vote for James Buchanan. He is a highly respected and valuable citizen.

Martin Barth, general agent for the L. & N. R. R. Co., at Gallatin, is a native of Bedford County, Penn., born in 1834, and the son of J. G. and Anna C. Barth. The father was a native of Darmstadt, Germany, born in 1802, and immigrated to the United States in 1830, locating at Baltimore, where he married. He soon moved to Bedford County, Penn. He was a musician by profession, being especially skillful on the violin and cornet. In 1866 he came to Gallatin, where he died in 1880. His wife was born in Darmstadt, Germany, in 1809; she came to America in the same year that her husband did, and is yet living. Our subject was educated in Pittsburg, Penn. In 1848 he entered a telegraph office in that city as messenger boy, and worked here for two years. The following six months he worked in Philadelphia. In 1851 he went to Louisville, Ky., and was assistant operator for four years, after which he went to Glasgow and took charge of the office. August 31, 1856, he married Mary F. Hawkins, a native of Kentucky, born in 1841, who bore him one child, still living: Harriett H. (Mrs. Benjamin F. Buckingham). Mr. Barth was in Glasgow four years, and from 1860 to 1864 was at Bowling Green, with the exception of about six months, was Sherman's operator in the late Rebellion. He was the first operator ever in Bowling Green, the office being established in 1860. In 1865 Mr. Barth came to Gallatin and assumed charge of the office at this place; he was express agent, ticket agent, operator and railroad agent for nearly eight years, when over work forced him to give up part. For the past ten years he has had assistance in the office. During the reign of cholera in 1873 he remained at his post, while nearly all the inhabitants of Gallatin fled elsewhere. Mr. Barth lost his wife in 1860, and in 1866 he married Miss Sallie Mitchell, of Union Town, Penn. He is conservative in politics, voting for principle and not for party. He is a member of the I. O. O. F., is a K. of P., and is one of the best agents on the Louisville & Nashville Railroad.

Dr. Humphrey H. Bate, a physician and surgeon, and a successful farmer of the First District, Sumner County, is a son of Humphrey and Anne F. (Weatherred) Bate, and was born in the house where he now resides, in 1844, being the eight of a family of nine children—three sons and two daughters now living. The father was of Welsh extraction, born in North Carolina in 1779, and died September 1, 1856. The grandfather, James Bate, was a son of Humphrey Bate. Our subject's father received a good common-school and business education, and when quite young was apprenticed to a ship builder and learned the carpenter's trade, which he followed for years; he also learned surveying, and was engaged with Col. Tipton in Sumner County and in West Tennessee for some time surveying. Mr. Bate was married twice, first to Miss Elizabeth Brineage, October 21, 1803, and by this marriage had six children. Mrs. Bate was born October 21, 1777, and died November 16, 1820; and September 7, 1811, he married our subject's mother. He moved to Sumner County before the death of his first wife, and soon after located on the farm where he now resides. In 1849 he moved to Texas and engaged in farming and surveying, but five years later he returned to Sumner County, where he spent the rest of his life. He was a man of marked energy and ability, and held the rank of colonel in the militia for a long time. Our subject's mother was born in Virginia, September 7, 1804, and died April 1, 1875. She was the daughter of William and Patience Weatherred. Dr. Bate's parents were both prominent members of the Missionary Baptist Church. Dr. Bate was educated chiefly at Rural Academy. He was a cousin of Gov. Bate, their mothers being sisters, and Dr. Bate's father was the grandfather of Gov. Bate. When only seventeen years of age, in April, 1861, he enlisted in the Confederate Army in Bate's Second Regiment of Tennessee Infantry, and was in the battle of Bull Run; he served a year in the Virginia campaign, then re-enlisted in the Tennessee Army, and at the battle of Shiloh received four severe wounds which incapacitated him for further service, and he has never entirely recovered from one. In 1866 he entered the medical department of the Nashville University and graduated in 1868, and after taking another course of lectures, commenced practicing medicine in Sumner County, and is now one of the leading physicians of the county, carrying an extensive and lucrative practice. October 27, 1869, he married Miss Martha A. Franklin, who was born near Hartsville in 1846, and died February 11, 1871. November 25, 1873, he married Miss Nannie D., daughter of William and Nancy S. (Cook) Simpson, of Tipton County. Two children, Humphrey and Anne, have been born to their marriage. Dr. Bate owns 300 acres of the old home farm near Castalian Springs, and is living in the house that Gov. Bate was born in, it having been built when the State was a part of North Carolina, and is one of the oldest brick residences of the county, and still in a good state of preservation. Politically Dr. Bate is a Democrat, and he is a Mason and a member of the Christian Church, his wife being an Old School Presbyterian. He is an influential citizen of the county and a popular gentleman and fine physician.

William Bates, an enterprising farmer of the Third District, was born in Wilson County, Tenn., June 21, 1843. He is the eldest of four children of John and Ann (Brown) Bates. The father was of Irish descent, born in 1820 in North Carolina, and settled in Wilson County about 1830. He was a farmer. Our subject enlisted in Company K, Eighteenth Tennessee. He took part in all of the great battles in Tennessee and Georgia. He was captured at Fort Donelson, and was exchanged. He was again captured at Atlanta, Ga., but made his escape and tried to join his regiment. He endured many hardships and privations; he had no food for eleven days. After his return home he engaged in farming on his father's place for about three years. June 20, 1867, he married Miss Sallie J. Britton, by whom he had seven children: James H., John Britton, Hinton Monroe, Tolliver, Eugene Head, William C. and Clara May. Two years after marriage Mr. Bates located on the Scottsville pike, remaining there seven years. He then moved to the east fork of Bledsoe Creek. In 1880 he settled at present place of residence. He was a Whig, but since the war has been a Democrat. He is a Master Mason and a respected, well known citizen. The entire family belong to the Baptist Church.

Alfred E. Bell, a well known farmer of the Ninth District, was born February 10, 1836, in Sumner County, the sixth of nine children of Patton and Jane (Gilbert) Bell. The father was born in Sumner County in 1808, of German descent. He was a farmer by occupation. His death occurred June 10, 1884. His grandparents came from Germany. His grandfather attained the unusual age of one hundred and six years. Mrs. Bell was born February 18, 1804, near Petersburg, Va., and came to Sumner County with her parents about 1820, and married April 28, 1827. The subject of our sketch married, November 22, 1855, Emeline C. Cline. To this union seven children have been born: Mary Jane

Amanda (now Mrs. Rutledge), Alfred P., Charley J. (deceased), Ellie Louisa (now Mrs. Garrison), Willie F., Jessie M. and Ada K. After marriage our subject purchased a farm of 150 acres near the Kentucky line. In 1865 he moved to the Third District, and farmed rented land for two years. He then came to present place of residence, and bought fifty acres, to which he has added until he now owns 300 acres of valuable land, well improved. At the outbreak of the war he enlisted and was elected captain, in which capacity he served through the campaign. He took part in the battle of Shiloh and many other severe contests. He was captured at Scottsville, Ky., and taken to Johnson's Island, in Lake Erie, September 25, 1863. He was retained there until June, 1865. He is a life-long Democrat, and cast his first presidential vote for James Buchanan. He is a prosperous agriculturist and esteemed citizen.

Bernice L. Bender, a substantial farmer of the Fourth District, was born in Sumner County, in 1857, being one of eight children, two sons and three daughters living: John S., of Wilson County; Sarah J., wife of J. C. Hubbard, of Smith County; Mollie E., wife of J. C. Frazier; Belle, wife of D. C. Douglas, and B. L. The parents were Bernice and Elizabeth (Smith) Bender. The father was born in North Carolina and came to Sumner County when a young man, locating in District No. 4 and established what is known as Bender's Ferry. He was married in Sumner County where he became a large land owner and leading farmer. He died in 1866. The mother was born in Davidson County in 1824, and is still living in Wilson County. Our subject having lost his father when only seven years old, was raised chiefly by his aunt, Mrs. Sarah Smith, and his brother-in-law, J. C. Hubbard, receiving his education in the common schools of Wilson County. He commenced life as a farmer and stock dealer, which he still continues with successful results. For three years he has lived on his farm of 150 acres of valuable land, seven and one-half miles southwest of Gallatin, and also owns a farm of 134 acres in Wilson County. He is a man of good business capacity. He was elected constable in 1882, and held the office for two years, and was deputy sheriff for a short time. He is strictly conservative in politics, adhering more to principles than to party. His first presidential vote was for J. B. Weaver in 1880. He is a consistent member of of the Methodist Episcopal Church South, and a man of undoubted integrity, liked and esteemed by all who knew him.

Col. Thomas Boyers, editor and publisher of *The Examiner* at Gallatin, was born in that city in 1826, and is the fourth of a family of twelve children born to Robert M. and Elizabeth (Banks) Boyers. The father was born in South Carolina in 1786, was of Irish extraction and a merchant by trade. In 1810 he came to Gallatin, Tenn., and traveled the distance on foot. He married in that city and afterward commenced merchandising which he continued for many years. His partner was Daniel Saffarrans. They were quite successful and invested their surplus capital in lands in Northern Mississippi, and at one time owned enough to make a strip one mile wide and 200 miles long. For some years Robert was in the commission business in New Orleans. He was one of the old citizens of Gallatin and died in 1870. His wife was born in Murfreesboro, N. C., and was of Swedish extraction. Our subject was educated in Nashville University and at an early age evinced a strong desire for journalism, and in 1847 became editor of *The Tenth Legion* in Gallatin, succeeding Gov. William B. Bate. In 1848 Col. Boyers and William M. Hutton founded *The American* in Nashville. In 1850 Mr. Hutton went to Memphis and became partner on the *Memphis Appeal*, and was succeeded on *The American* by Mr. Eastman, one of the ablest newspaper men in the State. In October, 1852, our subject married Mrs. Annie Brown *nee* O'Mahoney, a native of Ireland, born in 1826. They have three children living: Robert, Thomas and Annie (wife of Charles E. Baker). Robert is partner with his father in the *Examiner*, and Thomas is telegraph editor of the *Chattanooga Times*. In 1855 our subject retired from the *American* and returned to Gallatin where he established *The Examiner* and has since been its editor and publisher, with the exception of a few years during the "late unpleasantness." He took an active part in the war. In May, 1861, he was commissioned paymaster on ex-Gov. Isham G. Harris' staff, ranking as lieutenant-colonel. He filled the position during the war and also filled the same position on several minor staffs of volunteer service. He was with Morgan in Tennessee, and was at the battle of Murfreesboro; after said battle he was placed in command at Saltville, Va., and remained until the winter of 1865. At the close of the war he returned home, resumed his editorial work and has faithfully discharged his duty from that day until the present. Col. Boyers is a Royal Arch Mason, ancient member of the I. O. O. F. and Grand High Priest of the State at one time. In 1848 he was one of the charter members of Tennessee Historical Society. He is the oldest native born citizen living in Gallatin. Mrs. Boyers is a worthy and consistent member of the Presbyterian Church.

Robert Bryson, a substantial farmer and stock dealer living in the First District of Sumner County, is a son of James M. and Harriet M. (Hodge) Bryson. He was born in Sumner County in 1847, and was the third of a family of four children, viz.: George G., Anna R. (wife of Richard Alexander), our subject, and lady. The father was of Scotch-Irish ancestry, born in Sumner County in 1811, and was a son of Peter and Jean (Gillespie) Bryson. Peter Bryson was a native of North Carolina, and moved to Sumner County, when quite young, where he married and engaged in farming and blacksmithing until his death. James M. was raised at home, receiving few educational advantages, but through his own efforts acquired a great deal of general information. He married in January, 1839, and settled in the First District, where he lived until his death in July, 1884. He was entirely a self-made man, and one of fine character. He was captain of the militia during the general muster, and a volunteer in the Seminole war. The mother was born near Gallatin, Tenn., in 1819, and died in June, 1877. Both parents were members of the Old School Presbyterian Church, and highly esteemed in the community. Our subject was raised at home and educated at Rural Academy, and has given his time to farming and stock raising; he lives at the old homestead, owning 215 acres of productive land, well improved, seven miles northeast of Gallatin. Mr. Bryson is a man of energy and good business habits. His first presidential vote was cast for H. Seymour in 1868, and he has always been an active Democrat, and is an influential member of the Old School Presbyterian Church.

James W. Bullock, farmer and resident of the First District of Sumner County, is a son of James P. and Mildred (Didlake) Bullock. He was born in Winchester, Clark Co., Ky., in 1817, being one of twelve children, five of them living. The father was born in Virginia in 1789, and moved to Kentucky in boyhood, where he married in 1811, moving to Sumner County in 1849, and engaged in farming until his death in 1858. He was a man of ability and energy. He served as a volunteer in the war of 1812, under Gen. Harrison. In 1814–15 he was appointed clerk of the Clark County Kentucky Court, and held the office until 1845, when he was succeeded by our subject, who filled the office until 1851. David Bullock, our subject's grandfather, was the first clerk of the circuit and county court of Clark County, having been appointed to the office in 1793, and was succeeded by his son, James P. The mother of James W. was born in Virginia in 1790, and died in Summer County at the advanced age of eighty-six years. Both parents were members of the Christian Church. Our subject was raised and educated at home. July 30, 1846, he married Miss Susan, daughter of Nathan and Sallie R. Divine. They have two children: Sallie R., wife of Harvey Chenault, and Nathan Divine. Mr. Bullock moved to Sumner County in 1854, and settled on a farm where he now resides, owning 300 acres of rich land, highly cultivated and well improved, six and one-half miles east of Gallatin. He has obtained his handsome property by his own industry and good management; and is one of the best farmers in Sumner County. Politically he was formerly a Whig, but cast his first presidential vote for Van Buren in 1840; since the war he has been a Democrat. The entire family are members of the Christian Church. Mrs. Bullock was born in Mt. Sterling, Montgomery Co., Ky., in 1829. Her parents were natives of Virginia. He was of Irish, and her mother of French extraction.

Robert T. Bush, M. D. a practicing physician, surgeon and farmer, was born in Columbus, Ohio, in 1836, at his uncle's, Robert Neal, and is one of thirteen children born to Dr. Thacker V. and Narcissus (Neal) Bush. The father was born in Clark County, Ky., in 1797, and was of Scotch-Irish descent. At an early age he began studying medicine, attending lectures at Lexington, Ky., and at Cincinnati, Ohio. He established himself in business near Brownsboro, Ky., on a farm and remained here until some time between 1847 and 1850, when he moved to Sumner County, Tenn. He here purchased 327 acres near Castalian Springs, where he practiced dentistry in connection with his profession and farming. He afterward sold out and purchased a lot in Gallatin. After the war he sold this lot and went to live with his son, W. A. Bush, who lived on the upper Nashville pike, four miles west of Gallatin, where he died in 1871. The mother was born in Clark County, Ky., in 1802, and died on the farm in 1845. Our subject began his literary education at Rural Academy, Sumner County, and finished at Franklin College, Davidson County, Tenn. He then taught one term, and afterward engaged in the saw-milling business for three or four years. He then attended two courses of medical lectures at Nashville, and tendered his services to the military hospital at the same place, where he remained a few months. He then went as a supernumerary surgeon in the Seventh Tennessee Regiment to Virginia, and remained there about one year, when he came back to Tennessee. He then went in the same capacity to Mississippi in the Second Tennessee Cavalry. After five or six months' vacation interim of receiving his medical education at New York, he was assistant surgeon for three months at Soldiers' Retreat Hospital, situated at Alexandria, Va. After graduating he came back to Tennessee, and in a few years purchased the farm of 365 acres, where he now resides. He has practiced from that time up to the present date. In 1872 he married Miss Nettie E. Dobbins, daughter of Carson and Minerva E. (Roberts) Dobbins. She was born in 1846. As a result of the marriage two children were born: Robert is the only living child. Although commencing with very little of this world's goods, Dr. Bush has succeeded unusually well in all his undertakings. He has a large and lucrative practice, and his large farm is clear of debt, and is in a good state of cultivation. He is a Democrat, a dimitted member of I. O. O. F., Howard Lodge, and is also a member of the Masonic fraternity, King Solomon Lodge. He and Mrs. Bush are members of the Christian Church.

Alfred M. Burney, A. M., president of Howard Female College, Gallatin, Tenn., is a native of Williamson County, Tenn., and son of John and Matilda (Young) Burney. His parents were of North Carolina, Scotch-Irish descent, and moved to Hardeman's Cross Roads, Williamson Co., Tenn., in 1826, where the subject of our sketch was born June 4, 1833. In 1837 the parents moved to Maury County, Tenn., and settled for life near Harts Cross Roads, six miles east of Spring Hill. Having finished his education at Poplar Grove Academy, which rose upon the ruins of Jackson College and took its place, our subject was called by the trustees to the position of principal of the institution, in which he had been educated and began life as teacher of many of those who had been his schoolmates, some of whom were older than himself. In 1856 he founded McCain's Academy, six miles south of Columbia and conducted it successfully as a chartered institution under a board of trustees for five years. In the year 1858 he was united in marriage to Miss Martha M. Davis, daughter of Jas. Davis of that vicinity. She died July 1, 1861, and her infant son died on the 4th of the same month, after which the subject of this sketch returned to Maury County, Tenn., and went into the Confederate Army, having been appointed to the commissary department in Holman's battalion of cavalry, which was respectively under the commands of Gens. Wheeler and Forrest. At the close of the war he was elected principal of Mooresville Male and Female Institute at Mooresville, Tenn., and conducted this institution with the most flattering success for four years when he resigned to accept a similar position in the Robert Donnell Institute, Winchester, Tenn. During his residence at Mooresville he was united in marriage to Mrs. S. L. Nowlin, *nee* Orr, then of Waco, Tex., who was at that time spending a year with her mother to near Mooresville. In 1871 he resigned his position at Winchester, Tenn., to accept the presidency of Cumberland Female College, McMinnville, Tenn., which position he held for nearly ten years, voluntarily retiring from the college on account of his wife's health, with the unanimous endorsement of every member of the board of trustees, twelve in number. During his retirement he was strongly solicited to become the editor of the *Southern Standard*, a weekly journal published at McMinnville. Yielding to the wishes of his friends he entered upon the duties of editor and discharged them with an ability and vigor seldom witnessed in that field of journalism, boldly advocating the election of Gen. W. S. Hancock for the presidency, and Judge John V. Wright for governor of Tennessee in the campaign of 1880. In 1882, while temporarily engaged in teaching at Murfreesboro, Tenn., in a private school, he was elected president of Howard Female College at Gallatin, Tenn., and entered at once upon the discharge of the duties of that position with an energy and determination characteristic of his life accompanied with the most flattering and successful results. He is at the date of this writing closing his fifth year as president of Howard Female College, which is also the closing of the fiftieth year of the institution in its semi-centennial commencement excercises. Mr. Burney and his wife are members of the Cumberland Presbyterian Church, in which he has been a ruling elder for many years, having been moderator of the McMinnville Presbytery, a position seldom filled by any except ministers. He is also a member of the I. O. O. F., having filled every position in that order from secretary of a subordinate lodge to Grand Master of the Grand Lodge of Tennessee, and Grand Representative to the Grand Lodge of the United States. He is also a member of the order of F. & A. M., being at this date Worshipful Master of King Solomon's Lodge, No. 94, F. & A. M., Gallatin, Tenn. One peculiar feature in his history is that he never held a subordinate position, but always that of principal or president in his profession. He read a full course of law in Columbia, Tenn., preparatory to beginning its practice when the war broke out and changed the plans of his life. Another remarkable feature in his professional career is that he never sought a position and on retiring from the various positions held by him, he received the unanimous approval of every board of trustees with which he ever acted, and never had a single vote cast against an official act of his during his life to date. He made the money working at the carpenter's trade with which he educated himself, coming out at the end $100 in debt, which he paid off in a few months after he began teaching. For eighteen years after he left the paternal roof and until her death he never failed to visit his mother once a year regardless of distance, time, or expenses.

Oliver P. Butler (deceased), a merchant and farmer, was born in 1820, in North Carolina, and died at his home, seven and a half miles northeast of Gallatin in 1885. He was of Scotch descent, one of six children. He came to Tennessee at an early day with his parents, and settled at a point now known as Bracken, Tenn. He was a merchant at Fountain Head several years, and afterward engaged in farming at the same place. He had a complete and thorough medical education, but never practiced. In 1854 he married Mary Ann, daughter of Henry Sarver, of Fountain Head. To them were born two sons: Wm. F., who resides in Summer County, on the homestead, and John H., agent of the Adams Express Company at Kansas City, Mo. Mrs. Butler died about 1875. In 1879 our subject wedded Mrs. Susan M. (Brown) Parker, daughter of George T. and Amanda C. Brown, who resided in east fork of

Bledsoe Creek, eleven miles northeast of Gallatin. They were formerly of Virginia. Mrs. Butler was born on the farm now owned by Colby Chenault, eight miles northeast of Gallatin. By her former marriage there are three children: Clare, Washington T. and John R. Our subject was one of the most prosperous and successful farmers of the country. His education was secured chiefly by his own efforts. When he began life, he was the possessor of $1 but by energy and good judgment, amassed considerable wealth and valuable property. At one time he paid a security debt of $15,000 dollars. He was an enterprising, worthy citizen, well known and universally respected. He and his first wife were members of the church to which Mrs. Butler, William and John also belong.

Daniel and William Calgy, two enterprising farmers of the Third District of Sumner County, are natives of County Termaugh, Ireland, and were born about 1830 and 1840 respectively. They are the sons of Hugh and Mary (McCaulay) Calgy, natives of Ireland, and born in 1788 and 1794 respectively. The father followed agricultural pursuits for a livelihood, and in 1843 left his native country and came to the United States, preceded the year previous by his wife and son Daniel. He came to Gallatin, Tenn., and purchased 215 acres in the Third District, where he settled and passed the remainder of his days. His wife also inherited 150 acres, making in all 365. He died in 1854, and his wife in 1874. Of their four children only two are living: Daniel and William. Daniel was educated in his native county, and in Gallatin; at the early age of sixteen he left the parental roof and joined the Mexican Army, enlisting in Company I, First Tennessee Regiment, under Col. William B. Campbell, and was gone about four months. He afterward enlisted for three years in Company I, Third Regiment Tennessee, Capt. W. S. Hatton and Col. B. F. Cheatham commanders. He was discharged at Memphis in July, 1848. In 1855 he married Mary Avason, *nee* Hayse, a native of Hull, England, who died January 11, 1885. Mr. Calgy ran on the river between Nashville and Memphis, as an amateur engineer for four years. William Calgy was educated in Gallatin, and made his home with his mother as long as she lived, looking after the interests of the home place. Daniel and William have been residing on the old home place for twenty years, tilling the soil in partnership. In 1872 they erected a fine dwelling-house, it being a model of architecture and beauty. They now possess 368 acres, and are among the most influential farmers of Sumner County. October 11, 1866, William married Miss Maggie A. Witherspoon, a native of Crawfordsville, Miss., and the daughter of Dr. R. S. Witherspoon of Charlotte, N. C. The

Calgy Bros. are Democrats in politics, members of the Roman Catholic Church and are enterprising and substantial citizens.

James Campbell, a well known merchant, was born in Sumner County in 1816. He was one of fourteen children of Colin and Martha (Parish) Campbell. The father was of Scotch descent, born in 1792 in Virginia. He came to Sumner County when a small child with his parents, and located seven miles north of Gallatin. He enlisted in the war of 1812 in Capt. Wallace's company. After a year's service he returned home and married in 1814. His death occurred in 1860. He was a prosperous farmer. His wife was born in Virginia in 1794 and died in 1855. The subject of this sketch was educated in the common schools of his native county. He remained with his parents until his twenty-fifth year, when he began farming for himself, and continued until 1855, when he opened a grocery store at Castalian Springs. At the outbreak of the war he enlisted in Company E, Twenty-fourth Tennessee Regiment. On account of feeble health he served about one year. In 1869 he again embarked in the mercantile business. He has met with great success, receiving a liberal patronage. In 1872 he purchased a farm of 175 acres near the homestead. He was a Whig previous to the war, casting his first presidential vote for Harrison in 1840. He is now a Democrat and a Mason, belonging to King Solomon Lodge, No. 94, at Gallatin.

J. M. Cantrell, son of D. H. and A. L. (Gillespie) Cantrell, was born in Sumner County, Tenn., in 1837, and is a farmer and stock raiser by occupation. His father, who was of Irish descent, and a farmer by occupation, was born in Sumner County in 1801, and died in 1884. His mother was also born in Sumner County, about 1810, and died in April, 1886. Our subject received a fair education in the common schools, and assisted his father on the farm until twenty-five years of age. He enlisted in the army, and after the cessation of hostilities returned to his native county and worked on his father's farm for about a year. He was married in 1866 to Miss Cattie Milan, daughter of Andrew and T. Milan. She was born about 1842 in Sumner County, and her marriage resulted in the birth of four children: James M. (a merchant in Knoxville, Tenn.), Alice M. (attending school in Edgefield, Tenn.), Myra C. and Kittie C. Mr. Cantrell enlisted in the Confederate Army as a private in Company D, First Tennessee Cavalry, and participated in the battle of Shiloh. He has always been a Democrat in politics and is a member of the Masonic order. He, his wife and daughter Alice are members of the Methodist Episcopal Church South.

Dr. Edwin S. Carr, a physician and surgeon at Castalian Springs, Sumner County, was the only child born to the marriage of James C. and

Martha (Martin) Carr. He was born in Sumner County, February 2, 1853. Our subject's great-grandfather, Jackie Carr, was a native of Virginia, and one of the pioneers of Sumner County, being a man of prominence and ability. He wrote a history called "Early Times in Tennessee." His grandfather, Sewell Carr, was born in the part of Sumner County that is now Trousdale County. His father was born in Sumner County in 1828. He was raised and educated in the county, and was twice married: first to our subject's mother, in 1851; then to Miss Kate Harlan in 1855. He died in 1855. He was a man of good business qualifications, and an extensive dealer in live stock, and was a volunteer in the Mexican war, and a member of the Methodist Episcopal Church South. The mother was born in Sumner County in 1833, and died in 1853. She was a member of the Presbyterian Church. Our subject was raised by his grandfathers: Sewell Carr and Abram Martin. He was educated at White Creek Springs, Tenn., and in 1871 commenced the study of medicine under Dr. Woodson, of Gallatin. In 1872–73 he attended lectures at the Louisville University, and graduated from the Jefferson Medical College at Philadelphia in 1874, remaining in Philadelphia for six months as resident physician of the Presbyterian hospital. He then returned to his home and practiced until 1880, when he moved to Castalian Springs, and is regarded as one of the most successful physicians in the county and has a large and lucrative practice. Dr. Carr owns 170 acres of fine land, five and a half miles east of Gallatin on the Hartsville pike. January 14, 1875, he married Miss Eliza, daughter of Ben F. and Anna V. Jameson, of Sumner County, but natives of Kentucky. They have two children: Anna V. and James F. Mrs. Carr was born in Sumner County, in 1854. She is a faithful member of the Christian Church. Dr. Carr is a well posted man and has many friends.

William A. Chapman, farmer, was born in Sumner County in 1831, and is the son of Benjamin and Rebecca Ann (Bull) Chapman. At an early date one Philip Chapman was a merchant in England. He was the father of three sons and a daughter. One of his sons, Philip by name, went to Ireland, and some time in the first of the seventeenth century fled to the United States to escape religious persecutions. He first settled in New Jersey, and afterward in Bucks County, Penn. He had two sons and three daughters. James Chapman, the eldest son (our subject's grandfather), was a soldier and an officer of some prominence in the Revolutionary war. The tassel was shot from the hilt of his sword at the battle of Long Island. In 1773 he went to Prince Edward County, Va., and in December, 1797, he immigrated to Sumner County, Tenn., locating at King's Station, two miles south of Gallatin. He died in 1800.

Benjamin (subject's father) was born in Prince Edward County, Va., in the year 1788, and came to Sumner County with his parents and afterward settled on a part of the old home place, where our subject now lives. He afterward purchased 600 acres. He departed this life in 1861. He was a soldier in the war of 1812, and was at New Orleans under Gen. Jackson. Benjamin's wife was a native of Orange County, N. C., born in 1802. She died in 1848. They had two children who lived to be grown, our subject being the younger. He received his education in the schools of the neighborhood, and at Gallatin. In 1853–56 he made a trip through the Western States and had many thrilling adventures. February 16, 1858, he married Miss Mildred Fry who was born in Winchester, Ky., in 1832, and who is the daughter of Christopher Fry. They had four children: Cliffie, John F., Amanda E. and Sallie M. After marriage Mr. Chapman located on the old homestead and is residing there at the present time. The same tract has been in the Chapman family since 1798, it being one of the earliest settled places in the county. Mr. Chapman lost his wife December 3, 1881, and since then his most estimable daughter has been keeping house for him. Mr. Chapman is the possessor of 350 acres of land, and is one of the oldest native born citizens of Sumner County. He is very liberal, is a whole-souled gentleman and is highly respected for his many good qaalities. He is very conservative in politics, voting for principle and not for party. He and three children are members of the Cumberland Presbyterian Church; his daughter, Cliffie, is a member of the Presbyterian Church. In August, 1862, our subject enlisted in Company C, Fifteenth Regiment Tennessee Cavalry ("Ward's Ducks"), and participated in numerous severe skirmishes, being with Morgan in his famous raid through Kentucky, Indiana and Ohio. He was captured at Buffington Island July 19, 1863, and taken to Camp Morton and retained their until August, when he was taken to Camp Douglas and retained until March, 1865. He was then taken to Point Lookout, Md., where he was retained until after the surrender, being paroled June 9, 1865.

Lieut. Harvey Chenault, a prominent citizen and farmer of the First District, was born in Sumner County in 1837, being the fifth child of fourteen children, nine sons and four daughters living. The parents were David and Louisa (Quisenberry) Chenault, natives of Madison County, Ky. The father was of French ancestry, born in 1800. Our subject's grandfather was David Chenault, was a native of Virginia, and one of the pioneers of Madison County, Ky. He was a Baptist minister of ability, and possessed considerable means; he did a noble work in the church. David, Jr., was raised in Madison County; married in 1827, and moved to Sumner County in 1836; purchased a part of the "Old Greenfield tract" of land in the First District, where he spent the rest of his life farming, being one of the most extensive land owners in Sumner County. He was widely known and raised a large family of children, who inherited his many good qualities. He died in December, 1883. The mother was of German extraction and is still living at the old homestead, seventy-five years old, and a devout member of the Christian Church. Our subject was raised and educated at home. After attaining his majority he entered the mercantile business for a short time, and spent a year and a half in Texas. In 1861 he joined the Confederate Army, enlisting in Company K, Second Tennessee Infantry, as second lieutenant, and was soon promoted to first lieuteuant. He served in that regiment nearly three years; he was first in the Virginia campaign, and was then transferred to the Army of the Tennessee, taking active part in all battles that his command participated in—being in the battle of Acquia Creek, the second battle of the war. February, 1864, he was compelled to resign his commission on account of ill health. He then joined the cavalry and was sent to the Indian Territory, as quartermaster, for ten months, when he joined Douglas Texas Battery, and served until the surrender, when he returned home and resumed farming, after four years of gallant service. April, 1867, he married Miss Sallie, daughter of James W. and Susan M. Bullock. Six children were born to them, four sons and one daughter living: Anna D., William, Nathan B., Cleburne and Harvey. Mr. Chenault has always lived in the First District. In 1882 he purchased the old Gen. Winchester farm, known as "Crag Fort," six miles east of Gallatin, containing 500 acres of productive land. He is a good business man and a practical farmer, giving a generous support to all laudable enterprises. Politically he was formerly a Whig, casting his first presidential vote for John C. Breckinridge; since the war he has been a Democrat. Mrs. Chenault was born in Montgomery County, Ky., in 1846, and is a member of the Christian Church.

David Chenault, a substantial farmer and citizen of the First District of Sumner County, was born in Madison County, Ky., in 1833, and was the third child of a family of nine sons and five daughters, all living but one daughter, and all of the sons living in Sumner County but one. They are prosperous farmers and all owning adjoining farms, there being over 2,500 acres in one body, of the most fertile land in Sumner County. The father was of French descent, born in Madison County, Ky., in 1800, and a son of David Chenault, a native of Virginia, born about 1768, and died in 1852. He moved to Madison County, Ky., when ten years old, with his father, William Chenault, who was a native of France. He spent the rest of his life in Madison County, and was a man of wealth and prominence, and was a Baptist minister for over forty years. David Chenault, our subject's father, was married in 1827, and came to Sumner County in 1836, and purchased the farm on which stood the old Greenfield Fort, and he became one of the most successful farmers and extensive land owners in Sumner County. He was a man of fine character, industrious and charitable. He died in 1883. The mother was also a native of Madison County, and still lives at the old homestead in her seventy-sixth year, a faithful member of the Christian Church. The Chenaults are one of the most highly respected families in Sumner County. Our subject received a good common-school and business education. February, 1856, he was married to Miss. Martha Elizabeth, daughter of Horace and Mary (Brown) Head. Four sons and two daughters, out of the nine children born to this marriage, are living: Walker, Elizabeth (wife of Daniel C. Amos, near Bowling Green, Ky.), Lutie, Joe, David Horace and Frank. At the time of his marriage he was located in District No. 11, where he remained until 1858, when he settled below Gallatin, and in 1860 located on the farm where he now resides, and which he has since increased to 620 acres of land, well cultivated, and with a handsome brick residence on it. He is a man of fine judgment and kind heart, and a valuable citizen. He was formerly a Whig, and cast his first presidential vote for Fillmore in 1856, but since the war has been a Democrat. Mr. and Mrs. Chenault and three of the children are members of the Christian Church. Mrs. Chenault was born at Hickman, Ky., July 29, 1837; her father was a native of Orange County, Va., and her mother of Sumner County.

Milton W. Chenault, one of the leading farmers and citizens of the First District of Sumner County, is a son of David and Louisa (Quisenberry) Chenault, and was born in Sumner County in 1849, being the tenth child of a family of fourteen children, nine sons and four daughters living. He was raised at home, and received a good common-school and business education. February 26, 1874, he married Miss Nannie, daughter of Woodford and Mary Dunn, of Sumner County, formerly of Kentucky, where Mrs. Chenault was born in April, 1854. They have two sons and two daughters: Henry, Mary, Louisa and Milton W. Mr. Chenault first settled on what is known as the Sharpe farm, and in 1883 moved to the old homestead farm, where he owns 250 acres of valuable land, finely improved, and containing a handsome brick residence, situated ten miles northeast of Gallatin in a fine agricultural section, and is one of the most desirable homes in Sumner County. He is a man of fine business capacity and a progressive farmer, being well posted in the practical lessons of agriculture and stock raising, and applies modern machinery to his farming operatings. He gives a generous support to all charitable and religious enterprises. Politically, Mr. Chenault is a Democrat, casting his first presidential vote for Horace Greeley in 1872. Mr. and Mrs. Chenault are active members of the Christian Church.

Colby Chenault, a valuable citizen of the First District, engaged in farming and stock raising, is a son of David and Louisa (Quisenberry) Chenault, and was born in Madison County, Ky., in 1831, being the second of a family of fourteen children. He was raised and educated at home, and May 11, 1854, was married to Miss Araminta, daughter of B. S. and Nancy Harper, of Trousdale County, Tenn. They have nine children: James M., Alice E., Nannie L., Colby B., John W., David Seawell, Jacob Anderson, Sallie Ann and Ernest Emmett. Since his marriage he has been a resident of the First District, of Sumner County, and has lived on his present farm since 1867, owning 231 acres of land highly cultivated and well improved, ten miles northeast of Gallatin. Mr. Chenault rendered about thirteen months' active and gallant service during the late war (1862–63), under Gen. Morgan. He is a man of energy and good business qualifications, kind hearted and strictly honest. He was formerly a Whig in politics, and cast his first presidential vote for Gen. Scott, in 1852. He is a prominent Mason, and a valuable citizen. Mrs. Chenault was born in the part of Sumner County that is now Trousdale, in 1836, and is an active member of the Methodist Episcopal Church South.

William Chenault, a successful farmer and prominent citizen of the First District, of Sumner County, is a son of David and Louisa (Quisenberry) Chenault, and was born in Sumner County, in December, 1853, being the twelfth of fourteen children. He was educated at Rural Academy, and at the male academy, at Gallatin, and then completed a course of study at the Nashville Commercial College. May 3, 1882, he married Miss Lydia W., daughter of Col. Wm. H. and Sarah W. (McDaniel) Hall, both natives of Sumner County, the former a son of Gen. and ex-Gov. Hall. Mrs. Chenault was born in Sumner County, December 21, 1861. They have three children: Anna Louise, Mattie and Mollie Hall. Mr. Chenault first settled on east fork of Bledsoe Creek, and remained until 1886, when he moved to his present home, one mile south of the first place. He owns 240 acres of rich land nine miles east of Gallatin, on the Greenfield Pike. He is a thorough business man and energetic, and progressive in his ideas about farming, a kind neighbor and an upright citizen. His first presidential vote was for S. J. Tilden in 1876. Mr. and Mrs. Chenault are both consistent members of the Christian Church.

M. F. Chenault, one of the most successful young farmers of Sumner County, residing in the First District, is a son of David and Louisa (Quisenberry) Chenault; was born in Sumner County in 1856, being the thirteenth child of a family of fourteen children, nine sons and four daughters living. He was raised at home and received his education at Rural Academy and at Gallatin. When he attained his majority he commenced farming for himself and has proved that he has a practical knowledge of the business by his marked success. He owns 150 acres of valuable land in one of the most fertile sections of the county, ten miles northeast of Gallatin. Politically Mr. Chenault is an ardent Democrat, and his first presidential vote was for Gen. Hancock, in 1880. Mr. Chenault contributes liberally to the support of all educational and religious enterprises, and is exceedingly popular in his county.

Charles C. Chenault, a practical and progressive young farmer of the First District of Sumner County, engaged also in stock raising, was born in the county in 1858, being the youngest of fourteen children born to the marriage of David and Louisa (Quisenberry) Chenault. He was raised at home and received his early education at Rural Academy, finishing at Stonewall College, in Robertson County. After reaching his majority he turned his attention to farming, and by his energy and clear judgment has placed himself in rank with Sumner County's most enterprising and progressive farmers. He owns 280 acres of fine land in the First District, ten miles northeast of Gallatin. In politics Mr. Chenault votes with the Democratic party, his first vote for a president being cast for Gen. Hancock, in 1880. He is a consistent and useful member of the Christian Church and is a young man of influence and integrity.

Robert Collier, a well known and enterprising farmer of the Tenth District, was born in Shelby County, Ky., in 1831. He is one of six children of Thomas and Susan (Parker) Collier. The father was of Irish descent, born in Virginia in 1800, and emigrated west with his parents when a small child. He remained with them until his majority. Previous to the days of railroads he was engaged in hauling goods by wagons. In 1847 he moved to Sumner County and purchased a farm of 100 acres, eleven miles northeast of Gallatin. He settled there, tilled the soil in connection with his wagoning until his death in 1850. His wife was of Irish descent, born in 1803, ten miles northeast of Gallatin. She died in 1872, at subject's home, seven miles north of Gallatin. The subject of this sketch was principally educated at the Rural Academy, Sumner County. In 1856 he married Margaret A., daughter of George W. and Rebecca (Peyton) Parker, and granddaughter of John Peyton, one of the first surveyors of Tennessee. The marriage took place at the Parker farm, where Mrs. Sue M. Butler now resides. To this union thirteen children were born, of whom are living John P., Daisy, Patty M., David H., Susan, Elizabeth, Leon Hix and Maud. Those deceased are Lulu, Thomas Nathaniel, Claud and Parker. At time of marriage our subject purchased a farm of 175 acres near the homestead. Fourteen years later he bought the place upon which he now resides. In the fall of 1861 he entered the Confederate service, enlisting in the Forty-fourth Tennessee Regiment. In March, 1862, he went home on a furlough, and while at home became very sick with typhoid fever, on account of which he did not return to the army. He was a successful stock trader, shipping thousands of mules to New Orleans, and large numbers of cattle to Louisville, Buffalo and New York. He is one of the most progressive and prosperous agriculturalists of the county. He is a stanch Democrat, casting his first presidential vote for Pierce. Two of his daughters, Daisy and Patty, are members of the Old School Presbyterian Church.

T. J. Crenshaw, resident and farmer of the First District of Sumner County, is the son of John and Eliza Ann Crenshaw, and was born in Sumner County February 26, 1862, being the seventh born of eight children. Two sons and four daughters are living: Oria G., wife of Daniel Harper (deceased); Dabney; Elizabeth, wife of F. F. Harris; Martha F., wife of John R. Green; Thomas J., and Anna E. The father was born in Kentucky in 1819, being the son of Dabney Crenshaw, who was a native of Virginia. He received a limited education and moved to Sumner County when a young man, where he married, December 3, 1845, and farmed as a tenant until 1850, when he purchased a farm for himself where the family now resides. He was a man of good business ability and great energy, and held the office of magistrate for a number of years. He died in 1882. The mother was born in Sumner County in 1823 and died in March, 1881. Both parents were members of the Methodist Episcopal Church South, and highly esteemed in the community. The farm consists of 200 acres of fertile land, containing substantial improvements; part of the house was built in the year 1800, being one of the oldest houses in the county, and is two miles northeast of Castalian Springs. Our subject was raised at home and educated at the common schools in the county, and has charge of the old farm. In politics he is a Democrat and his first presidential vote was cast for Cleveland. Dabney Crenshaw was married in October, 1872, to Miss Susan Browning, and they have five sons and three daughters. Our subject is a young man of good character and is enterprising and energetic, and a most useful citizen.

S. E. Cummings, a farmer of the Ninth District, was born January 19, 1830, in Clark County, Ky. He is the second of eight children born to Malachi and Edith (Brooksher) Cummings. Both parents were also natives of Clark County, and of English descent. The father was born in 1802; a prosperous farmer. He moved to Sumner County, Tenn., in 1841, and died March 2, 1842. His wife was born January 10, 1802. The subject of this sketch was quite young when his father died. He remained on the farm and assisted his mother in raising a large family. December 22, 1872, he married Miss Sarah E. Fonville, a native of Sumner County, of French-English origin, born in June, 1836. Their union resulted in the birth of three children: John E., Thomas E. and Mabel. By his wife Mr. C. received fifty acres of land, and purchased another fifty, making a fine farm. It is situated on the Red River Turnpike, four and a half miles from Gallatin. He is one of the county's most energetic and enterprising agriculturists and worthy citizens. He is a member of the Methodist Episcopal Church South. He was formerly a Whig, but now affiliates with the Democratic party.

James Darnall, farmer and stock raiser of the Second District of Sumner County, is a son of John S. and Elizabeth (Dassy) Darnall, and was born in Sumner County in 1827, being one of nine children, seven living. The father was born in Maryland in 1784; was raised in that State and married there in 1809, moving to Sumner County in 1819, and continued farming in that county until his death in 1852. He was a volunteer in the war of 1812. The mother was also a native of Maryland, born about 1782, and died in 1854. Our subject had limited educational advantages. October 19, 1854, he married Miss Amelia T., daughter of James and Jane Hamilton, both natives of Tennessee. Mrs. Darnall was born in Sumner County in 1836, and they had ten children, four sons and two daughters living: Ida, Taylor, Robert Lee, Ernest, Effie and William T. Mr. Darnall has been living on his present farm since 1859. He owns 205 acres of very productive land, pleasantly located three and one-half miles southeast of Gallatin. He has been a man of frugal and industrious habits. In politics has been a life-long Democrat; his first presidential vote was cast for Gen. Cass in 1848. Mrs. Darnall is a member of the Methodist Episcopal Church South.

Thomas J. Day, proprietor of the Day House, and partner in Day & Allen's livery stable, was born in what is now Trousdale County, Tenn., in 1831; son of Isaac and Elizabeth (Scott) Day. The father was born in 1804, in North Carolina, of Irish ancestry. He died in 1885. His first wife was a native Tennessean, and died in 1841. His second wife was Nancy Stubblefield, and she is also dead. Thomas J. remained with his parents until the age of nineteen years. In 1851 he wedded Martha J. Allen, and shortly after this event he became a partner in a wool factory and cabinet shop at Hartsville, a business in which he has ever since continued. His partner in this enterprise was Arch Allen, who has always continued with him from the first. In 1861 they secured control of the stage line between Gallatin and Hartsville, and are now running two daily stages between these points, and also between Hartsville and LaFayette, carrying the mails on each line. Since 1864 Mr. Day has lived in Gallatin. In 1885 his livery barn, together with eighteen horses, burned; but with commendable pluck he immediately rebuilt and restocked, and now has a finely equipped livery barn. His first wife died February 18, 1874. May 2, of the same year, Mrs. Maggie V. (Sweetland) Powell became his wife, and they have one son, Archie. Mrs. Day by her first husband has four children: Annie, Eddie, Minnie and Carrie. In 1880 Mr. Day began keeping hotel. He is an Odd Fellow, a Democrat, and Mrs. Day is a Missionary Baptist.

A. B. C. Dickenson was one of the early settlers of the First District of Sumner County. He was born in Virginia in 1817, and is a son of James I. and Nancy (Brown) Dickenson, being the fifth of six children born to their marriage, only the youngest two surviving. The father was of English descent, born in Virginia in 1774; was raised and educated in that State, and married there in 1801, moving to Sumner County in 1818, settling on the farm where our subject now resides. He died September 11, 1827. The mother was born in Virginia in 1785, and died February 21, 1864, a member of the Methodist Episcopal Church South. Our subject was raised by his mother, and educated at Rural Academy and at Hart College, then spent several years teaching. He remained on the farm with his mother until his marriage to Miss Susan, daughter of Ephraim and Susan Pussley, December 7, 1846. Five children were born to them; one son and two daughters are living: Nancy V., wife of J. W. Whiteside; Ephriam P. and Leonora A., wife of Walter Boensch. Mr. Dickenson owns 180 acres of rich and well improved land, two miles northeast of Castalian Springs. When he first built his present home it was almost a forest, but is now under a high state of cultivation. He is one of Sumner County's most enterprising farmers, and is a man of strict integrity, and an ardent advocate of education and prohibition. His first presidential vote was cast for Van Buren in 1840. Mr. and Mrs. Dickenson are both members of the Methodist Episcopal Church South. He was elected steward of the Bethpage Church April 7, 1849, and was elected recording steward of Green Grove Church in August, 1853, and has attended every quarterly meeting but four for thirty-two years. He is a man of influence and fine moral character.

J. B. Donelson, of Gallatin, is a native of this county, his birth occurring in November, 1850. His father, Gen. Daniel S. Donelson, was born in 1801 in Sumner County, Tenn., and at the age of fifteen years was appointed to the West Point Military School through the influence of Gen. Jackson, graduating with the first honors of his class when in his twentieth year. Declining an appointment in the army he returned to the "Hermitage," his home in his native State, and lived with Gen. Jackson until his marriage with Miss Margaret Branch in 1830. He farmed extensively, acquiring a homestead of 1,139 acres, and several times was elected to the State Legislature, at one time serving as speaker of the Lower House. On the breaking out of hostilities between the North and the South he was appointed adjutant-general and in erecting the fort near Dover it was named Donelson in his honor. Later he was appointed brigadier-general and assigned a command in West Virginia. He distinguished himself in the battles of Perryville, Cheat Mountain and Murfreesboro, at the latter engagement having a horse shot dead from under him. By exposure he brought on illness so that a part of the time he was not in active field duty. He was, however, promoted to major-general for bravery and meritorious conduct. He died, lamented, April 17, 1863. A brother of Gen. Donelson was a candidate for vice-president on the Fillmore ticket in 1856, and was United States minister to France under President Jackson. His wife was born in 1814, and was a daughter of John Branch, a governor of North Carlina. She died in 1871 after bearing eleven children, nine of whom are yet living. J. B. Donelson, the immediate subject of this sketch, was educated in his native State and Florida. He began clerking in a boot and shoe house in Nashville in 1873 and in 1875 embarked in the trade on his own responsibility. Two years later he came to Sumner County and began farming and has continued at that and stock dealing until the present. He is a Democrat and a member of the K. of P. and Iron Hall fraternities and he and wife belong to the Missionary Baptist Church. To his marriage with Miss Alexander, which occurred in 1874, two children have been born: Rebecca and Alexander.

H. C. Dorris, farmer and owner of saw mill in Sumner County, District No. 8, was born in Robertson County, in 1843. He is one of eight children of Roland B. and Eveline (Jones) Dorris. The father, of Irish origin, born in 1807 in Robertson County, was an able Baptist minister and missionary. He died in 1872. The mother, a native of the same county, died when our subject was very small. Educated in Robertson and Sumner Counties, our subject began for himself when twenty-three years old, by engaging in the saw mill business. In 1865 he married

Sopha W., daughter of William and Emma Clark, and native of Sumner County. Their eight children are Eddie, Roland B., Clark, Levy B., Henry C., Vernen, Oscar and Eleanor. Politically Mr. Dorris is a Democrat. His wife and son, Roland B., are members of the Methodist Episcopal Church South.

Cullen E. Douglass, a farmer of the Ninth District, was born May 29, 1825, in the district where he now resides. He is the fifth of six children born to William Howard and Sarah (Edwards) Douglass. The father was born in 1782 in Sumner County of Scotch descent; a farmer and at one time an extensive slave trader. He died July, 1834. His wife was born October 4, 1788, on the farm upon which our subject lives. Her father came to the county at an early day. Mrs. Douglass departed this life March 5, 1865. The subject of our sketch married Miss Harriet Newell Bain April 4, 1848. Their union resulted in the birth of ten children, Henry E., Sarah E. (now Mrs. Brinck), William A., Eliza B., John R. B., Nannie, Delia, Juliet Glass (now Mrs. Zdanowitz), R. Edwards and Sophia. Mrs. Douglass was an estimable and energetic woman. Her death occurred December 20, 1862. Our subject wedded Miss Mary E. Estes. Eight children were born to this union: Robert Estes, Harriet B. (deceased), J. Glass, Cullen E., Mary, William E., David and Irene. Mr. Douglass has been a school director, magistrate and commissioner for the poor for the past twenty years. For a number of years he has been an elder and deacon in the old school Presbyterian Church, to which his family all belong. He is a strict temperance man and never uses tobacco. He is a successful and enterprising agriculturist. His farm contains 260 acres of the most productive soil. On his place was originated the noted Douglass peach. The farm is known all over the country as Variety Grove. Mr. Douglass was originally a Whig, casting his first vote for Henry Clay. He is conservative, but takes most interest in the Prohibition party.

Capt. C. S. Douglass, A. B., A. M., superintendent of public instruction of Sumner County, was born in that county in 1839, and is the son of Col. Young N. and Benetta (Rawlings) Douglass. The father was of Scotch-Irish descent. At an early date three brothers, natives of Scotland, immigrated to the United States; one settled in Middle Tennessee, one in Virginia and one in North Carolina, Stephen A. Douglas being of the northern branch; James Douglass, our subject's grandfather, being of the North Carolina stock. He was born in North Carolina in 1762, and when quite young came to Sumner County, where he married in 1777. He died in 1851, aged eighty-nine. Col. Young N. Douglass was born in Sumner County in 1805 and followed the occupation of a farmer. He married in 1834, and afterward located in Gallatin and began merchandising. He afterward engaged in farming, and was very successful in this occupation. He died in 1865. He was captain of one of the first military companies organized in the county. He was afterward known as Col. Douglass. His wife, Benetta (Rawlings) Douglass, was a native of Sumner County, born in 1813, and the daughter of Dr. Benjamin Rawlings, who was a pioneer physician of Middle Tennessee. Mrs. Douglass died in 1849. Mr. Douglass was twice married, his second wife being D. Killebrew, *nee* Green. There were six children born to the first union, our subject being the third. He received his rudimentary education in the schools of his native county, and his collegiate education at Center College, Danville, Ky., graduating from that institution in 1860, from which he received the degree of A. B. In 1884 the same institution conferred upon him the degree of A. M. After completing his schooling he commenced the study of law. About this time hostilities between the North and South commenced and he entered the army. He organized Company H, Thirtieth Regiment Tennessee Infantry, and was at once commissioned as adjutant, with title as first lieutenant. At the battle of Fort Donelson he was captured, taken to Camp Chase, and from there to Johnson's Island, being retained seven months. He was then released, and at the reorganization of the army joined Company H, Thirtieth Regiment Tennessee Infantry of Robertson County, and was elected captain. He was afterward appointed as adjutant-general, and served in this capacity the remainder of the war. He participated in all the principal battles and many severe skirmishes, being in eighteen regular pitched battles. He was wounded in the left arm and had a horse shot from under him at Jonesboro. He was a brave and skillful officer and did much hard fighting. July 23, 1865, he married Miss Susan Graham, a native of Sumner County, Tenn., born in 1845, and the daughter of Dr. Alexander Graham. To them were born two children: Ada and St. Clair. In 1871 Capt. Douglass, in conjunction with Prof. C. W. Callender, organized the Sumner High School in Hendersonville at a cost of $2,100. At the end of two years Prof. Callender was elected superintendent of public instruction, and our subject assumed the principalship of the school, holding this position seven years, and also filled an unexpired term in the male school in Gallatin. In 1880 he was elected to his present position by the county court. In 1884 and 1885 he was principal of the normal school in Gallatin. He is a member of the Teachers' State Association of Tennessee, and in 1883 he was president of the association. He was vice-president of the same at one time, and is now a member of the executive committee. He is a Democrat in politics, and in 1878 ran for the Legislature, but was defeated by sixteen votes. He was Worshipful Master of the Masonic fraternity, a member of the K. of P., and he and wife are members of the Methodist Episcopal Church South. He has been superintendent of the Sunday school for fifteen years. He is a prominent and influential citizen, and one of the leading educators of the time.

Reuben Douglass, a prominent farmer and stock dealer of the Eighth District of Sumner County, is a son of Wiley J. and Eliza (Watkins) Douglass, and was born in Sumner County in 1831, being one of a family of five sons and one daughter, four living. The father was of Scotch extraction, born in Sumner County in 1792, and the grandfather, Reuben Douglass, was a native of North Carolina and one of the earliest pioneers of Sumner County. Wiley J. was married twice, first to our subject's mother in 1819. She was born in Sumner County in 1802 and died in 1832. In 1844 he married Miss Grimm. They had three sons and two daughters. He was one of Sumner County's most influential citizens and large land owners, and died in 1866. Our subject was raised and educated in Sumner County and in Gallatin, and has always been a farmer and stock raiser, owning 150 acres of good land, six miles northwest of Gallatin. In 1861 Mr. Douglass enlisted in the Confederate Army, Company B, Fifteenth Tennessee Cavalry, under Gen. Morgan, being with him on his famous raid through Indiana and Ohio, and was captured at the same time in 1863, taken to Camp Chase, Ohio, then to Camp Douglas, Ill., and a short time before the surrender was taken to Point Lookout for exchange, but by that time the war closed, and he returned to Sumner County after four years of gallant service. In May, 1881, he married Mrs. Margaret Turney, *nee* Davis. Politically he was formerly a Whig, and his first presidential vote was for Gen. Scott in 1852, and since the war has been very conservative in politics. Mr. and Mrs. Douglas are active and useful members of the Methodist Episcopal Church South. He is well known throughout the county, and liked and esteemed by all as an upright man and a true friend.

William Read Duffy, a resident of the First District of Sumner County, engaged in stock raising and farming, is a son of Michael and Cornelia (Read) Duffy, and was born in what is now Trousdale County, in 1849, being one of five children, three living: William R., Hon. Hugh C., living near Cynthiana, Ky., and Micha Ella. The father was a native of Ireland, and came with his father, Charles Duffy, to the United States when about six years old. They located in Sumner County where he was raised, and he commenced life as a merchant and general trader at Hartsville with his brother, Pat Duffy, the firm being M. & P. Duffy, and they continued the business for many years. Our subject's father was a man of good business capacity, and at one time represented his county in the Legislature, and at the time of his death was tax collector. He died at Castalian Springs, in 1858. The mother was born in what is now Trousdale County in 1819, and was a daughter of Capt. William and Polly (Bledsoe) Read, and is still living near Hendersonville, a member of the Methodist Episcopal Church South. She was married in 1860, to George W. Terry. Our subject was raised by his mother, but, during the war, was with his uncle, Frank Rogan, and was educated at the neighboring schools, finishing at Rural Academy. He commenced farming on his own responsibility when only seventeen years of age, and has since successfully continued, with the exception of a few years—1876 to 1879—spent in Texas and other Western States. Mr. Duffy owns 216 acres of a farm of 336 acres six and a half miles east of Gallatin, and it is one of the best farms in that section. He has been quite extensively engaged in stock raising in connection with his farming, and has met with success. Mr. Duffy's first presidential vote was cast in 1872 for H. Greeley. He is a most worthy citizen of Sumner County.

John G. Dunn, farmer and stock dealer, near Hendersonville, Tenn., was born in Sumner County, August, 1826. He is one of seven children of Albert G. and Amanda (Gowen) Dunn. The father, of Irish and Scotch origin, was born near Nashville, Tenn., in 1804. Since 1825 he has farmed near Hendersonville. The mother, born in 1806 where the asylum is now located, near Nashville, died in 1868. With common-school advantages and those of Robertson Academy, in Davidson County, our subject began for himself as farmer when eighteen years of age. In 1846 he married Susan, daughter of William and Elizabeth Shaw, and a native of Sumner County. She died in February, 1848. In December, 1849, he married Margaret D., daughter of Thos. and Sallie (Smith) Watson, and born in Wilson County in 1834. Their three children are Mary L., Sallie W., and Harry S., passenger conductor from Pensacola, Fla., to Repton, Ala., who began running a train when twenty years old. In 1885 his second wife died; she was a member of the Methodist Episcopal Church. A Whig previous to the war, Mr. Dunn has since become a Democrat. His children are all members of the Methodist Episcopal Church South.

J. Edwards, farmer and stock raiser, near Saundersville, was born in Norfolk County, Va., in March, 1815. He is one of five children of Thos. and Mary (Bartee) Edwards. The father was born in England in May, 1765, and came to Rutherford County in 1818 as a farmer; he died in 1849. The mother, of French origin, was born in Norfolk County,

Va., in 1782, and died in 1857. With common-school advantages, he began for himself, at eighteen, as salesman for J. R. Daniel & Co., of Murfreesboro. Two years later he took a like position with John W. Walker & Co., general merchandise, Nashville, of which firm he became partner. In 1848 he married Sarah E., daughter of Thos. and Calpurnia (Gray) Keenan, and born in Courtland, Ala., in 1829. Their four children are Sarah A., wife of John F. McCreary, traveling for Goodell, Lite & Jones, Nashville; William H., farmer; Mary B., wife of J. W. Foster, lumber dealer, White Bluff, Tenn., and Jos., Jr., bookkeeper for Cowan & Co., Nashville. Previous to the war a Whig, he has since been a Democrat. His wife and two daughters, Sarah and Mary, are members of the Presbyterian Church. Since 1859, when he bought his present 316 acres, he has lived in Sumner County.

Maj. M. S. Elkin (deceased) was a legal practitioner of Gallatin and a native of Scott County, Ky. He was born in 1840, and was the son of Robert and Lucy (Quisenbery) Elkin. The father was a native of Kentucky and came to Sumner County about 1848, where he has since resided. His wife was a native of Kentucky, and of French descent; she died in 1863. After her death Mr. Elkin married Mrs. Lucy Morris, *nee* Prestage, of Virginia. To the first marriage were born five children, our subject being the eldest. He was but eight years of age when his parents came to Sumner County. He was educated at Gallatin and at Cannelsburg, Penn., where he attended school two years. When the war broke out between the North and South he abandoned his studies and entered the army. November, 1865, he married Miss Mattie C. Moore, a native of Logan County, Ky., born in 1845, and the daughter of Josiah and Mary S. Moore. This union resulted in the birth of four children: Willie Conn, Lucy, Mary S. and Milton S. Immediately after the war Mr. Elkin commenced the study of law under Col. John W. Head, and in 1866 was admitted to the bar. He then commenced practicing and for a number of years was a law partner of Maj. W. S. Munday. Maj. Elkin rose very rapidly in his profession, and soon became an able lawyer and an eloquent speaker. The last fifteen years of his life he ranked as one of the best advocates of his profession in Sumner County. He was logical in his arguments and convincing in his manner of speech. He died December 27, 1884, while yet in the prime of life. When Mrs. Elkin was two years of age she was taken by an uncle and aunt—W. B. Conn and wife. Mr. Conn was a native of Burford County, Ky.; he died November, 1860, aged seventy-eight. His wife, Martha (Herndon) Conn, was born in Scott County, Ky., in 1821, and is now living with Mrs. Elkin. Maj. Elkin was a member of the K. of P., the

K. of H., also member of the Masonic fraternity, being Worshipful Master. He was city attorney of Gallatin for one term. He was a member of the Missionary Baptist Church, of which his wife is now a member.

Rev. M. R. Elliott, attorney-general for the Tenth Judicial District, was born in Lawrence County, Ala., in 1835. He is one of seven children of Samuel and Frances (Ratcher) Elliott. The father, of Scotch-Irish origin, was born in Wilson County, Tenn., in 1804. A farmer and cotton-planter by occupation, he went to Lawrence County, Ala., when a boy and began farming, and, although offered office, he clung to his favorite pursuit and lost all his wealth by the war. He was director for the Memphis & Charleston Railway for several years. He died in 1872 at his home in Lawrence County, Ala. The mother, of Irish descent, was born in Morgan County, Ala., about 1812, and died in 1842. Our subject received his literary education in Virginia and graduated from the Lebanon Law School in 1857. He began practice as partner of Gen. Robert Hatton, of Lebanon, Tenn. In 1860 he married Margaret, daughter of William and Eveline (Douglass) Franklin, and born in Sumner County in 1837. Their four children are William F., physician in Hendersonville, Tenn.; Jennie M., wife of J. W. Knight, druggist, Gallatin, Tenn.; Samuel R., clerk in a drug house in Bowling Green, Ky., and Benjamin D., at college in Hartsville. Enlisting in 1862 as private in Capt. Russworm's company, he soon was appointed ordnance officer and was in the battle of Hartsville. After Morgan's capture, on account of ill health, he was assigned to post duty. After the war he practiced his profession in Sumner County until, on account of his wife's health, he moved to his present home. Our subject was an elector in the Bell and Everett campaign of 1860, and was nominated by the Democratic party to represent Sumner County in the State Legislature, but he declined on account of his wife's health. In August, 1886, he was elected to his present office. Mr. Elliott is a minister in the Methodist Episcopal Church, of which denomination all his family are members. He is a brilliant speaker and ranks as one of the best orators in Tennessee.

Dr. John W. Franklin, physician and farmer of the Fourth District, is a son of John and Elizabeth (Rawlings) Franklin, and was born in Sumner County in 1819, being the ninth child in a family of seven sons and three daughters. The father was of Irish ancestry, born in Sumner County in 1776. The grandfather, James Franklin, was a native of West Virginia; he went to Eastern Kentucky when a young man, where he had an elder brother, and finally moved to what is now Sumner County, where he erected a station, Camp Fort, and made his future home. Our subject's father had no educational advantages, but was a man of clear judgment and general information. He was married in 1795. In early life he followed flatboating to Natchez and other southern points. He was one of Sumner County's largest land owners and planters and a wealthy citizen, and was sheriff of the county at an early day. He died in 1832. The mother was a native of Sumner County, being about four years younger than her husband. She died in 1866, a member of the Methodist Episcopal Church South. Dr. John W. Franklin was raised at home until about fourteen years old, when he was sent to Hallowell's Quaker School, at Alexandria, Va., where he remained four years; then returned home and began the study of medicine under Dr. John J. Franklin, and eighteen months later entered the Transylvania Medical University, at Lexington, Ky., where he graduated in 1841. February 10, 1842, he was married to Miss Florida, youngest daughter of Rev. Dr. Silas M. and Maria W. Noel, of Frankfort, Ky. Two sons and one daughter were born to them: Adele, wife of George L. Van Bibber, of Bel Air, Md.; John A. (deceased), and Dr. Edward N., of Gallatin. Mrs. Franklin was born at Frankfort, Ky., in 1826, and died in January, 1848. May 3, 1849, he married Miss Sarah F., daughter of Thomas A. and Lucy Baber, who was born in Sumner County February 17, 1831. Her parents were both natives of Virginia; her father was born in 1796, her mother in 1804. Six sons and three daughters were the result of this union; one daughter died. The children were Lucien B., of Nashville; Ernest; Thomas B., freight cashier of the Baltimore & Ohio Railroad, at Wilmington, Del.; Blanche; James W., of Maryland; Robert L.; Benjamin H. and Mabel. Dr. Franklin commenced the practice of medicine in 1842 at Memphis, Tenn., where he remained until 1845, when he moved to Gallatin, Tenn., and has since lived in Sumner County, with the exception of one year, 1847-48, which he spent in New Orleans. In 1852 he bought the farm where he now resides, four miles west of Gallatin on the Nashville pike, and has continued the practice of medicine in connection with farming. He has been very successful as a physician and has had an extensive and lucrative practice, and is one of the leading physicians of the county. Dr. Franklin owns 162 acres of very productive land with a commodious brick residence and other substantial improvements. Early in 1861 he was appointed surgeon of the Seventh Tennessee Regiment, but was compelled to return home the same year on account of ill health, and was soon after placed in the brigade staff and entered the Virginia campaign. Politically he has always been a Democrat and cast his first vote for Martin Van Buren.

in 1840. Dr. Franklin is a Mason, and one of the two oldest members of the I. O. O. F. of Sumner County, and is a member of the State Medical Association and of the American Public Health Association. Dr. and Mrs. Franklin are active members of the Old School Presbyterian Church. He is a man of culture and an able physician, and is exceedingly popular in his town and county.

Ernest Franklin, farmer, was born in Sumner County in 1854, and is one of twelve children (two of whom are dead) born to Dr. John W. and Sarah Baber Franklin. The father was born in Sumner County in 1821 where he now lives. He is a farmer and a practicing physician of considerable note. He has practiced his profession for thirty-five or forty years with great success. The mother was born about 1840 or 1841 and is still living. Our subject received his education at Gallatin and Nashville. At the age of twenty-five he engaged in the dry goods business at Gallatin where he remained two years. In 1880 he married and moved on his wife's farm ten miles northeast of Gallatin where he has since resided. His wife, Georgia Brown, was born in Sumner County in 1862 and is the daughter of George and Elizabeth (Woodson) Brown. To our subject and wife were born two children: Betty Woodson and John Thomas. Mr. Franklin is an industrious, enterprising young man and in the past four years has done much to improve the farm. He is a stanch Democrat and cast his first presidential vote for S. J. Tilden. He is a member of the Presbyterian Church and his wife a member of the Methodist Episcopal Church.

Ed. N. Franklin, M. D., practicing physician and surgeon of Gallatin, was born October 20, 1846, in that city, and is the youngest of a family of three children born to the union of Dr. John W. and Florida (Nolen) Franklin. The father was born in Sumner County, Tenn., and was of English descent. He received a good literary education at Howell's College, Alexander, Va., and his medical education at Transylvania University, Franklin, Ky. After practicing for some time he was obliged to give it up on account of ill health and return to Gallatin. About 1849 he purchased a farm of 300 acres four miles from Gallatin, where he located and is now living engaged in farming and stock-raising. He has the best drove of Jersey cattle in Sumner County, also fine racing stock. His first wife, Florida Nolen, was a native of Frankport, Ky. She died in 1847. After her death he married Miss Sarah Baber and by this union had nine children. Our subject's grandfather, John Franklin, was a native of North Carolina, who came to Sumner county at a very early date and was one of the largest land holders in the county. Our subject was an infant when his mother died and was then taken by his uncle, John Armfield. His education was received at Forest Home, Ky., being a graduate of that institution. In 1866 he commenced the study of medicine with his father and in 1869 graduated as an M. D. at the University of Penn, Philadelphia. He located at Galveston, Tex., being placed in charge of the Marine Hospital. At the end of ten months he received word that his uncle was taken suddenly ill and he left his practice and hastened to his bedside in Nashville. The Doctor was a constant attendant on his uncle as long as he lived, which was two years after he was taken ill. January 3, 1872, Dr. Franklin married Miss Nannie Hillman, daughter of Daniel Hillman, who was known as the "Iron King" of the South, being the most extensive iron manufacturer south of the Ohio River. He owned four large furnaces, one large rolling mill, was a man of remarkable business capacity and a man of great wealth. Mrs. Franklin was a native of Kentucky and bore her husband four children: Florida, Grace, Hillman and Charles. The Doctor remained in the "Rock City" until 1880 when owing to ill health he came to Gallatin. The Doctor has a lucrative practice and is one of the leading physicians of Sumner County. He is a member of the American Public Health Association, State Medical Association, and in 1885 was vice-president of Sumner County Medical Association. He is a member of the K. of P. Lodge, No. 21. In connection with his profession the Doctor is greatly interested, and is a dealer in, fast stock, especially running stock. Mr. Franklin is a member of the Episcopal Church.

John C. Frazier, farmer and stock raiser, of the Fourth District of Sumner County, is the son of George and Elizabeth (Cage) Frazier and was born in Sumner County in 1835, being an only child. The father was of Scotch-Irish ancestry, born in Mississippi about 1816, and received a good education. He was twice married; first, to our subject's mother, in 1834, and in 1839 to Ann Eliza Cage, a cousin of his first wife. One child was the issue of this marriage, but it died. He was a planter and a life resident of Mississippi, where he died in 1840. The mother was born in Wilson County, Tenn., in 1817, and died in 1835. John C. Frazier was raised partly in Mississippi and partly in Sumner County, by different relatives, receiving his early education in Sumner County, then entered Cumberland University at Lebanon, Tenn., with the intention of taking a scientific course, but was forced by ill health to abandon the idea. He completed his education at Franklin College, July 19, 1860. Mr. Frazier married Miss Mary E., daughter of Bernice and Ann E. Bender, of Sumner County. They have two sons and two daughters: William B., Elizabeth S., Bright B. and Birdie Belle. He first located in Mississippi until 1863, then moved to Sumner County, and has since lived here and in Davidson County, engaging in farming and stock-raising, and owning a beautiful farm five miles southwest of Gallatin on the Nashville Pike. Mr. Frazier has displayed energy and sound judgment in his farming operations, and has met with marked success. He was formerly a Whig in politics, but is now a Democrat. His first presidential vote was for M. Fillmore in 1856. He was formerly a member of the I. O. O. F. Mr. and Mrs. Frazier and their oldest daughter, are prominent members of the Christian Church. Mrs. Frazier was born in Sumner County in 1842. He is a useful citizen, and a man of fine moral character.

Henry Fry, a well known farmer and stock raiser of Sumner County, residing in the Fourth District, is a son of Abraham and Isabella (Kingland) Fry, and was born in Pennsylvania in 1822, being the fifth of eleven children—nine still living. The father was of Dutch descent, born in Pennsylvania in 1795, and died in 1867. He spent his entire life in that State engaged in farming, and was married when about twenty years old. The mother was born in same State three years later than her husband, and died in 1882. Our subject was raised and educated at home. In 1845 he married Miss Margaret, daughter of Isaac and Martha Fry, of Rush County, Ind., and by this marriage had eleven children, six sons and four daughters living: John (of Gallatin), William Henry (of Bedford County), Isaac, Henan, Abraham, Albert, Sarah Ann (deceased), Clarinda (wife of Prady Mitchell), Martha (wife of Henry Furmer, of Pennsylvania), Elizabeth (wife of James Evans, of Gallatin, Tenn.), and Belle. He first located in Washington County, Penn., and farmed there until 1852, and when the excitememt about finding gold in California was so great, he went out there, and spent two years mining, meeting with some success; then returned to his family, and in 1870 moved to Sumner County, purchasing a farm of 370 acres, with a handsome residence on it, seven miles southwest of Gallatin. Mr. Fry has acquired a large part of his property through his own efforts, being industrious and a good manager. He introduced into his county the rearing of thoroughbred Clydesdale horses in connection with his farming. Mr. Fry was formerly a Whig, and cast his first presidential vote in 1840 for W. H. Harrison, and since the war he has been a Republican, and stands well in his community.

R. G. Gillespie, a well known farmer of the Ninth District, was born July 15, 1826, in Sumner County. He is the eldest of two children born to Jacob and Nellie (Graham) Gillespie. The father was born in October, 1779, in Roane County, N. C., of Irish ancestry. He was a soldier of the war of 1812. When he first came to Sumner County he settled at a town called Cairo (which is now extinct). At that time there were but few settlers. The mother was also a native of North Carolina, of Irish descent. With her father (who was an officer of the Revolutionary war) she moved to Mercer County, Ky., and then to Sumner County. Her death occurred in 1867. The subject of our sketch was educated in Sumner County. October 26, 1853, he married Miss Susan Harris, who bore him five children: George Marian (deceased), Bright Harris, Jacob, Benjamin Blake, Nellie Graham (now Mrs. Head), Frank Bates and Mattie Ann (deceased). Mrs. Gillespie's grandfather, Squire Walton, came to Davidson County at a very early day, and settled near Goodlettsville. At the age of twenty-six our subject moved to his present place of residence, purchasing 205 acres of valuable land, to which he has since added 72 acres. It is located on the Red River Turnpike, six miles from Gallatin. Mr. Gillespie is a life-long Democrat, and cast his first vote for Franklin Pierce. He is a Master Mason. Mrs. Gillespie and daughter are members of the Methodist Episcopal Church South.

George M. Gillespie, farmer, and son of Jacob and Nellie (Graham) Gillespie, was born on the farm near Gallatin, in Sumner County, in 1828, and is one of two children born to his parents. The father was born in 1773 in North Carolina, and came to Williamson County, Tenn., where he remained but a short time. He then came to Sumner County, and located where our subject now resides. He died here in 1864. The mother was born in 1790, in North Carolina, was of Irish descent, and died about 1866. Our subject received his education in the common schools of Sumner County, and remained with his parents as long as they lived. At the death of his father he came in possession of 600 acres of land, on which he is now living. In 1859 he married Harriet Jane Duffer, daughter of William and Rebecca Duffer. Mrs. Gillespie was born at Station Camp, seven miles west of Gallatin, in 1836. Eight children were the result of this union: Aldrich Oma (Mrs. James Bright), Belmont, Queen (Mrs. David Kerley), Susan D., William, Jacob, Thomas, George and James Graham. Oma, Bell, Queen and Susan are members of the Christian Church. Mr. Gillespie, by hard and careful work, has improved the farm, so that he has it in a good state of cultivation, with good fences and buildings. He is a Democrat, and cast his first presidential vote in 1848.

Louis A. Green, of Gallatin, was born in 1836 in Sumner County, Tenn., a son of Z. F. and Mary Jane (Brown) Green, and grandson of Zachariah F. Green, who was a native of Ireland. The father was born in 1808, and was a farmer by occupation. He married in 1830, his wife being five years his junior, and in 1839 moved to Texas, where he afterward died. Mrs. Green afterward married M. R. Moore, and died in 1866. Until sixteen years of age Louis A. lived with his mother, then clerked for a number of months, farmed, traded and engaged in diver's occupations. In 1860 he wedded Eliza Key, who died in September of the same year. The breaking out of the war served, in a measure, to divert his mind from this great loss. He enlisted in Company I, Fifty-fourth Regiment of Confederate Tennessee Infantry, which was later consolidated with the Forty-fourth Regiment, and was a participant in the battles of Chickamauga, Knoxville, Petersburg and other important engagements. He received a severe wound in the left arm which necessitated the removal of five inches of bone, and this effectually ended his military career in the field, but he was detailed in the quartermaster's department. After the war he resumed farming and speculating, and has so continued until the present with much success. He is a Democrat, an Encampment Degree Odd Fellow and an ancient member of the K. of P. He married, in 1870, Miss Ella Green, of Columbus, Miss., and they are the parents of five children: Nellie, Elizabeth, Louis, Robert and Zachariah.

Isaac N. Guthrie, one of Sumner County's most extensive farmers and stock raisers, residing in the Fourth District, is a son of James and Elizabeth (Gibbs) Guthrie, and was born in Franklin County Ky., in 1810, being the fifth born of eleven children and the only one living. His father was born in Virginia in 1779 and died in 1840. His grandfather, Thomas Guthrie, was a native of Virginia, and a volunteer in the war of independence. He moved to Woodford County, Ky., in 1782, where he died in 1837. Our subject's father received but a limited education. He was married in 1802, and was a farmer and hotel-keeper, and a man of considerable means. The mother was born in Virginia in 1780 and died in 1859. Both parents were members of the Baptist Church. Isaac N. Guthrie was raised and educated at home, and July 6, 1832, he married Miss Mary Beauchamp, of Spencer County, Ky. Five children were the issue of this union, four sons living: James I., Isaac N., Jr., Nathan N. and Henry Clay, all of whom served in the Confederate Army. Mrs. Guthrie died September 15, 1844, and May 8, 1845, he married Miss Martha A. Montgomery, of Shelby County, Ky. Eight children were born to this marriage; three sons and three daughters living: George N. (of Gallatin), Elizabeth J. (wife of Jacob Livar), Emma L. (wife of Legrand Scott, of Davidson County), Frank, Willie M. and Mary Beauchamp. Mrs. Guthrie died July 30, 1877, and March 25, 1879, he married Mrs. Margaret E. Taylor, a daughter of Thomas and Margrie Hardin, of Logan County, Ky. Mrs. Guthrie was born in that county in 1832. Her father was a native of Casswell County, N. C., and her mother of Baltimore, Md. Mr. Guthrie first located in Shelby County, Ky., where he was a merchant for many years and also a farmer. In 1848 he moved to Sumner County, and continued to merchandise at Gallatin in connection with farming until 1860, and since then has given all of his time to farming and breeding thoroughbred shorthorn cattle, Southdown sheep, Berkshire hogs and Percheron trotting horses, and has met with great success. Mr. Guthrie owned at one time 583 acres of valuable land in Sumner County, but his farm now contains only 350 acres, having given some to his children. He has a handsome brick residence on his farm, four miles west of Gallatin, on the Louisville & Nashville Railroad. In 1865 Mr. Guthrie was elected magistrate, and held the office for twelve years. He was formerly a Whig, and cast his first presidential vote for Henry Clay in 1832. Mr. Guthrie has been a prominent Mason for many years, and was also clerk and treasurer of the Baptist Church at Gallatin, Tenn. Mrs. Guthrie belongs to the Methodist Episcopal South. Mr. Guthrie was appointed by President Jackson postmaster at Shelbyville, Ky. He is one of the most influential citizens of the county, and has been active in all measures that would promote the interests of his town and county.

William Hall, clerk of the Circuit Court of Sumner County, was born in said county, March 17, 1848, the only son of William H. and Sarah W. (McDaniel) Hall. The father was of Scotch-Irish origin, born in 1813 in Sumner County, a farmer by occupation. His father, William Hall (subject's grandfather), was born in Surrey County, N. C., in 1775, and when ten years of age moved with his father to Sumner County, near Bledsoe Lick, now Castalian Springs. He was one of the first white settlers of Middle Tennessee and became very conspicuous in State affairs. He was for five terms a member of the Legislature, also of United States Congress. In 1829 he was made governor of Tennessee upon the resignation of Samuel Houston, by virtue of his being at that time speaker of the State Senate. William H. Hall (subject's father) was a prosperous farmer and business man, and owned about 300 acres of land in Sumner County and 500 in Macon County, Tenn. His death occurred in 1883. His wife was born in Sumner County, January 8, 1828, at the village of Cairo on Cumberland River; was married in October, 1845, and became the mother of four children, one son and three daughters, all of whom are living. She died in February, 1882. Our subject was educated at Rural Academy, Sumner County. At the age of eighteen he became a salesman in a store at Christian Springs, where he worked two years, and then taught school one session. The following year he was in a hotel in Louisville. In June, 1872, was employed as teller in the Sumner County Deposit Bank, and remained three years, but failing health forced him to seek outdoor work, and he engaged in farming. In 1879 he gave up farming and engaged in milling in a custom flouring-mill on Bledsoe Creek in Sumner County, at what is known as the Lower Branham Mill. In 1881 he began the manufacture of ax handles; the next year he went to Dixon County, continuing in same business. May, 1884, he was appointed deputy circuit court clerk of Sumner County, and in August, 1886, was elected to the position which he now holds. He is an efficient public officer and thorough gentleman. October, 1874, he married Miss Mary, daughter of James A. Mentlo. Mrs. Hall was born in Sumner County on June 22, 1857. To this union have been born four children: Susie, Wincenna, James M. and William Alexander. Mr. and Mrs. Hall are esteemed members of the Christian Church. Hr. Hall is a Democrat, a member of the I. O. O. F. and the G. C.

William Harper, farmer and stock raiser, was born in Sumner County, Tenn., September, 1843, and is one of a family of two children born to S. and S. (Easley) Harper, both natives of Virginia. The father was born in Culpeper County, in 1780, was of English descent, a farmer and stone-mason by occupation, and died in 1872. The mother was born in 1789, and died in March, 1877. Our subject was educated in the schools of Sumner County, and at the age of twenty-one began working for himself on his father's farm. In 1863 he married Miss Minerva A. Childress, a native of Sumner County, born in 1843, and the daughter of John and Elmira Childress. This union resulted in the birth of five children: Sallie I., W. J., Ella, Jesse L. and Earl P. Mr. Harper is a Democrat, a member of the Masonic fraternity, also of the K. of H., and his wife and three daughters, Sallie, Willie and Ella, are members of the Methodist Episcopal Church South.

Capt. Geo. Harsh, one of Sumner County's most useful and influential citizens, is a son of Phillip and Madeline (Kahler) Harsh, and was born in Schuylkill County, Penn., in 1827. The father was a German, born at Frankfort-on-the-Main, in 1798, and immigrated to the United States when he was about fourteen years old. He settled in Pennsylvania, where he married in 1820, and in 1839 moved to Cincinnati, O., where he remained two years, then moved to Nashville, Tenn. He was by profession a very fine physician and surgeon and upon moving to Nashville, engaged in the practice of medicine. He received two diplomas in his profession, one from Germany, having returned to his native country to complete his studies. The latter part of his life he turned his attention to the homœopathic school of medicine, and was the first to introduce that practice in Nashville. He remained in that city until 1860, then purchased a farm four miles from there and spent the rest of his life quietly. He died in 1871. He was a prominent mason. The mother was a native of Schuylkill County, Penn., born in 1803, and died in 1884. She was a member of the Lutheran Church. Capt. Harsh was raised and educated at home; when fourteen years old he began as a clerk in a mercantile house of his father's at Lebanon, Tenn., and was afterward in Gallatin until 1847, when he entered the Mexican war in the Third Tennessee Regiment as second lieutenant, ex-Gov. W. B. Bate being first lieutenant. He served in that capacity until the close of the war, when he returned home, but soon after spent some time traveling in the North, and acted as cashier of the mercantile house of John Purdue, of LaFayette. In 1849 Capt. Harsh returned to Gallatin, and in 1850 went to Lebanon; in 1851 he married Miss Mary S. O. Guthrie, who died in 1855, and in 1856 he married Miss Tobithia Newby, of Smith County. They had ten children, eight of them living: Phillip W., a minister in Texas; Mary A., wife of W. W. Brown; Nathan J.; Callie E.; Lee Cheatham George; R. N. Herbert and William G. Mrs. Harsh died in 1868, and in 1869 he married Mrs. James K. Polk, daughter of William T. and Mary A. Edmonds, of Memphis. Three children were born to them, two living: Thomas Walker and Alex Cyrus. After his first marriage he remained in Lebanon two years, then spent five years in Smith County, engaged in farming and milling. In 1858 he went to Nashville and engaged in brewing a short time; then was in the grocery business until the war commenced, when he entered the Confederate Army as captain of Company E, First Tennessee Infantry, and was in active service until the battle of Shiloh, when he was captured and imprisoned at Nashville about three months, when he was paroled and did not re-enter the service. In 1866 he established with his brother a government store at Nashville, the firm being Harsh Bros. In 1872 he established another store in New York City, of which his brother had charge until his death in 1873, when the business was discontinued, and in 1874 Capt. Harsh purchased a farm in Sumner County of 440 acres, four miles east of Gallatin, where he has since resided, with the exception of two years spent in the grocery business at Nashville. The farm is well cultivated, with fine improvements on it, the dwelling being one of the handsomest in Sumner County. He is a man of very fine business qualifications and of strict integrity. He is a director of the Nashville Plow Company, vice-president of the Farmers' & Traders' Bank, of Gallatin, president of the Gallatin and Bledsoe Creek Turnpike, and was magistrate for a number of years in Davidson County. He is a warm advocate of education, and has given his children the best advantages. He is generous and enthusiastic in disposition. Politically a Democrat, his first presidential vote was for Gen. Cass. He is a Knight Templar and a Mason. Mrs. Harsh was born in Obion County, raised in Memphis, and was first married in 1871 to James K. Polk, a nephew of ex-President Polk, by whom she had one child, James K. Polk. She is a member of the Christian Church.

Harris Brown, clerk of the Sumner County Court, was born in said county in 1858. He is one of four (three living) children born to William B. and M. J. (Harris) Brown. Both parents were of English descent and natives of Sumner County, born in 1825 and 1838 respectively. The father was an agriculturist. In 1861 he enlisted in Company D, Second Tennessee Regiment of Cavalry, Bennett's brigade, and was elected orderly sergeant. At the battle of Harrisburg, Miss., in 1863, he received a wound in the leg, from the effects of which he died a few days later. In 1883 his widow married the Hon. W. G. Pond, an ex-member of the State Legislature. The grandfather of subject, George T. Brown, was a native of Albemarle County, Va. He came to Sumner County at an early day, and was magistrate of the First District for thirty years. Harris Brown received an excellent education at the University of Tennessee, at Knoxville. He graduated in 1877, with the highest honors of his class; also of the military department, being captain of Company A, the banner company of the school. He returned to his native home and taught school two years. In 1879 he became bookkeeper for C. Levy & Bro., Gallatin, remaining with them two years. In 1881, in partnership with his brother-in-law, J. H. Butler, he established a grocery store, continuing in the business fifteen months. From 1883 to 1885 he clerked for C. Levy & Bro. In August, 1886, he was elected to his present position by a majority of 206 over two of Sumner County's strongest men. April 29, 1881, he married Miss Carrie H., daughter of John A. Patterson. Mrs. Brown was born in Sumner County, in 1859, and is the mother of two children: John P. and William T. Capt. Brown is a man of fine morals, a worthy, respected citizen. He is a stanch Democrat and cast his first presidential vote for Hancock, in 1880.

M. J. Hassell, farmer and stock dealer in District No. 8, Sumner County, was born in February, 1827, in that county. He is one of five children of Jennett and Jane (Pervine) Hassell. The father, of Scotch origin, was born in Chowan County, N. C., in 1789, and came to Sumner County when a boy and began farming. He was in the Creek war under Gen. Jackson, and died in

1868. The mother was born near Gallatin, Tenn., in 1780, and died in 1866. Besides the ordinary common-school course our subject attended Lebanon University. When twenty-one years of age he began farming in Sumner County. In 1848 he married Ann E., daughter of Bright B. and Sallie Harris, and born in Sumner County in August, 1828. Their six children are Eliza M.; Mattie J., wife of William K. Walton, Gallatin, Tenn.; Jennett B., farming; Isaac W., lawyer in Springfield, Mo.; Charles G., farmer, and Tyry H., merchant and physician. Mr. Hassell is a Democrat; since 1882, justice of the peace, and since 1880, poorhouse commissioner. He is a member of the F. & A. M. order, and he, his wife, Isaac, Eliza and Mattie are members of the Methodist Episcopal Church South. He is a member of the church in which the first Methodist Episcopal conference there was held, under Bishop Asbury. The deserted old church is now a barn on his farm.

Prof. W. A. Haynes, A. B., B. D., is a native of Cornersville, Giles Co., Tenn., born in 1834, and the son of David and Rebecca (Warren) Haynes. The father was born in 1800, in Giles County, Tenn., was of Irish extraction and a farmer by occupation. He remained in his native county until about 1840, when he moved to Kentucky, and then to Illinois, where East St. Louis now is. He died in 1848. His wife was born in Bedford County, Tenn., in 1808, and died in 1845. They had nine children (seven of whom are living), our subject being the fourth. He was quite young when his parents died, leaving him to care for himself. At the age of seventeen he entered the Cumberland University, at Lebanon, Tenn., and completed the full course, both literary and theological. He graduated in 1859 as A. B. and B. D. During the civil war he enlisted in Company C, Eighteenth Regiment Tennessee Infantry (Confederate Army), and at the time of the reorganization he was transferred to Company C, Thirteenth Regiment, and was elected chaplain of the company. At the end of the first year Prof. Haynes returned home and he and J. D. Kirkpatrick organized Company C, Bennett's regiment, J. D. Kirkpatrick being elected captain and Prof. Haynes first lieutenant. He took part in seventeen battles, and at Hartsville was wounded in the right arm, which disabled him for three years. He remained, however, in service until the close of the war, when he returned and entered the teacher's profession at Laquard's, where he taught three years. December 30, 1866, he married Miss Mittie Cowen, a native of Wilson County, born in 1830, and the daughter of James Cowen. They had four children: Sallie, Docia (deceased), Katie and Pearl. In 1867 Prof. Haynes moved to Brownsville, W. Tenn., and was elected principal of the Brownsville Male Academy, where he remained ten years, with the exception of one year, when he was in charge of the Baptist Female College. In 1877 he came to Gallatin and the same year was elected president of the Howard Female College and held the position five years. During his years of teaching the Professor has also had charge of churches of his faith, the Cumberland Presbyterian doctrine. For the past nine years he has conducted services in Beach Church, ten miles west of Chattanooga. It has the largest attendance of any church in Sumner County. Prof. Haynes is a fine scholar and an eloquent and forcible speaker. He is a Democrat in politics, but was a Whig previous to the war, voting for Fillmore in 1856. He is a member of the following orders: Masonic, I. O. O. F., K. of P., K. of H., L. and K. of H., Iron Hall and the G. T. His grandfather, John Haynes, was a native of North Carolina and immigrated to Giles County about 1800. He was a soldier in the Revolutionary war.

Hon. Charles R. Head, one of the leading attorneys of Gallatin, and senior member of the law firm of Head Bros., was born in Sumner County, Tenn., in 1846, and is one of a family of seven children, five of whom are living, born to Hon. John W. and Evaline B. (Brooks) Head. The father was born in Sumner County in 1821, and was of English descent. His education was received by untiring efforts on his own part and while still quite young he began the study of law. As time would permit, he diligently and faithfully applied himself to that study. He was a member of both Houses of the Legislature. In 1858 he was attorney-general and reporter, and the author and publisher of three volumes of Head's Reports, which are valuable documents to the lawyers of Tennessee. He was judge of the court of arbitration with Senator A. O. P. Nicholson, chief justice in 1873. October 2, 1874, he was elected as congressman for the Fourth Congressional District, and on the 10th of the same month he died. Judge Head was a self-made man in the true sense of the word, was a man of unusual ability, and a wise and discreet counselor. His wife was born in Smith County in 1822, and is now living in Gallatin. His father, Henry Head, was a native of Virginia, and at a very early date immigrated to Sumner County and settled in District No. 1. Charles R., our subject, received his education at Gallatin, and in Forest Home Academy in Kentucky. In 1867 he began studying law with his father and soon entered the law department of Cumberland University, at Lebanon. He and his father afterward formed a partnership, the firm being known as John W. Head & Son. After the death of his father, Charles and his brother Lee formed a partnership under the firm title,. Head & Bros. Charles is city attorney of Gallatin and county attorney of Sumner County. The Head Bros. are attorneys for the Louisville & Nashville Railroad, and also for Dunn's commercial agencies. In 1868 Charles married Miss Sophia Childress, daughter of E. H. Childress of Nashville. Mrs. Head died in 1870, leaving one child, Adrian C. In 1874 Mr. Head married Miss Alice Burford, a native of Smith County, born in 1849, and by her had these children: John W., David, Lee, Elizabeth, Allen and Alice. Mr. Head is a member of the I. O. O. F., Lodge No. 13, of the K. of H., K. of P., and he and wife are members of the Methodist Episcopal Church South.

Hon. Lee Head, judge of the county court of Sumner County, and junior member of the firm of Head Bros., was born in Sumner County in 1849; son of Hon. John W. and Evaline B. (Brooks) Head. (For further particulars of parents, see sketch of Chas. R. Head.) Our subject received his education at Kentucky's military institute, and at the Cumberland University at Lebanon, graduating from the law department in 1871. He immediately joined his brother Charles and his father in the law office in Gallatin and commenced his practice. In 1873 and 1875 he was elected to the Lower House of the State Legislature and served on the judiciary committee and chairman on committee on elections. In 1878 he was elected judge of the county court of Sumner County and has been elected each succeeding year since. In 1881 Lee married Miss Nellie Gillespie, a native of Sumner County, born in 1862, and a daughter of R. G. Gillespie. To them were born two children: Graham and Charles R. Mr. Head is a member of the K. of H., the K. of P. and he and wife are members of the Methodist Episcopal Church South. Head Bros. are Democrats in politics.

Dr. James M. Head, Sr., a practicing physician of the Tenth District, was born in Sumner County, Tenn., in 1818. He is one of the twelve children born to Henry and Elizabeth (Sandford) Head. The father was of English descent, born in Albemarle County, Va., in 1770, and came to Tennessee about 1804. He leased and located on a farm, one and a half miles from Cairo, where our subject was born. Ten years later he moved two miles north of Castalian Springs, where he purchased a 300 acre farm. He died in 1855. His wife of Scotch origin, born in Albemarle County, Va., in 1777, and died in 1873. The subject of this sketch received his literary education at the Rural Academy, Sumner County, and remained with his parents until his eighteenth year. He then began the study of medicine with Dr. M. D. D. F. Sharpe. Two years later he attended a five months' course of lectures at the Transylvania Medical College, Lexington, Ky. After several months' practice he returned to the college, and graduated in the spring of 1841. He came home and bought a farm of fifty-three acres, upon which he now resides.

In 1841 he married Bathenia P. Branham, who was born in 1825, and died in 1885. Eight children were born to this union, two of whom died in infancy, and six are yet living. Those living are Milton E., a member of the Christian Church—he married Elizabeth Yager about 1868; Flora, married Dr. J. L. Vertress in 1869; Altie is a member of the Christian Church. John Brodie is an M. D. He married in 1871 Miss Virginia Perkins. Henry O. was married in 1877 to Sallie Wilson of New Orleans. James M., a lawyer, of Nashville, married in 1885 Miss Minnie Chevvy of that city. Our subject enlisted in the Confederate Army in 1861, as surgeon of the Thirtieth Tennessee from Sumner County. He took part in the battle of Fort Donelson, and was captured. After six months' imprisonment he was released. He was afterward in the battles of Vicksburg and Port Hudson, and many minor engagements. He returned home in 1863, and since which time his attention has been given to farming and his professional duties. He has an extensive and lucrative practice, and is recognized as one of the most able physicians in the county. He lost considerable wealth by the war, owing to the emancipation of the slaves. He now owns 600 acres of valuable land. His first presidential vote was cast for James K. Polk. He has always been a stanch Democrat. He was a member of the P. of H., Greenwood Lodge, No. 24. He was Master of lodge and overseer of State Grange. No man in the county is more widely known, or respected than Dr. Head.

James House, banker and merchant of Gallatin, was born in Sumner County, Tenn., in 1832, a son of James, Sr., and Ann (Baker) House. The father was born in 1795 in Burtee County, N. C. When sixteen years old he came with his father, mother and six brothers to Sumner County, locating in the Third District, near Pilot Knob. He learned the tailor's trade, but after his marriage, in 1829, he began farming. He settled on a hundred-acre tract of land, two miles north of Gallatin, which was given him by his father-in-law, Isaac Baker. Mr. House was one of the most successful agriculturists in the county, and became possessor of 500 acres and considerable wealth. His first wife, and mother of our subject, was a native of South Carolina. She died in 1834. Three children were the fruits of this union. The second wife was Nancy Crenshaw, who bore him seven children. Her death occurred in 1856. Mr. House departed this life March 4, 1866. The subject of this sketch received his education in the common and high schools of Gallatin. In 1849 he became an apprentice to the tinner's trade, at which he worked three and a half years. He then went to Murfreesboro, going into the stove and tin business with F. G. Mackey. Sixteen months later he sold his interest and returned to Gallatin and established a grocery store, continuing in that line two years. In 1858 he again engaged in his regular trade, to which he has almost exclusively given his attention. With the exception of Messrs. Jo. Natcher and J. Nickelson, our subject is the oldest continuous business man in Gallatin. In 1860 he married Miss Eunice R., daughter of Rev. Luke P. Allen. Mr. House is a native of Sumner County and father of Emma L., wife of Robert G. Connell; James B.; William H.; Annie; Ernest B.; L. Allen; Walter T. and Rufus M. In 1862 our subject enlisted in Company D, Duke's regiment, Morgan's command, and was assistant forage-master, a position of the time. He participated in the battles of Woodbury, Bradyville and Chickamauga; was in the Kentucky raid in 1862 and in the Kentucky and Ohio raid in July, 1863. He, with a company of men under Capt. Davis, was at Bardstown, detached from the main command to make a demonstration on the Louisville & Lexington Railroad. While Morgan was crossing the Ohio River at Brandensburg nearly the entire detachment was captured on Twelve-Mile Island, twelve miles above Louisville. He made his escape back into Kentucky, thence out to the Confederate lines with a few comrades, traveling in the night and lying by in the woods during the day. January, 1864, he returned home on account of feeble health. In 1884 he was elected president of the Gallatin Bank. He is a life-long Democrat, an old member of the I. O. O. F. and K. of P. He and his wife have been connected with the Methodist Episcopal Church South since 1865. Mr. House has been a church officer since 1866. He is a thorough gentleman and a worthy, esteemed citizen.

Capt. J. B. Howison, farmer, stock raiser and banker of Gallatin, was born in Prince William County, Va., and is the son of James and Amanda M. (Farrow) Howison. The father was born in Prince William County, Va., in 1804, and was of Scotch descent. He always resided in the same county in which he was born, and cultivated the soil. He died in 1874. The mother was born in 1815 and was of English descent. She died in 1867. Our subject received his academic education in his native county and his collegiate education at Alleghany College, West Virginia, where he was in attendance at the breaking out of the war. He at once abandoned his studies and enlisted in Company B, Third Regiment, Wise's legion (Confederate Army), and afterward joined the Sixtieth Regiment, Virginia Infantry, and was elected first lieutenant. At the end of the first year he joined the Sixth Regiment Virginia Cavalry, and was elected to the same office. The last eighteen months of the war he commanded the squadron of two companies, D and H, being ranked as captain. He fought at Brandy Station, second Manassas, Gettysburg, Spottsylvania C. H., Culpeper C. H., Rappahannock, Slaughter Mountain, Cedar Creek and numerous severe skirmishes. January 11 he was wounded by a shell in the shoulder, which disabled him for one year. When seventeen years of age he commenced teaching school and taught one year. In 1866 he left his native State and came to Sumner County, where he resumed teaching. May 1, 1872, he married Miss Alice M. Fitzgerald, a native of Memphis, Tenn., born in 1852. They have five children: Eunice, Henry F., Emma, James Allen and Charles L. In July, the same year of his marriage, he went in partnership with his father-in-law, H. Fitzgerald, in the large cotton-mill of Gallatin. In September the mill burned down with a loss of $25,000 to Mr. Howison and leaving him $15,000 in debt. At the time of the fire Mr. Howison was in Alabama engaged in the lumber business, and it was there he met with marked success, making $25,000 the first year. In 1881 he returned to Gallatin and purchased 275 acres. In June, 1884, when the Farmers' & Traders' Bank was organized Capt. Howison was elected president, which position he now holds. He is also a member of the new livery and feed stable of Gallatin, the firm being known as Pierce, Howison & Burford. Mr. Howison is also engaged in raising thoroughbred mares, running and trotting stock, and is speculating in buying and selling mules and horses. Since 1881 he has been engaged in merchandising in Gallatin, handling farming implements, hardware and groceries. Mr. Howison is a man of marked business ability and is upright and honest in all his dealings. He is a Democrat, a K. of P. and he and wife are members of the Presbyterian Church. He is school commissioner of the Twenty-second Division.

W. A. Hunter, farmer and retired druggist, was born in Warren County, Tenn., in 1837, and is one of a family of four children born to the union of Thomas J. and A. Hunter, natives of North Carolina and Warren County, Tenn., respectively. The father came to Warren County when a small boy. He died in 1840. The mother was born in 1815 and died in 1883. Our subject was educated in Nashville and was apprenticed at the age of fourteen to learn the drug business. In 1865 he married Miss C. P. Gaildroth, a native of Jackson County, Tenn., born in 1859, and the daughter of Joseph and Martha Gaildroth. This union resulted in the birth of four children: William A., Addie A. (deceased), Mattie A. (deceased) and Josephine A. Mr. Hunter was engaged in the drug business in Nashville for twenty years, and is now living on his farm in Sumner County, Tenn. He is and has always been a Democrat in politics.

J. R. Hutchison, farmer and stock raiser, was born in Sumner County, Tenn., in 1826, and received his education in the county schools. At the age of fourteen he began working for himself in a blacksmith shop, learning the trade. He worked at this for about ten years, and then built a distillery and began the manufacture of whisky. In 1845 he married Margaret J. Hamilton, a native of Sumner County, born in 1828, and the daughter of Capt. Harry and Jane Hamilton. She bore him three children; Buena Vista (deceased), William A. (farmer), and J. H. C., school-teacher. Mrs. Hutchison died in 1852. In 1861 Mr. Hutchison enlisted in Company E, Seventh Tennessee Infantry, Confederate Army, and was soon elected first lieutenant. In 1862 he was discharged and came back to his native county where he engaged in farming. In 1863 he married Mrs. Catherine Davis, a native of Sumner County, born in 1828, and the fruits of this union were two children: Montgomery (farmer) and Daniel B., now attending school. Mr. Hutchison has been a Democrat all his life, was deputy sheriff in 1853–55, and is a member of the Masonic lodge. Mrs. Hutchison and son, J. H. C., are members of the Cumberland Presbyterian Church. The parents of our subject were James and Margaret (Frazer) Hutchison. The father was a native of Scotland, born near Edinburgh in 1794, and was a farmer by occupation. He moved to Davidson County about 1800, and at the end of one year he came to Sumner County, where he died in 1845. His wife was a native of Sumner County, born in 1800, of English descent, and died in 1836.

Capt. J. H. Joyner, M. D., farmer, stock raiser and physician, is a native of Sumner County, born in 1828, and is one of a family of six children born to Robert and Mary (Hargrove) Joyner, natives of North Carolina, of English descent, and born in 1802 and 1803 respectively. The father was a farmer by occupation and moved to Sumner County, Tenn., in 1810. He died in 1851. The mother died in 1881. Our subject was educated in the common schools of Sumner County, and graduated from the medical department of the University of Louisville in 1850. He then came back to Sumner County and began the practice of his profession at the age of twenty-two. His father died shortly after he came home, and after his death our subject lived with his mother until the breaking out of the war. In 1862 he enlisted in the Forty-fourth Tennessee Infantry, Confederate Army, as private, and was soon elected captain. After the battle of Corinth he was discharged and came home, where he began the practice of his profession. In 1865 he married Mary C. Perry, a native of Davidson County, born in 1834, and the daughter of Zachariah and Jane Perry. Two children: John E. (deceased), and M. Emma, were the fruits of this union. Emma graduated at the Howard Female College, at Gallatin, in June, 1886. Mr. Joiner is one of the largest stock raisers in Sumner County, and is now an extensive land owner. He is a Democrat in politics, but previous to the war was a Whig. He is a member of the Masonic fraternity and organized the Goodletsville Lodge in 1856, of which he was appointed Worshipful Master by the Grand Lodge. Capt. Joyner is an excellent physician and a prominent citizen. He, his wife and daughter are members of the Cumberland Presbyterian Church.

Maj. W. H. Joyner, dry goods merchant, of Gallatin, is a native of Sumner County, born in 1834, and the son of Robert and Mary (Hargrove) Joyner. The father was born in 1802 and a farmer by occupation. In 1810 he came to Sumner County and settled in the Sixth District, known as Joyner's district, named in honor of him, where he purchased 640 acres of land. He was one of the first settlers in the county and died about 1851. His wife was born in North Carolina in 1803 and came to Sumner County, Tenn., when a mere child. She died in 1881. They had six children, four of whom are now living. Our subject received his education in the common schools of Sumner County and remained at home until the breaking out of the war, when he organized Company B, Eighteenth Tennessee Regiment (Confederate Army) and was elected captain. He participated in the battles at Fort Donelson, Franklin, Chickamauga, Murfreesboro, Missionary Ridge, Atlanta and was in many severe skirmishes. He was captured at Fort Donelson and sent to Johnson Island. He was retained about nine months when he was exchanged and afterward rejoined his command. At the battles of Chickamauga and Murfreesboro he was wounded, shot in the leg at the former and two ribs broken at the latter place. When the army was reorganized he was promoted to the rank of major, which position he retained until the close. He returned home May 22, 1865, after an absence of just exactly four years. October 3, 1865, he married Miss Eliza Goodlett, a native of Davidson County, born in 1842 and the daughter of Rev. A. G. Goodlett. To them was born one child, James, who is a student in the commercial college at Nashville. In 1866 Mr. Joyner located in Gallatin and the same year was appointed deputy sheriff. In 1868 he was elected sheriff and served four years. In 1872 he was proprietor of Peyton's Merchant Mills and the following year established a livery and sale stable in Gallatin, and also speculated in stock. In 1883 he established a dry goods store in connection with his stable. In 1885 his stable was burned and since then he has given his entire time to his store. He is very conservative in politics, voting for principal and not for party, but rather favors the Democratic principles. His first presidential vote was cast for Fillmore in 1856. He is a member of the following orders: Masonic, I. O. O. F., K. of H., K. of P., and he and wife are members of the Methodist Episcopal Church South, he being one of the stewards.

S. E. Lackey, farmer and trader, is the son of William M. and Martha A. (Hocker) Lackey. The father was born November 25, 1815, in Madison County, Ky., and is of Irish descent. He is a farmer and followed this occupation for some time in his native county. In 1846 he moved to Lincoln County, Ky., where he has since resided. His wife is a native of Madison County, Ky., born August 28, 1822. To them were born two children, our subject being the only one living. He was born in Madison County, Ky., in 1841, and received his education in the schools of Lincoln County and at the University of Virginia, Charlotteville, where he attended two sessions. He was at the above mentioned institution at the breaking out of the war and in the summer of 1862 he enlisted in Company B, Sixth Regiment Cavalry (Confederate Army) under Gen. Buford. He was in the battles of Perryville and Murfreesboro and after the latter fight was transferred to Morgan's command, being with him in his famous raid through Kentucky, Indiana and Ohio. He was captured at Cheshire, Ohio, was taken to Camp Chase, then to Camp Douglas, and retained in both prisons about seven months. He escaped and afterward was one of twenty-three who captured the town of St. Albans, Vt., which created such great excitement at the time on our northern frontier. In October, 1864, on demand for extradition by the United States, for himself and comrades, he was tried and acquitted and demand for extradition denied by the British Government. He was, however, exempt from the general amnesty proclamation of President Johnson, but was afterward included and in 1866 returned to his native State and began trading in stocks. He has been engaged in the same business more or less ever since. In November, 1869, he married Miss Susie K. Alexander, a native of Gallatin, Tenn., and the daughter of James and Nancy J. Alexander. Three living children were the result of our subject's marriage, viz.: William W., Samuel E. and Mattie Alma. In 1870 Mr. Lackey came to Gallatin, where he has since resided. He resides in the suburbs of Gallatin on a beautiful stock farm in which he takes a pardonable pride. He is a Democrat in politics, casting his first presidential vote for Seymour and Blair in 1868. He is a member of the Masonic fraternity, the K. of P., the K. of H., and he and wife are members of the Missionary Baptist Church.

Mrs. Sarah Edmonia Lane, proprietor of a private boarding-house in Gallatin, is the oldest child born to the union of Zachariah F. and Mary

Jane (Brown) Green (for further particulars of parents see sketch of Louis Green). Our subject was born in Sumner County, Tenn., in 1832, and in 1848 was united in marriage to William R. Lane, a native of Sumner County, born in 1824, and the son of Bennet and Catherine Lane. To our subject and husband were born five children, who lived to be grown: Zachariah B., who is a farmer in Sumner County; Susan Elizabeth, deceased wife of William Allen; Martha W. (deceased); Sallie C., wife of Berry E. Love, and Miss W. Anna. William R. Lane was a farmer by occupation, and for many years was constable of his district. He was a soldier in the Mexican war, enlisting in Company I, First Regiment Tennessee Infantry, and after returning home never engaged in any active employment, his health being destroyed while serving his country. He died in 1863. In 1872 Mrs. Lane commenced keeping a private boarding-house on the public square. In 1874 she assumed charge of the Sindle House, and for six years was the mistress, and proved a success as such. In 1880 she moved on the public square, and in 1885 moved where she now resides. Mrs. Lane is a lady of fine taste, and one who is well skilled in looking after the culinary department and the management of a first-class boarding-house. Mr. Lane was a Royal Arch Mason, a Democrat in politics, and a member of the Methodist Episcopal Church South. Mrs. Lane is also a member of the same church.

P. A. Langford, farmer and stock dealer of the First District of Sumner County, was born in Clay County, Tenn., in January, 1847, being one of nine children, three sons and five daughters living. The parents were Eryin F. and Pamelia (Gates) Langford. The father was of Irish descent, born in Tennessee in 1812, and was the son of Stephen Langford, a native of Virginia. He was married August 13, 1840, and spent his entire life in his native county, farming and dealing in stock. He was colonel in the militia. He died September 25, 1860. The mother was also a native of Tennessee, born November 14, 1825, and is still living in Clay County, near her birthplace, a devout member of the Christian Church. Our subject was raised and educated at home, and has good business capacity. February, 1867, he commenced merchandising at Butler's Landing; in December, 1868, he went to Texas, and returned in about two years. May 10, 1876, he married Miss Alice, daughter of Van and Lucy Allen of Sumner County. They have two children: Frank and Irene. Mr. Langford remained in Clay County until 1883, when he moved to Sumner County, and purchased a farm of 155 acres finely improved, and desirably located, five miles east of Gallatin. Although Mr. Langford is comparatively a young man he is one of the most progressive farmers of Sumner County, and is extensively engaged in dealing in, and shipping stock to Southern points. He is a strong Democrat; his first presidential vote was cast for H. Seymour in 1868. Since 1871 he has been a member in good standing of the Masonic lodge. Mrs. Langford was born in Smith County, near Dickson's Springs, in 1854. Her parents were both natives of the same county. Her father was of Irish extraction, being a son of Robert Allen, who for several terms was a member of Congress while living in Smith County. Her mother was a daughter of William Young, a native of Virginia, born in 1797, afterward a prominent and wealthy citizen of Smith County, Tenn.

A. A. Lewis, postmaster at Gallatin and assistant publisher of the *Tennesseean*, was born in 1825 in Sumner County, a son of Andrew and Sidney V. (Boyers) Lewis. The father was of English-Irish descent, and a native of Dickson County, Tenn. About 1824 he moved to Sumner County, but in a short while returned to his native county, where he died about 1828. He was a farmer and a blacksmith. His wife was of English-Irish and Scotch-Welsh origin, was born in 1795 in South Carolina. After Mr. Lewis' death she married Harbert Wallace, now deceased. Her death occurred in 1881. Of four children, our subject is the only surviving one. He received a liberal education at Gallatin, at which place he became an apprentice in a printing office, and for four years worked on *The Gallatin Union*, published by D. C. Gaskill. He was afterward journeyman printer in other places. About 1855, in partnership with Martin Van Buren Hale, he established the *Tenth Legion* at Gallatin, and about 1859 he became associate editor with Robert Duncan of the *Courier and Enquirer* at same place. In 1861 he entered the provisional army as clerk in the paymaster's department, under Col. Boyers, who was assistant paymaster of the Army of the Tennessee. The latter portion of 1862 our subject was appointed chief clerk under Paymaster-General Col. William Williams, of the provisional army of Tennessee. He resigned in 1864 and returned home. In 1848 he married Miss Emeline P., daughter of R. S. Follis, of Allen County, Ky., where Mrs. Lewis was born in 1825. She died in 1886. Six children were born to this union, of whom are living Sidney R., Ella C., Frank W., Alberta A. and Lula O. In 1872 Mr. Lewis and son, Sidney R., established *The Tennesseean*, a newsy and ably edited county paper with a weekly circulation of about 1,500. It is Democratic in politics and fearless. In June, 1886, Mr. Lewis was appointed and commissioned by President Cleveland as postmaster at Gallatin. After assuming charge of the postoffice, his son Frank became associate editor of *The Tennesseean*, and has since been published by the Lewis Brothers. Our subject is a life-long Democrat, voting for Lewis Cass in 1848. He is a member of the Methodist Episcopal Church South, a Royal Arch Mason, and connected with the I. O. O. F., Scarlet degree.

Capt. Samuel Lyon, miller of Gallatin, was born to the union of Hamilton and Frances (Royse) Lyon, in Hamilton County, Ohio, in 1836. The father was born at Georgetown, Penn., in 1805, and was a blacksmith by trade. In 1825 he moved to Cincinnati, Ohio, where he married. For the past thirty years he has lived in Johnson County, Ky. His wife, Frances Royse, was a native of Maine, and departed this life in 1843. Our subject made his home with his father until twenty years of age, he receiving his education in the common schools and at Farmer's College, in Hamilton County. At the age of sixteen he commenced learning the iron molder's trade, working as an apprentice about four years. In 1857 he came to Tennessee, and worked in Gallatin, Chattanooga, Nashville and Murfreesboro. At the breaking out of the war he found Tennessee rather unpleasant for him as he was a strong Union man. Accordingly he went to Kentucky, and in 1861 enlisted in Company L, Second Kentucky Cavalry (United States Army), remaining in service nearly four years. He was in the battle of Shiloh, Resaca, Perryville, Murfreesboro, Chickamauga, Atlanta, Savannah and numerous minor engagements. He was with Sherman in his famous march to the sea, and in 1863 was commissioned as sergeant, later, of the same year, he was commissioned first lieutenant, and the following year was made captain, and served as acting assistant inspecting general and acting assistant adjutant-general, on the staff of Gen. E. H. Murray, commanding first brigade, Kirkpatrick's cavalry division, during the last year of his service. He was one of the fortunate ones, for although four horses were shot from under him he escaped without a wound. Two years after the war Capt. Lyon went into the oil business, prospecting and boring for oil in southeast Kentucky. In 1867 he came to Gallatin, and assumed charge of the Gallatin Flouring Mills. The mill was erected in 1854, and in 1881 Capt. Lyon added a saw. The mill has a capacity of 50 barrels of flour, 25 barrels of hominy, and 150 barrels of meal. Capt. Lyon purchased the mill in April, 1887, and is now sole owner and proprietor. In 1867 he married Miss Julia B. Barker, of Gallatin, the daughter of Henry J. Barker, and to them were born four children: Henry, Charles, Lizzie and Hurst. Capt. Lyon is a Republican in politics, and cast his first presidential vote for Abraham Lincoln. He is a Mason, a member of the K. of H., K. of P., a Good Templar, and his wife is a member of the Episcopal Church.

J. B. Malone, liveryman, is a native of Tennessee, born in 1844, a son of James N. and Keturah (Hannah) Malone. The father was of

Irish descent, born in what is now Trousdale County, this State, in 1806, and his father was a native of Virginia, immigrating to Middle Tennessee at a very early date. James N. Malone is yet living in this county, and is one of its oldest and most respected citizens. His wife was born in 1806, and died in 1884, after bearing five children, four of whom are yet living, viz.: Pattie, J. B., Minerva J. (Mrs. Joseph Andrew) and John W. J. B. Malone received a fair education in youth. May 3, 1861, he enlisted in the Second Tennessee (Confederate) Regiment, and was a faithful servant of his country. He participated in the battles of first Manassas, Shiloh, Richmond (Ky.), Perryville, Murfreesboro and Chickamauga, at the last named battle being severely wounded by a canister-shot through both legs, from the effects of which his right knee has always remained stiff. After remaining on an ambulance on the battle-field nearly three weeks, he was taken to the hospital at Marietta, Ga., where he suffered untold agony from erysipelas. For five years after the war he walked with crutches. By speculating in live stock he made considerable money, and for the past fifteen years has been in the livery business. December 16, 1885, he married Miss Kate, daughter of Prof. H. B. Todd, of Franklin, by whom he is the father of one infant daughter. He is a Democrat, has served two terms as county trustee, and is a first-class citizen.

Capt. J. N. McKoin, farmer and stock dealer, near Gallatin, District No. 9, Sumner County, was born in Clarksville, Tenn., in December, 1842. He is one of the six children of John G. and Mary J. (Baker) McKoin. The father, of Scotch-Irish origin, was born in Logan County, Ky., in 1812, and a furniture dealer by occupation. In 1830 he moved to Montgomery County, and was a director of The Planters' Bank at Clarksville, and also alderman. He is now retired from business. The mother, of Scotch origin, was born in Todd County, Ky., in 1822, and died about 1876. Educated in Stewart College, Clarksville, Tenn., in 1861 he enlisted in Company E, First Kentucky Cavalry, Helm's regiment, and was made sergeant. After his year's time was out he joined Williams' battalion for eight months as private, when he was commissioned captain. After forming a company in Kentucky, he was at Fort Donelson, Brice's Cross Roads, Milton and Tupelo. He was wounded at Hewey's Bridge, and still has in his possession the ball that wounded him. He was captured at Brice's Roads in 1865, and was detained a prisoner until the close of the war, when he returned to Montgomery County and engaged in agriculture. In June, 1869, he married Emma S., daughter of Henry and Mary A. Lugg, born in Robertson County in January, 1851. Their three children were Lena (deceased) John G. and

Henry S. in school. In 1879 Mr McKoin bought 300 acres of land, on which he has since resided. He is a self-made man, a Democrat in politics and a member of the Masonic fraternity.

Capt. J. H. McLaren, trustee of Sumner County, was born April 21, 1836, in Amelia County, Va., the only child of John W. H. and Avery Tilda (Hamblen) McLaren, both of whom were also natives of Amelia County, Va. The father was of Scotch descent, born in 1793, and married in 1833. In the fall of 1836 he started for Texas, but owing to illness stopped in Wilson County, Tenn., and settled there. His death occurred in 1838. His wife was of Irish extraction. Her second marriage was with R. R. Barton; she died in 1860. Our subject's educational advantages were very limited. He began farming on his own responsibility at the age of twenty. In 1855 he married Miss Docia A., daughter of James Cowen. She was born in Wilson County in 1836, and became the mother of seven children, viz.: Jesse B. (deceased); Mattie J., wife of D. B. Evertson; Sallie H., died in 1876, aged fifteen years; John S. J., who is his father's deputy; Mollie C.; Oldham C., and Addie D. After marriage our subject was engaged in farming and milling. In 1862 he enlisted in Company B, Forty-fifth Tennessee Regiment Infantry, and was elected third lieutenant of that company. At the battle of Shiloh he received a wound in the right knee by the bursting of a shell. After the battle he was promoted to the rank of captain and at the reorganization of the army was discharged owing to disability. After the war he resumed his former occupation. In 1871 he came to Gallatin and contracted to build one mile of the Cincinnati & Nashville Railroad in Sumner County. In 1874 he was elected constable, and served as such until 1880 when he resigned and became candidate for the office which he now holds. He has been elected four times, the last time receiving a plurality of nearly 800 votes over three other candidates. He has made an efficient and able officer. When he assumed charge of the office in 1880 the county was $24,000 in debt, and at present has a surplus of several thousands of dollars. He is a Royal Arch Mason, a member of the I. O. O. F., K. of H., K. & L. of H., K. of P., Iron Hall and A. O. U. W. He and his wife belong to the Missionary Baptist Church.

Lieut. J. A. Mentlo is a son of Dr. W. and Mary (Alexander) Mentlo and was born in Macon County, Tenn., in 1833, being one of two children, and the only child surviving. The father was born in Barren County, Ky., March 1, 1804, and died February 23, 1870. He was a son of Daniel Mentlo, who was a native of Virginia and one of the pioneers Barren County, Ky. Our subject's father was a man of ability and energy; he was a physician by profession, and graduated at Lexington,

Ky., and soon became one of the leading physicians in this county. He moved to Hartsville when about eighteen years old, and began the practice of medicine. He married March 18, 1828, and in 1838 went to Gallatin, but three years later moved to the country, not far from Gallatin, where he purchased a large tract of land and remained on it until his death. The mother was born in Smith County, May 11, 1811, and died October 10, 1865, a devout member of the Christian Church. Our subject was raised at home attending the neighboring schools, but completing his studies at Bethany, Va. October 20, 1852, he married Miss Susan, daughter of John and Mary Branham, and three of the five children born to them are living: Mary, wife of Wm. Hall, of Gallatin; Nannie, wife of Wm. H. Dunn, and Susie M., wife of Sam M. Anderson, of Louisville, Ky. He has since resided at the old homestead farm, owning 624 acres of valuable land, containing a handsome brick residence. It is four miles south of Gallatin, on the Hartsville pike. In 1862 Mr. Mentlo enlisted in the Confederate Army, in Company C, Bennett's battalion, as first lieutenant and remained one year, he participated in the battle of Shiloh, and was then discharged on account of the expiration of his commission, and was soon after captured and held as a prisoner at Gallatin and Louisville for three months, and was then paroled. Mr. Mentlo is an extensive land owner and a well posted farmer. He is liberal in his support of all charitable and religious enterprises and is a true Democrat. He is a Knight of Pythias, a Knight of Honor and Knight of the Golden Cross, and with his wife belongs to the Christian Church. Mrs. Mentlo was born in Sumner County in 1833.

James N. Mitchener, a prominent farmer and citizen of the First District, was born in Sumner County in 1827, and was one of fourteen children born to William B. and Elizabeth (Caudle) Mitchener. The father was of Dutch extraction, born in North Carolina in 1775, and moved to Sumner County when a boy, being one of the earliest settlers of the county. He was twice married, first to Mary Brien when he was just twenty-two years old. They had four children; after her death he married our subject's mother. He died in 1851, a highly esteemed citizen and a member of the Methodist Episcopal Church South. The mother was born in North Carolina in 1785, and died in 1849. Our subject was raised and educated in Sumner County. In November, 1848, he married Miss Narcissa, daughter of Samuel and Mary Wilkes, residents of Sumner County, but natives of North Carolina. Three of the four children born to them are living: Ann E., wife of T. J. Glenn; Lorilla Jane, wife of D. P. Dickenson, and Franklin C. Mrs. Mitchener died in 1855, and in July, 1856, he married Miss Cinderella, a sister of his first wife. Five of the eight children born to this marriage are living: John and Nancy Ellis (twins), the latter died; Samuel L. and Louisa L. (twins), the latter is the wife of A. J. Dickerson; Jeff Davis (deceased); Ulysses and Narcissa L. (twins), the latter deceased, and Cordelia C., wife of F. F. Hamilton. Mr. Mitchener has lived in Sumner County since his marriage excepting two years, 1858–59, that he spent in Henry County, and has lived on his present farm since 1862. He owns 155 acres of Sumner County's fertile land, well improved. He is a man of energy and undoubted integrity, and with the exception of eighteen months has been a magistrate in his district since 1865, also constable for a number of years, and was at one time lieutenant and captain of the militia. In politics he has been a life-long Democrat, casting his first presidential vote for Gen. Cass in 1848. Mrs. Mitchener was born in Sumner County in 1829. They are both earnest members of the Methodist Episcopal Church South and valuable citizens of the county.

Elihu N. Mitchener, a well known farmer and citizen of the First District, was born in Sumner County in 1829, being the eleventh born in a family of fourteen children. The parents were William B. and Elizabeth (Caudle) Mitchener. The father was of Dutch ancestry, born in North Carolina in 1775, and was twice married. His first wife was Mary Brien, and they had four children. After her death he married the mother of our subject. He was one of the early settlers of Sumner County, having moved to the county when it was a dense forest. He was an energetic man of fine character, and a consistent member of the Methodist Church. He died in 1851. The mother was born in North Carolina in 1785 and died in 1849.

Our subject was raised under the parental roof, and educated at Coram's Hill. He remained at home until he married Miss Nancy W., daughter of William and Sallie (McDaniel) Moss, September 15, 1857. Four sons and three daughters were born to this marriage: Robert M., Sallie E. (wife of Henry Gibbs), James N., William M., Kate C., Elihu W. and Nannie Pearl. Before his marriage Mr. Mitchener purchased the old home farm, where he has since resided, with the exception of five years in Wilson County, from 1858 to 1864. Mr. Mitchener owns 300 acres of valuable land ten miles southeast of Gallatin; all of this he has acquired by his frugal and industrious habits and good management, and he is now one of the most progressive farmers in Sumner County, and a man known for his honesty and integrity. He has been a life-long Democrat, and cast his first presidential vote for Franklin Pierce. Mr. and Mrs. Mitchener are faithful members of the Missionary Baptist Church. Mrs. Mitchener was born in Sumner County in 1834; her father was born near Fort Blunt, E. Tenn., in 1788, and was a volunteer under Gen. Jackson in the war of 1812. His mother, Jemima Barton, was born, raised and married in Fort Barton in E. Tenn., and died in Wilson County in 1833; he died in 1869.

Hon. D. A. Montgomery, farmer and school-teacher, is a native of Sumner County, born in 1852, and one of a family of three children born to John and Margaret (Taylor) Montgomery. The father was born in Sumner County, in 1826, of English descent, and a farmer by occupation. The mother was also a native of Sumner County, born in 1827 and of English descent. Our subject received his early education in the county schools and later attended Cumberland University at Lebanon. In 1873 he began work for himself, and in February, 1874, he married Miss Callie A. Kirkpatrick, daughter of Taylor and Mildred Kirkpatrick. She was born in Sumner County, Tenn., February, 1855, and by her marriage became the mother of one child, Robert S. Mr. Montgomery has been a Democrat all his life. He was elected justice of the peace in 1883, which office he now holds. He represented Sumner County, in the State Legislature in 1886, and received the largest number of votes any man received in Sumner County. He is one of the county's best citizens and has the respect of all. He and Mrs. Montgomery are members of the Cumberland Presbyterian Church.

John Morris, a native of the Emerald Isle, was born in 1837, and is one of six children born to Bartlett and Mary Morris, natives of Ireland, who died in 1863 and 1857, respectively. Our subject received his early education in Ireland, and at the age of twelve left his parents and immigrated to the United States, locating in Wheeling, Va. He worked on the railroad there for about eighteen months, and then went to Belmont County, Ohio, and began working on the Central Ohio Railroad, as section foreman. He then went to Pittsburgh, Penn., where he was engaged as foreman on the slack waters for about two years. About 1855 he came to Stewart County, Tenn., and from there to Laura Furnace. He then came to Nashville as train master. He was married in Nashville, in 1865, to Miss Ann Morrissey, a native of Canada, born in 1847, and the daughter of John and H. Morrissey. To this union were born eight children, viz.: John B., William H., Mary E., Margaret, Ellen, Agnes, Martin J. and Edna. Mr. Morris has always been a Democrat in politics and he and family are members of the Catholic Church.

William F. Moss, farmer and manufacturer of hickory handles, was born in Green County, Ky., in 1838, and is one of eleven children (six dead), born to Benjamin T. and Elizabeth C. (Duke) Moss. The father was born in 1792, in Virginia, and was a soldier in the war of 1812. After the war he came to Kentucky, and was married in this State. He died in 1849. The mother was also a native of Virginia, born in 1794, and she too is dead. Our subject was educated in Green and Warren Counties, Ky. He remained at home and worked on the farm until the breaking out of the late civil war, when he enlisted in the Confederate Army, Company L, Duke's regiment, Second Kentucky Cavalry, and remained with Morgan until his capture. When the company broke, our subject swam the Ohio River at Buffington's Island, into West Virginia, made his way to Greenbrier, W. Va., where he took the train for East Tennessee. Here he with others joined the army under Gen. Wheeler's command, and was captured while on a raid with Wheeler through Middle Tennessee. He was taken to Camp Morton, in Indiana, and was held until the spring of 1865. After his release he came back to Warren County, Ky., and worked on the farm for his brother, David J. Moss, for one year when he moved to the farm now owned by Mrs. Ernest Franklin, Sumner County, Tenn. In 1879 he purchased the farm near Bethpage, where he now resides. In 1862 he married Luke A. Allen, a native of Allen County, Ky., born in 1845, and the daughter of Luke P. and Annitta (Perkins) Allen. Nine children were the result of our subject's marriage: William B., Maggie Fletcher, Elizabeth C., Thomas Luke, Jennie H., Annitta, Ulysses Duke, Henry Fisk and Allen Woodson. There were also twin boys who died in infancy. Mr. Moss is a well-to-do farmer, and owns 200 acres of land nearly all of which is in blue-grass. He is a Democrat in politics and cast his first presidential vote for John Bell, candidate for the Whig party. He is a member of the I. O. O. F., R. H. Barry Lodge, No. 176, and is also a Good Templar. Mr. and Mrs. Moss and the eldest four children are members of the Methodist Episcopal Church.

Maj. W. S. Munday, attorney at law at Gallatin, is a native of Albemarle County, Va., and first saw the light of day in 1827. He is the son of Walker B. and Patsey (Smith) Munday. The father was born about 1807, was of English descent, living in Virginia at the time of his marriage. About 1829 he immigrated to Sumner County, Tenn., but the last thirty years of his life were passed in Kentucky. He died in 1876. His father was a drum major in the Revolutionary war. Mrs. Patsey Munday was born in Virginia and was also of English descent; she died in 1879. They had nine children, our subject being the eldest. He came to Sumner County, when a small lad and received his education in the common schools of that county. At the age of sixteen he was elected clerk of the county court and served eight years giving universal satisfaction. He was the youngest man ever elected to any county office in

Sumner County. When twenty years of age he commenced the study of law, Judge John J. White being his preceptor. He began practicing in Nashville, with Hon. McMurry as partner, but at the end of one year, not being satisfied with the location, returned to Gallatin where he has since resided. In 1857 and 1858 he was senator for Sumner and Smith Counties. Previous to this in 1852 he married Miss Almira Turner, a native of Gallatin, and the daughter of Capt. John G. Turner. One child blessed this union named William O. In November, 1861, he was commissioned by Geo. Harris to muster State troops, and succeeded so well that he was afterward appointed to the rank of major in the commissary department, with orders to report to Brig.-Gen. Daniel S. Donelson in northwest Virginia. In 1863 Donelson died, and Maj. Munday was appointed as chief of subsistence of the purchasing bureau in the State of Tennessee, which position he held until peace was declared. June, 1865, he returned home after four years' absence. Maj. Munday is one of the oldest practicing attorneys in Gallatin, and is one of the leading lawyers of the Sumner County bar. He has a fine library, one of the best in Gallatin; is a member of the I. O. O. F., Lodge No. 13. In 1862 he lost his wife, she being about twenty-two years of age. In 1866 he married Virginia James who died in 1877, and in 1881 he married Mary K. Thompson, a native of Rutherford County, and a member of the Presbyterian Church.

Prof. A. B. Murray, principal of Sumner High School, is a native of Sumner County, Tenn., born in 1854, and a son of William and Mary (Bugg) Murray. The father was born on the eastern shore of Maryland in 1823, and was of Irish extraction. When eighteen years of age he left his native State and went to Natchez, Miss., and from there to New Orleans a few years after. In 1844 he became private secretary of Mr. John Armfield, of New Orleans, La., who was a member of one of the largest business firms in the South. William worked for Mr. Armfield eight years, and during the summer months would reside in Sumner County, Tenn., and pass the winter season in New Orleans. He was married in 1850, and in 1852 purchased 199 acres, which he increased to 359 acres, all lying in the Fifth District, where he located and passed the remainder of his days. He died in 1883. His father, Michael Murray, was a native of Ireland. The mother of our subject was a native of Sumner County, born in 1828 and died in 1872. She was the daughter of Anselm B. and Tobitha (Smith) Bugg, very early settlers of Sumner County. Tobitha's grandfather, Daniel Smith, settled in the county in 1784, where Harry Smith now resides. To William and Mary (Bugg) Murray were born six children, our subject being the second. He received his academic education in the schools of Sumner County, and his collegiate education in the Cumberland University of Lebanon, Tenn., where he graduated June 10, 1875, receiving the degree of A. B. In 1877 he entered the teacher's profession and purchased C. W. Callender's interest in the Sumner High School at Hendersonville, and for the following three years was joint principal with Capt. C. S. Douglass. In 1880 Prof. Murray purchased Capt. Douglass' interest, and from said date our subject has been principal and sole superintendent of the above mentioned institution. The school will average about ninety pupils of a ten months' session each year. It is one of the best educational institutions of Sumner County, is a credit to the county and to the present superintendent. Prof. Murray takes an active part in the educational work of Sumner County, and is one of the leading educators of that county. He is well fitted for the position he now occupies, giving universal satisfaction as an instructor and disciplinarian. He is a Democrat in politics and cast his first presidential vote for S. J. Tilden in 1876. He is a Master Mason, a member of the Presbyterian Church, being an elder in the same, and is superintendent of the Sunday-school.

Joseph Natcher, boot and shoemaker in Gallatin, is a native of Carlisle, Cumberland Co., Penn., born January 18, 1823, and the son of George and Nancy (Kline) Natcher. The father was born in Cumberland County, Penn., was of German-Welsh descent, and a wagon-maker by trade. He was born, reared and passed his life in the same county. He died in 1828. His wife was a native of Philadelphia. After the death of her husband she married Frederick Sano, who was killed at Key West during the late war. She died in 1835. Our subject was five years old when his father died and only twelve when his mother passed away. What education he received was obtained outside of the schoolroom, as he had not attended school more than one year during his life. When quite young he served an apprentice in a blacksmith shop at Harrisburg, Penn., where he remained three years, but owing to his health was obliged to give it up. About 1841 he commenced learning the shoemaker's trade in Carlisle, and here worked for three years. In July, 1845, he came to Gallatin and worked a few months as journeyman for one Buckingham, after which he purchased Buckingham's stock and commenced business on his own responsibility. In 1852 he married Miss Caroline Lawrence, a native of Sumner County, born in 1828. Previous to this, during the war between the United States and Mexico, he joined the patriotic band, enlisting in Company I, First Tennessee Regiment, under Col. William B. Campbell and Col. S. R. Anderson. He fought at Monterey and Vera Cruz, but served only a few days over twelve months when he returned and at once re-enlisted in Company K, Third Regiment, under Col. B. F. Cheatham, William Hatton, captain, and Gov. Bate, first lieutenant. He was gone nearly two years, and at the termination of hostilities, went to Hartsville, thence to Arkansas, and in 1851 returned to Gallatin and opened up a shop, and here has continued to reside. He is counted among the oldest citizens, and is respected by all. By his marriage Mr. Natcher became the father of five living children: William H., who is bookkeeper at Bowling Green, Ky.; Ada, wife of George Philips; George, merchant; Clarence M., shoemaker at Gallatin and Capitola. Mr. Natcher is a man who attends strictly to business and is a skillful workman. He is a Democrat in politics and an ancient member of the I. O. O. F. His wife is a member of the Christian Church.

Jonas Nickelson, proprietor of the foundry and machine shops of Gallatin, is a native of Rhode Island and was born in 1821. He is the son of John and Jane (Williston) Nickelson. The father was born in New England in 1782, and in his younger days was a baker by trade; the latter part of his life was passed in cotton manufacturing. He died in 1834. His wife was a native of the Eastern States and died at the age of seventy-two. They had eleven children, six of whom are living, our subject being the eighth child. He was educated in Massachusetts and when eleven years of age commenced working in a cotton factory. At the age of eighteen he was assistant superintendent, and at the age of twenty-one was superintendent or overseer, being very skillful in the adjustment of machinery. In 1849 he came to Lebanon, Tenn., as superintendent of the carding and spinning department in a cotton factory, returned north in 1857, came to Gallatin in 1852 to take charge of adjusting the machinery in the carding and spinning department of Gallatin cotton factory; went to Gibson County, Tenn., in 1854, remained there until 1855, when he returned to Gallatin and took an interest in foundry and machine works at that place, and immediately entered upon the manufacturing of threshing machines, horse-power, fanning mills, corn shellers, chilled and cast plows and job work in general. He has been in the same business ever since and is one of the solid business men of Gallatin. He has added much to the prosperity of that city. The coming year he intends manufacturing hay presses. February 24, 1859, he married Levina M. Chase, a native of New Hampshire, born in 1828, and a member of the Missionary Baptist Church. Mr. Nickelson is a Democrat, a member of the Iron Hall Golden Cross, and has been alderman of Gallatin for several terms.

Samuel Nickelson (deceased), late manufacturer of woolen goods in Gallatin, was born in Salem, Mass., in 1814, son of John and Jane

(Williston) Nickelson. (For further particulars of parents see sketch of J. Nickelson.) At the age of seven our subject went to Newton Upper Falls in Massachusetts, and was employed in the cotton factory, learning carding and spinning. When a youth he was quite skillful and afterward became superintendent. About 1839 he went to Covington, Ky., where he resided two years. In 1841 he went to Lebanon, Tenn., and was employed as superintendent of the cotton-mills. 1848 he passed in Massachusetts, and the following year he went to California, it taking him 169 days to make the trip. He lived in the Golden State three years and during this time worked in the gold mines. He was among the first influx of immigrants to the State after the discovery of gold. He returned to Lebanon in 1852, and October 4 of the same year he married Miss Dorthula V. Phipps, a native of Lebanon, Tenn., born in 1826, and the daughter of W. R. D. Phipps, of Yazoo County, Miss. To them were born seven children: Albert O. P., who is in the government employ in Indian Territory; William R. D., an M. D. of Pastoria, Ark.; Samuel, Leola V., Ophelia and Victoria (twins), and Edwin F. In 1854 Mr. Nickelson went to Pulaski, Tenn., and began manufacturing cotton goods, which he continued until 1864, when he moved to Cambridge, Mass., and from there to Gallatin in 1868, where he erected a woolen-mill known as the Eagle Woolen Mills. In December, 1874, the mill was burned, and the following year Mr. Nickelson erected another, or the present one. Mr. Nickelson also owned twelve acres in Gallatin and a beautiful home. He also owned 335 acres in Alabama. He died June 5, 1877, and after his death his oldest son operated the mill. Mr. Nickelson was a Democrat in politics, a Mason and a Baptist in belief, although his family were members of the Presbyterian Church. He was a man of much public spirit, a Christian gentleman and a good citizen.

A. Parham, farmer and stock dealer, was born in 1825, in Granville County, N. C. He is one of six children of George and Elizabeth (Brinkly) Parham, the former a farmer, born about 1785 in Granville County, N. C., and the latter born about 1795 in the same county. Their deaths were in 1878 and 1880 respectively. Our subject was educated in Granville County and Sumner County, Tenn., where they came in 1835. He began for himself when of age, on his father's farm, but soon bought 100 acres adjoining his old home, and superintended both farms. In 1873 he married Lovey, daughter of Britton and Mary Rogers, and born in 1838 in Sumner County. Their two children are Annie B., at school, and George. Mr. Parham is a Democrat politically, and since 1882 has been a justice of the peace. His wife is a member of the Primitive Baptist Church.

M. B. Perdue, a well known farmer of the Tenth District, was born September 12, 1846, in the northern portion of Sumner County. He is one of nine children of Green P. and Matilda J. (Mattox) Perdue. The father was born in 1814 near our subject's home. At the age of twenty-six he married and settled on a farm given him by his father, near the homestead, where he died in 1884. His wife was born in the same vicinity, and now resides on the farm where Mr. Perdue died. Our subject was educated at Cross Plains, Robertson Co., Tenn. After attaining his majority, he taught winter school for seven years and farmed in the summer. In 1877 he sold a 200-acre farm which had been given him by his father, and purchased 100 acres seven miles northeast of Gallatin, where he has since devoted his time to agricultural pursuits. In 1871 he wedded Zoeintha, daughter of Rodney B. and Polly Durham, of Sumner County. Three sons and three daughters have been born to this union, Cotton Warren, Daisy A., Green, Erma Queen, Herbert Rodney and Virgil Blair. Ada Marshall died in 1876, in infancy. Our subject has been for several years a successful stock dealer and farmer. His place, which contains 350 acres, is highly cultivated and improved. He is a stanch Democrat, and is connected with the Masonic order and Bethpage Lodge. He and his wife are consistent and esteemed members of the Methodist Episcopal Church South.

A. D. Peyton, dealer in groceries, queensware and hardware, was born in Rutherford County, Tenn., in 1860. Capt. Thomas D. Peyton, his father, was born in 1831 in the same county as our subject, and was a son of John Peyton, who was a native of Wilson County, this State. Thomas D. resided in his native county until 1878, when he moved to Nashville, merchandising until 1880, when he moved to Sumner County and engaged in agricultural pursuits. During the late war he was captain of Company E, Forty-fifth Confederate Regiment of Infantry and as such led his command at Shiloh. Owing to ill health he was compelled to resign his commission at the reorganization. He and wife were parents of ten children, five yet living. A. D. Peyton is the fifth child. He secured an academical education in his native county and at nineteen years of age graduated at the Goodman Business College, Nashville. For two years he was employed as traveling salesman from Nashville wholesale houses, but in 1882 engaged in farming in this county at which he continued three years. In 1886 he established his present business, which has prospered from the beginning. Miss Willie S. Bell, daughter of Maj. Robert Bell of Wilson County, became his wife, December 20, 1882. He is a Democrat and a member of the K. of P., and he and his wife belong to the Methodist Episcopal Church South.

D. M. Phillips, of the Tenth Civil District of Sumner County, is a native of Tennessee, his birth occurring in 1823. He is one of a family of seven children born to Martin and Sarah Phillips. The father, a native of South Carolina, was born in 1793, and at the age of fourteen years came to Tennessee, residing the first seven or eight years in Smith County. Later he removed to DeKalb County, where he died in 1867. His wife was a native of the Old Dominion, born in 1795; died in DeKalb County, this State, in 1885. The subject of this sketch made his home with his parents until the age of twenty-two years, when he began farming upon his own responsibility. In 1868 he moved to this county, purchasing the 600-acre farm where he now resides, to which he has since added considerable. Mr. Phillips is one of the best and most successful farmers and stock raisers in the county; is a Democrat and a worthy citizen. In 1862 he entered the Confederate service and was on detailed service until he was paroled, some thirteen months after his enlistment. In 1845 he married Susan Martin, who died in 1859, leaving one son—Alexander T. In 1860 Mrs. Elizabeth (Turner) Morgan became his second wife, and to their union have been born five children: Minnie, Nelson M., Joe D., Anna and James M.

F. F. Pierce, one of the most extensive stock dealers of Sumner County, and member of the firms of Pierce, Howison & Burford, and Pierce & Burford, of Gallatin, also Pierce, Lyle & Co., of Nashville, was born in 1844 in Alleghany County, Penn. He is a son of Daniel and Elizabeth (Ketchum) Pierce, both of whom were natives of Pennsylvania, and of English descent. The father was born near Pittsburgh in 1807, a farmer and banker. His entire life was spent in his native State, where he died in 1881. His wife died in 1877. The subject of this sketch received a good common-school education in his native county, followed by a course at Wyer's Military Institute at Westchester, Penn. February 2, 1869, he married Miss Hannah, daughter of Perry A. Lytle, who was born in Allegheny County, Penn., in 1847. To this union three children have been born: Alvin, Elmore and Lizzie. In 1869 our subject came to Sumner County and purchased 400 acres of land in the Third District, two miles from Gallatin, on the Gallatin and Lebanon pike, and began farming and speculating. In 1882 the firm of Pierce & Burford was formed. In 1884 Pierce, Lyle & Co. was established in Nashville. They speculate in all kinds of live stock. May, 1886, the livery stable of Pierce, Howison & Burford was erected. It is made of brick and frame, 188 feet long and 48 feet wide, and cost $4,000. They have sixteen horses, ten single and four double vehicles. It is a first class stable in every particular, and is receiving a liberal patronage.

Mr. Pierce takes great interest in the improvement of the stock in the county. He owns some fine stock, two Gen. Thomas, two Blackwoods and one Scott Thomas. He is a director in the Farmers' & Traders' Bank, and a K. of P. He is a Republican, and voted for U. S. Grant in 1868. He and his wife are actively connected with the Missionary Baptist Church, Mr. Pierce having been the Sunday-school superintendent more than a year. He is an energetic, prosperous and highly esteemed man.

Hon. W. G. Pond, farmer, stock-dealer and merchant in Fountain Head, Sumner County, was born there in 1883. He is one of seven children of Richard and Ann M. (Guthrie) Pond. The father, of Scotch-Irish origin, was born in Robertson County in 1808. For thirty years he was justice of the peace where he lived. After 1830 he lived in Sumner County until his death in 1879. The mother, also of Scotch-Irish blood, was born in Sumner County in 1815, and died in 1862. With common school advantages our subject engaged in merchandising at twenty years of age. In 1857 he married Nannie J., daughter of Thornton and Fannie Lain, and born in 1839 in Wilson County. Their four children are W. G., clerk in his father's store; C. Y., farmer; Fannie A., wife of W. F. Butler, and John L., farmer. In January, 1882, his wife died. In May, 1883, he married Mrs. M. J. Brown, daughter of G. B. and Mary G. Harris, and born in Sumner County in 1835. Enlisting in Company E, Thirtieth Tennessee Regiment as private, in 1861, he was soon made first lieutenant, and then assistant commissary with the rank of captain; captured at Fort Donelson, he was imprisoned at Johnson's Island six months, and then exchanged at Vicksburg, Miss. After following the flag until it went down he was paroled at Jonesboro, N. C., in 1865, and came back to his native county penniless and began merchandising. Always a Democrat, he represented Sumner County in the Lower House in 1874. He is a Mason, and his wife is a member of the Christian Church, while his children, Willie and Fannie, are members of the Methodist Episcopal Church South. Mr. Pond has been so successful as to acquire 600 acres of fine land, and a good business worth about $40,000.

Allen L. Pryor, an agriculturist of the Tenth District, was born in White County, Tenn., in 1816. He is one of seven children of John and Massey (Taylor) Pryor. The father was of English descent, a native of Virginia. He located in White County about 1815, and remained there until 1828 or 1829, when he moved to Sumner County and purchased a 100-acre farm nine miles north of Gallatin, near South Railroad Tunnel. A year later he went to Overton County where he died about 1850. The mother was of French-English origin, a native of Virginia, and died about 1863. The subject of our sketch was educated in the common schools of Sumner County. At the age of eighteen he became an apprentice to the spinning-machine trade, under Squire Wm. Matthews. After four years he began working for himself at his trade, in Sumner County. In 1854 he bought a farm of 105 acres, upon which he now resides. He has since added to the place until it now contains 320 acres. In 1845 he married Elizabeth, daughter of William and Anna Tally, of Sumner County. Mrs. Pryor was born in 1825, in Virginia, and died in 1863, a member of the Cumberland Presbyterian Church, and mother of six sons and five daughters: Wm. T. (a resident of Collin County, Tex.), Lycurgus, John E., Ann Eliza, Lucy, Elizabeth and Alice; those deceased: Dewitt, Katherine and two infant boys. December 25, 1871, our subject wedded Margaret, daughter of Isaac and Adeline McWhirter, of Sumner County. Mrs. Pryor was born in Hardeman County, Tenn., in 1835. Subject is a Democrat, and cast his first presidential vote for Martin Van Buren. With the exception of two children, the entire family belongs to the Cumberland Presbyterian Church. Lycurgus is a member of the Methodist Episcopal Church.

J. Y. Robb, clerk and master of the chancery court, was born in Sumner County, Tenn., August 15, 1832, and was appointed by Judge George E. Seay, to his present position in September, 1882. He is the youngest of a family of seven sons and three daughters born to Joseph and Ann (Motheral) Robb. The father was of Scotch-Irish descent, born April 11, 1781, in Mecklenburg County, N. C. He came to Sumner County about 1799, where he taught school a number of years. He then began cultivating the soil in the Tenth District, in connection with which he established a dry goods store in Gallatin. Very soon after he came to Tennessee, he connected with Shiloh Church, the first Presbyterian Church organized in Middle Tennessee, and was a ruling elder in the same until his death. He died November 11, 1811. His wife, also of Scotch-Irish origin, born in 1791 in Sumner County, and died July 3, 1846. Our subject received his education at Transmont Academy, Gallatin. October 22, 1856, he married Miss Clara, daughter of Wm. and Penelope Lauderdale. Their union resulted in the birth of Charles W., a physician at Goodlettsville, Davidson County; Wm. L.; Nella and Bessie. Mr. Robb is a Democrat and cast his first presidential vote for Buchanan in 1856. He is a member of the Presbyterian Church; has been an elder in the same since 1872. His wife, Charles and Nella are also members of the same church.

H. W. Robb, a farmer of the Second District of Sumner County, was born in Wilson County, Tenn., in 1815, and is a son of John and Jane (McKearney) Robb. The father was of Irish ancestry born in North Carolina in 1785, where he was raised, and married there in 1806, and in 1808 moved to Wilson County, Tenn., where he engaged in farming until his death in 1864. The mother was born in North Carolina in 1785, and died in 1874. Our subject was raised and educated in Wilson County, and in 1850 married Miss Margaret, daughter of John and Margaret Palmer of Wilson County. They had four sons and five daughters: Jane, Sallie, Martha, Ellen (wife of Malone Swaney), John (of California), Charles, Frank, Margaret and William. Mr. Robb remained in Wilson County until 1859, when he came to Sumner County, and located on his present farm five miles east of Gallatin. He owns 265 acres of land, well cultivated and improved. Mr. Robb has always been a hard working, industrious man, and has accumulated his property by his own efforts. He is a good citizen and a kind neighbor. Before the war he was a Whig but is now a Democrat. Mrs. Robb was born in Wilson County in 1828, and is an earnest member of the Christian Church.

J. C. Rodemer, contractor, and also supply merchant with store in Gallatin, is a native of Frederick, Va., born in 1839, and the son of Christopher and Anna (Ruloff) Rodemer. The father was born in Baden, Germany in 1813. When quite young he left his native country and immigrated to the United States, settling in Virginia. He married and afterward lived in Maryland and Kentucky. In 1858 he came to Sumner County and settled near Gallatin. He followed contracting on railroads the greater portion of his life. He worked on the Louisville & Nashville Railroad for three years. He died in 1858. His wife was born in Prussia and since the death of her husband has lived in Sumner County. Of their seven children (five now living) our subject is the eldest. He received his education in an academy at Cumberland, Md., and at the age of thirteen commenced working on contracts with his father. After the death of his father he succeeded him in the business at which he has since been engaged. He has worked on the Baltimore & Ohio, the Parksburg Branch, Virginia, the Louisville & Nashville, the Nashville & Northwestern, and was contractor on the Tennessee & Pacific, Glasgow Branch, Memphis & Knoxville, Elizabethtown & Paducah (Cumberland, Ohio), Owensboro & Russelville, Nashville & Tuscaloosa, Knoxville Extension of Lebanon Branch of Louisville & Nashville, Cincinnati Southern, Middle & East Tennessee Central, and numerous pikes. In 1866, directly after the war, Mr. Rodemer married Miss Mary Ida Walsh, who was a native of South Carolina. She died in 1868. Mr. Rodemer is a Royal Arch Mason and Council Mason and is a highly respected citizen. He is a member of the Methodist Episcopal Church South. He has been successful, and carried out and completed all his contracts.

Charles B. Rogan, of the Eleventh District, of Sumner County, is a son of Frank and Martha L. (Read) Rogan, and was born in Sumner County in 1839, being the fifth of nine children, two sons and one daughter living. The father was of Irish descent, born in Sumner County in 1798. Our subject's grandparents, Hugh and Ann (Duffy) Rogan, were natives of Ireland; the grandfather was born in Glenntown, Donegal County, in 1747, and the grandmother was born in Lisduff, County Tyrone, and were married in 1775. Mr. Rogan immigrated to the United States in the last ship that came over before the war of independence, and landed at Philadelphia where he soon found employment with a Quaker by the name of Downey, and in a short time enlisted as a marine on the American ship, "Philadelphia," but was deceived by Downey about the time the ship was to sail, and reached Philadelphia the day after it left. Mr. Rogan then followed the Colonial Army south with the intention of enlisting, but finding the army retreating, he went direct to what was known as The Hornet's Nest, a settlement of Irish Presbyterians in North Carolina, for protection, and soon after joined a surveying expedition, as guard, to run the line between North Carolina and Virginia, now Tennessee and Kentucky, reaching what is now Trousdale in December, 1779, where they camped until spring, then moved to where Nashville now stands, and, under the North Carolina laws granting 640 acres of land to those who raised corn on the Cumberland River, he raised a crop of corn and carried it to the bank of the river for transportation, and through the assistance of others who had taken advantage of the same law, obtained a flatboat and agreed to transport their crops together. But his associates, after loading the boat with their crops, poled down the river, and upon reaching the point where Mr. Rogan had his, they refused to permit him to load it, claiming that the boat was loaded to its full capacity. He, being baffled in his efforts and outraged at the deception, remained with his crop on the bank and watched the boat moving down the stream, but before it was out of sight the entire party, with the exception of a negro, were ruthlessly and brutally murdered by a band of Indians, who fell suddenly upon them from the forest. Mr. Rogan, soon after this narrow and fortunate escape, joined Gen. Daniel Smith and a small party, who were defeated at Crag Font Bluff by Indians. He then made his home with Col. Isaac Bledsoe, of Bledsoe Lick, now Castalian Springs. (For his brave defense of that place, read Carr's history of "Early Times in Tennessee.") He was actively engaged with every expedition sent against the Indians from that section. Some years later Mr. Rogan started back to Ireland to bring his family to the new settlement, but reaching Virginia he was told by a relative that his wife had married another man, and being disappointed he immediately returned to Tennessee, but, years later, receiving a direct message from his wife that the statement in regard to her marriage was false, he started at once to Ireland (in 1796) to see his family, after an absence of twenty-one years. He went via Wilmington, N. C., where he took on board a cargo of flaxseed, but on nearing the coast of Ireland was caught in the storm that destroyed the French fleet, and was compelled to throw his cargo overboard. Mr. Rogan then joined his family, and they soon after returned to the United States and settled in Sumner County on land that he had received for his "corn" grant, and a portion of this land has ever since remained in the hands of his descendants. He was a brave soldier and an industrious farmer, and died in 1814 after a remarkably exciting and eventful career, and was one of the most intelligent, useful and daring pioneers of the State. Frank Rogan, our subject's father, was raised and educated at home. In 1833 he married Miss Martha L. Read, a granddaughter of Col. Isaac Bledsoe, and a daughter of Capt. William Read. He was a farmer, and a life-long resident of the farm where he was born. He was a man of brilliant intellect, and honored for his integrity and courage. He died in 1885. The mother was born near Enon College, Trousdale County, in 1802, and died in 1862. Our subject received his early education at Rural Academy, and finished his studies at St. Mary's College in Kentucky. In 1861 he enlisted in the Confederate Army, in Company K, Second Tennessee Regiment, under W. B. Bate, and entered the Virginia campaign, being in the first battle of Bull Run. In January, 1862, he re-enlisted, and at once joined the Tennessee army, and engaged in the battles at Shiloh and Chickamauga; afterward was placed on Gen. Bate's staff, where he remained until the close of the war. November 18, 1866, he married Miss Victoria, daughter of Matthew and Angeline Cecil. In 1868 he settled on his present farm where he owns 213 acres of fine land ten miles northeast of Gallatin. Politically Mr. Rogan is an ardent Democrat; his first presidential vote was for John C. Breckinridge. Mr. and Mrs. Rogan are both members of the Catholic Church. She was born in Kentucky in 1847.

D. A. Rascoe, a farmer and merchant in Cotton Town, Sumner County, was born there in February, 1826, one of eleven children of Thomas H. and Sarah H. (Combs) Rascoe. The father, a farmer by occupation, and born about 1800, near Gallatin, died in 1879. The mother was born in Ohio, came to Sumner County when a small child, and died in 1861.

Our subject attended Rural Academy, part of the time as assistant teacher, and began teaching when about twenty years of age. In 1859 he married Amanda, daughter of Isaac and Mary Baker, and born in Sumner County in 1841. Their children are Willie E., wife of Fred Weatherbee, of Boston; Thomas H., a farmer; Isaac, deceased; Hettie E.; Alexander C., clerking in California; Mary B., David L., Winfield S. and Bessie H.—the last three in school. Mr. Rascoe, wife, Willie and Hettie are all members of the Church of Christ.

Harmon J. Shafer is a son of David and Catherine (Sloggy) Shafer, and was born in Pennsylvania in 1840, being the youngest of five children, two sons and two daughters living. The father was of French extraction; born in Pennsylvania in 1807, lived in his native State nearly all of his life, and was a good business man, and was a butcher and stock trader at Pittsburgh for a great many years, and was postmaster at New Castle, Penn., during Polk's administration. He became a man of considerable means. In 1875 he came to Sumner County on a visit, and died here. The mother was also a native of Pennsylvania, and was born in 1806 and died in 1877. Our subject was raised and educated in Pennsylvania. In 1865 he married Miss Margaret A., daughter of John and Mary Haffey, of Pittsburgh, where Mrs. Shafer was born. They had six children, one son and three daughters living: David Charles, Margaret, Ellen, Kate and Ida Lewis. Mr. Shafer commenced business as a stock dealer at Pittsburgh, which he continued until 1867, and in 1869 moved to Sumner County and located south of Gallatin on the Cumberland River. In 1882 he purchased his present farm of 304 acres of rich land, five miles west of Gallatin, between Nashville and Gallatin pike. Politically, he is a Democrat; his first presidential vote was for McClellan in 1864. Mrs. Shafer is a member of the Catholic Church; he is a valuable citizen of the county.

J. M. Shute, a very successful farmer of the Fifth District, was born where he now resides in 1832, and is a son of Lee and Margaret (Dunn) Shute. The father was born in Davidson County, Tenn., in 1797, and was of German descent. He was married in his native county, and in 1831 came to Sumner County, purchased 320 acres of land in the Fifth District, where he settled, and engaged in agricultural pursuits. He afterward possessed 840 acres in Sumner County. He died in 1879. His wife was born in Davidson County, Tenn., in 1811, and died in 1852. They had eight children, three of whom are living. Lee's father, John Shute, settled on the old home place, where he passed his life. Lee's grandfather was a native of Pennsylvania, and at a very early date immigrated to where Goodlettville is now standing. It was then Mansker

Lick. He afterward moved to Richland Creek, near Nashville, where he settled and died. Our subject was educated in the common schools of his county, and in addition attended the literary department of Cumberland University at Lebanon for one year. He attended Washington Institute, in Davidson County, two years, and the Tennessee Institute about the same length of time. In 1853–54 he was in attendance at the law department of Cumberland University for ten months. In 1855 he entered the teacher's profession, and taught two years. He then commenced his career as a farmer. During the civil war he enlisted in 1861 in Company A, First Battalion of Tennessee Cavalry (Confederate Army), and participated in the battles of Shiloh, Thompson Station, Murfreesboro, Pulaski, Lebanon, Franklin and Barbersville. He was captured at Jackson, W. Tenn., and taken to Alton, Ill., where he remained one month. He was again captured at Kingston Spring, and was taken to Camp Chase, Ohio, and retained six months. He was paroled in 1864, and returned home. After peace was declared he resumed farming on the old home place. In 1867 he married Miss Martha Donelson, a native of Sumner County, born in 1847, and the daughter of Gen. Daniel S. Donelson. The fruits of this union were four children: Margaret Lee, Mary D., John Branch and Martha B. Mr. Shute's father erected a large and commodious brick house in 1858, one of the best in the county. Our subject now owns 400 acres, and is one of the substantial farmers of the county. He is a Democrat, a Royal Arch Mason, and he and wife are members of the Presbyterian Church.

James A. Soper, farmer of the Third District, is a native of Sumner County, born in 1843; son of James and Julia A. (Boon) Soper, both natives of Sumner County, Tenn. The father was born in 1819, and was a farmer by occupation. His father (subject's grandfather), John O. Soper, was a native of Maryland, who immigrated to Sumner County, Tenn., where he settled and remained until his career ended. The father of our subject married in Sumner County, and in 1850 he moved near Cole's Ferry, where he now resides, being one of the old citizens of Sumner County. His wife was born about 1815, and she too is living. They had four children only two of whom are living, our subject being the second child. He was educated in the common schools of his native county, and in 1861 enlisted in Company K, Eighteenth Regiment Tennessee Infantry (Confederate Army), and participated in the battles of Fort Donelson, Murfreesboro, Chickamauga, Missionary Ridge and Dalton. At Fort Donelson he was captured and taken to Camp Butler, Ill., where he was retained about eight months, and then exchanged at Vicksburg, when he immediately joined his command. At Atlanta, August, 1864, he was captured and taken to Camp Chase, Ohio, where he was retained about six months. In February, 1865, he was paroled in Rome, Ga., and returned home May, 1865. December, 1867, he married Miss Melissa Ophelia Gourley, a native of Sumner County, and the daughter of Samuel and Rebecca Gourley. To our subject and wife were born three children: Annie, Edwin and Maud. Mrs. Soper died February, 1877, and in August, 1879, Mr. Soper married Mary E., sister of his first wife. To this union were born two children: Harmon and Samuel. In 1880 Mr. Soper located where he now resides. He has a good farm of 173 acres, and is an enterprising and successful farmer. In politics he is a conservative, voting for principle and not for party. Mrs. Soper is a member of the Methodist Episcopal Church South.

Dr. W. R. Tomkins, cashier of the Bank of Gallatin, was born in 1837, in Gallatin, Sumner Co., Tenn., a son of J. R. A. and Mary (Madding) Tomkins, both of whom were of Irish descent. The father was born in 1800 in South Carolina, and when six years of age came with his father, John Tomkins, to Gallatin, where he commenced merchandising at an early age, and was for many years one of the leading and most prosperous business men of the place. He was president of the cotton factory a number of years. In 1871, when the Bank of Gallatin was organized, with a capital stock of $75,000, he was elected president, and his son, Joseph M., became cashier. Both died in 1879. Mr. Tomkins owned 600 acres of land near Gallatin, and was one of the most esteemed citizens. His wife was born in Robertson County, Tenn., and married in Sumner County. She was the mother of five children, of whom only John A. and our subject survive. Her death occurred in 1846. Dr. Tomkins received a thorough literary education at Central College, Danville, Ky. At the age of twenty-two he began the study of medicine. In 1859 he graduated at the Nashville University as an M. D. In 1861 he again graduated and received the same degree at the University of New York, New York City. During two years of the war he was assistant surgeon in the hospitals at Nashville. After the restoration of peace the Doctor began his practice, which he continued with success until 1879, when he was appointed cashier of the bank in his deceased brother's place. In 1865 the Doctor married Miss Mary, daughter of R. S. Payne. One child was born to this union, Lewis M., who received a fatal injury from a falling brick wall October 6, 1886, and died twenty-two hours afterward. He was a young man of exemplary habits, beloved by all. The day of his funeral all the business houses were closed in respect to his memory. The Doctor's second marriage was with his sister-in-law, Miss Alice Payne, who bore him one child, William R. His third union was with Miss Ida Lewis, of St. Louis, by whom he has one child, Charles. Mrs. Tomkins is an earnest member of the Methodist Episcopal Church South. The Doctor owns 440 acres of valuable land in Sumner County, and is one of the most able and solid business men of Gallatin. He is a Democrat, a member of the Masonic fraternity, King Solomon Lodge, No. 94. He also belongs to the K. of H. and K. of P.

Gen. William Trousdale (deceased) was born in Surry County, N. C., in 1790, and was of Scotch-Irish descent. When eight years of age, he came with his father, James Trousdale, to Sumner County, Tenn., and located on 640 acres, which James received for services rendered during the Revolutionary war, and on which a portion of Gallatin is now standing. William was a pupil of the Rev. Gideon Blackburn and of John Hall, two of Tennessee's early and most honored educators. In 1813, although a mere boy, William abandoned his books and as a private volunteer, entered the army. Soon after reaching the Indian country, he was elected third lieutenant. He participated in the battle of Tallahatchee, fought by Gen. Jackson's side at Talladega, and when his term of service expired returned home and resumed his studies. In 1814, in response to a call for volunteers, he joined the patriotic band and was at the battle of Pensacola, where he captured a cannon. He also took part in the battle of New Orleans, and when peace was restored he returned home and again began his studies. He read law and was admitted to the bar in 1820. He married Miss Mary Bugg, a native of Virginia, born in 1808. In 1835 he was elected senator to the State Legislature, and in 1836 became major-general of the State militia. The same year, at the head of a gallant regiment of mounted men, he went to Florida, where he was engaged in three battles. In 1837 he was the Democratic nominee for Congress, and was defeated by a small majority, although the Whig majority was large. In 1840 he was Democratic elector in the presidential contest, and in 1847 he was appointed by the President as colonel of infantry in the United States Army. June 13 he landed at Vera Cruz with his regiment; July 13 he was at Pueblo, and August 13 he reached the valley of Mexico. He was at the battle of Molino-del-Rey, also at the battle of Chapultepec. He was twice wounded and had a broken arm, but continued on duty. He commanded the Third Division of the army on the return home. In 1849 he was elected governor, Neill S. Brown being the Whig candidate. He filled this honorable position with credit and distinction. In 1853 he was appointed by President Pierce as minister plenipotentiary to Brazil, and after four years at Rio Janeiro, he returned home by way of Europe and visited Italy, France and England. He died in March, 1872. He was a gentleman in the fullest sense of the word, a faithful and incorruptible public servant and an able professional man. His wife came to Sumner County, when only six years of age. She died in 1883. Their son, Hon. J. A. Trousdale, is a legal practitioner at Gallatin.

Charles W. Trousdale was born at Gallatin in 1838, and is a son of ex.-Gov. Wm. Trousdale of Tennessee. He was educated in his native town, and in the city of Rio de Janeiro, when he accompanied his father, the United States minister to Brazil during the administration of President Pierce. After his return from South America, Mr. Trousdale studied law with his father, and was admitted to the bar in 1860. In 1862 he joined Ward's regiment of Tennessee Cavalry, Morgan's command, was elected first lieutenant of Company A, and served with that company until the battle of Chickamauga. Being wounded in that battle, and permanently disabled for field service, he was assigned to post duty; and served as assistant adjutant-general on the staff of Gen. Marcus J. Wright, at Atlanta, and with Gen. W. W. Macall, at Macon, Ga., until the close of the war. Mr. Trousdale married in 1860, Eleanor, daughter of Eli Odom of Sumner County. She died in 1866, leaving one child, a daughter. Since 1870 Mr. Trousdale has lived at his home in Gallatin.

J. N. Turner, an enterprising farmer and stock raiser of District No. 11 in Sumner County, is a son of Nelson B. and Elizabeth (Bunton) Turner and was born in Sumner County in 1839, being the youngest of seven children, three sons and two daughters surviving, and all living in Sumner County. The father was born in Virginia in 1797, and came to Sumner County with his parents when only nine years old, and was one of the pioneers of the county. He was married at the age of twenty-six and died May 31, 1874. He was colonel of the militia during the muster, and a farmer by occupation and a member of the Christian Church. The mother was born in Sumner County in 1805 and died in June, 1842. Our subject was raised at home and educated at Rural Academy. In May, 1861, he enlisted in the Confederate Army in Company I, Second Tennessee Infantry, under Gen. Bate, and served in the Virginia campaign and was in the first battle of Bull Run. In February, 1862, he re-enlisted for the war and entered the Army of the Tennessee, was in the battles of Shiloh and at Perryville, Ky., where he received a severe wound in his left leg, that caused its amputation a few days after. He remained with a private family in Kentucky for some time, and was then in prison in Camp Butler until he recovered, when he was placed in the quartermaster's department, where he remained until the war closed, when he returned home after four years' gallant service. October 17, 1865, he married Miss Pattie, daughter of David P. and Alice Bullock, of Sumner County, formerly of Kentucky, where she was born in 1844. They have three sons and three daughters: James E., Erskine B., Alice B., Pattie B., Anna H. and David Bullock. Mr. Turner first located on a farm on Cumberland River in the Third District, but in 1875 moved to his present farm that consists of 343 acres of Sumner County's best land, eight miles northeast of Gallatin; he also owns 462 acres in the Third District. He is one of the most extensive land owners and enterprising farmers in the county, and is a man that exerts a good influence. He is an enthusiastic Democrat and cast his first presidential vote for John C. Breckinridge in 1860. Mr. and Mrs. Turner are active and faithful members of the Christian Church.

T. S. Vaughn, M. D., whose residence is on Cole's Ferry pike, two and a half miles from Gallatin, is a native of Wilson County, Tenn., born in 1820, and the son of Rev. M. S. and Sarah R. (Vaughan) Vaughan. The father was of Welsh descent, born in Georgia in 1797, and when a child went to Alabama. He was married in Wilson County, Tenn., and located at Blount Springs, Ala., after marriage. At an early age he took an interest in politics, and soon became one of the leading politicians of Alabama, and one of its most influential citizens. He was one of the framers of the constitution of the State, and afterward served in both branches of the Legislature for several years. About 1832 he moved to Wilson County, Tenn., and in 1839 entered the ministry, advocating the Cumberland Presbyterian faith. He was both a circuit and local minister, having charge of one church eighteen years. He was also a teacher by profession, being for twenty-four years principal of the La Guardo Academy. He was a thorough student, and a gentleman in every sense of the word. He died in 1871. For several years he was engaged in surveying cotton lands in Mississippi for the Federal Government. He served through the war of 1812. His wife was born in 1798, in Wilson County, Tenn. She died in 1873. They had nine sons, only two of whom are living: T. S. (our subject) and Edmund D., who lives near La Guardo, engaged in agricultural pursuits. Our subject obtained his literary education at the La Guardo Academy, and when twenty-three years of age went to Lake Providence, La., and was hired as bookkeeper in a wholesale and retail dry goods store. He was there five years, when he returned and commenced the study of medicine. He went to the medical school at Lebanon, Tenn., where he remained eighteen months, and in 1851 he graduated at the University of Louisville, Ky., as an M. D. The following year he lived in Sumner County and practiced medicine. He then went to La Guardo and practiced medicine and sold drugs. In 1855 he went to Jackson Port, Jackson Co., Ark., and resided there ten years, devoting his time and attention to his profession and meeting with good success. In 1863 he came to Sumner County and purchased 186 acres and in 1869 sold out, after which he purchased 186 acres where he now resides. The Doctor looks after the interests of his farm and does some practicing yet, but has been trying to abandon his practice for some years. Previous to the late war he married Miss Mildred A. Lane, a native of Sumner County, born in 1832, and the daughter of Bennett Lane. Dr. Vaughan is a Democrat, a Royal Arch Mason and his wife is a member of the Cumberland Presbyterian Church.

Josiah Walton, farmer and stock dealer, District No. 8, Sumner County, was born there in 1829. He is one of nine children of Josiah, Sr., and Sarah (Walker) Walton. The father, of Welsh origin, was born in Sumner County in August, 1788, and was chairman of the county court several years, and private secretary of Andrew Jackson in 1818. He died in August, 1857. The mother, of Irish origin, was born in Davidson County in 1792, and died in May, 1876. With a common-school training our subject began clerking, at his majority, in a grocery in Nashville. In October, 1868, he married Mary F., daughter of Jas. R. and Nancy A. Drake, and born in Davidson County in 1850. Their children are Mary A., Sarah P. and Suella, all in school; and Hattie L. (deceased), William I., Emma E. and Laura E. (deceased). Mr. Walton served in Company B, Ninth Tennessee Cavalry, of the Confederate Army, enlisting in 1862. A Whig in politics previous to the war, he became a Democrat. From 1876 to 1882 he served as justice of the peace. Mr. Walton and two daughters, Mary and Sarah, are members of the Methodist Episcopal Church South, and his wife of the Cumberland Presbyterian Church.

Joseph Weisiger, Jr., engaged in stock raising and farming in the Fourth District of Sumner County, is a son of Joseph and Mary A. (Kincaid) Weisiger. The mother was a daughter of Judge John Kincaid, of Kentucky, an ex-member of Congress. Our subject was born in Danville, Ky., in 1850, being the second of nine children, five living. The father was of German descent, born in Danville, Ky., in 1825. The grandfather was also named Joseph and was a native of Kentucky and a practicing physician at Danville until 1853, when he moved to Texas and remained there until his death in 1881. The father was raised at Danville and received a good collegiate education, being a graduate of Center College at that place. In early life he engaged in the drug business at Frankfort, Ky., and then at Danville, but later has been a farmer. He was married in 1847; moved to Sumner County in 1870, and has since then resided in the county near Hendersonville, engaged in farming.

The mother was born in Lincoln County, Ky., in 1826, and died in 1884, a member of the Old School Presbyterian Church. Our subject received a collegiate education at Danville, and came with his parents to Sumner County in 1870. In December, 1871, he married Miss Fannie C., daughter of John W. and Eveline Head. They had five children, three living: Eva, Etta and William. Mrs. Weisiger died January 19, 1884, and in May, 1886, he married Miss Callie, daughter of John B. and O. E. Baker. Mrs. Weisiger was born in Sumner County in 1864. Mr. Weisiger first settled at Hendersonville where he remained until 1877, then moved to his present farm, one mile and a half southwest of Gallatin on the Nashville pike, where he owns eighty-three acres of land, and is quite successful in both farming and stock raising. He is kind and charitable in disposition and in politics a Democrat; his first presidential vote was for Horace Greeley. Mr. and Mrs. Weisiger are both members of the Old School Presbyterian Church.

H. S. Wherry, of Willis & Wherry, farmers and stock dealers, in Sumner County, was born there in 1847. He is one of eleven children of John J. and Jane (Smith) Wherry. The father, of Scotch-Welsh origin, was born near Gallatin, Tenn., about 1816. A farmer by occupation, he was appointed tobacco inspector at New Orleans by Andrew Jackson, holding the position about three years. He died in November, 1875. The mother, of Welsh descent, was born in Sumner County about 1816, and is living on her farm near Gallatin. With the advantages of St. Mary's College, and Forest Home Academy near Louisville, our subject began farming for himself at the age of twenty-one. Five years later he spent two years as salesman in a clothing store at Nashville, and then began his present career of farming. In December, 1876, he married Cecelia, daughter of Stephen C. and Mary (Bradford) Willis, and born in Sumner County in 1850. Their five children are John S., Harry S. and Robert E., in school, and Jennie M. and Georgie E. Mr. W. is a Democrat and a member of the F. & A. M. fraternity, and his wife is a member of the Presbyterian Church.

Samuel Wilson (deceased), farmer, and son of John and Anne (Meek) Wilson, was born in Sumner County, Tenn., about 1800. He was one of eight children, all of whom are dead. The father was born in North Carolina and came to Sumner County at an early age, locating on a farm where our subject was born. He remained there until his death. The mother was also a native of North Carolina and died on the farm in Sumner County. Our subject was educated in the common schools and at the age of about twenty-five began farming for himself. This he continued on the same farm until his death in 1849. He had married Nancy Moore, daughter of Israel and Elizabeth (Wallace) Moore, in 1824 or 1825. She was born in 1804, and as a result of her marriage, ten children were born: Louisa (widow of Joseph Wallace), James A., John M., (deceased), Melissa, (wife of Alvin K. Seago), Mary Jane (wife of Samuel Thornhill), Richard, S. Frank and three children, deceased. At the time of his death our subject owned 500 acres of good land and was a very successful farmer. He was a Democrat and a good citizen. Mary Jane, Melissa, James and Frank are church members. The first and last named are members of the Old School Presbyterian Church. Melissa is a member of the Baptist Church and James is a member of the Cumberland Presbyterian Church.

Thomas F. Witherspoon, cashier of the Farmers' & Traders' Bank at Gallatin, was born in 1825, in Lexington, Ky., a son of Dr. John R. and Sophia (Graham) Witherspoon. The father was of Scotch origin, born in 1774 in Williamsburg District, S. C. He was a second cousin of John Witherspoon, one of the signers of the Declaration of Independence. Dr. John R. graduated in the literary department of Princeton College, in 1794; soon afterward attended the Transylvania University at Lexington, Ky., and graduated as an M. D. He married near Lexington, where he resided and practiced until 1826, when he moved to Green (now Hale) County, Ala., where he died in 1852. During his residence in Alabama he was a planter. His wife was born in 1792 in Lincoln County, N. C., and died in 1866. She was a sister to William A. Graham, who was a United States senator, governor of North Carolina for two terms, Secretary of the Navy during President Fillmore's administration, and was candidate in 1852 for Vice-president on the ticket with Gen. Winfield Scott. Our subject was educated at Mobile, Ala., but owing to ill health did not graduate. In 1851 he married Miss Catherine, daughter of the noted divine, Rev. L. D. Hatch. Mrs. Witherspoon was born in Newbern, N. C., in 1828. Their union resulted in the birth of five children: Walter, a merchant of Gallatin; Fannie; Thomas A., a graduate of the Naval Academy at Annapolis, now holds a position in the Patent Office at Washington, D. C.; Robert S., a salesman in Nashville, and Martha. In 1854 our subject went to Mobile and engaged in the commission business. During the war he was in the commissary department and after the restoration of peace located at Greensboro, Ala. In 1867 he returned to Mobile, and the following year, with his family, went to California, where for five years he was engaged as a planter. In 1873 he moved to Gallatin, and was immediately employed as assistant cashier in the Sumner Deposit Bank, which position he retained until 1884, when the Farmers' & Traders' Bank was organized, and our subject became cashier. He is a Democrat, and a member of the K. of H., a man of honor and integrity, highly esteemed by all. Mrs. Witherspoon and three children are members of the Presbyterian Church.

W. H. Worsham, merchant in District No. 8, Sumner County, was born in Robertson County, in 1853. He is one of eight children of Robert and Abby (Dorris) Worsham. The father, born in Pittsylvania County, Va., in 1828, and reared on a farm, has been merchandising at Worsham, Tenn., for about sixteen years past. The mother was born in 1832. Having attended the common schools, he began for himself when of age as salesman for Truett Sons, and for Morgan in Rosebank and elsewhere, where he was employed five years. In December, 1881, he married Elizabeth, daughter of W. W. and Sarah A. Douglass, and born in Sumner County, in July, 1858. Their three children are Lula F., Robert D. and Henry B. Mr. W. is a Democrat politically, and a member of the F. & A. M. order. Since 1879 he has been engaged in his present successful business.

Dr. Thos. M. Woodson, practicing physician and surgeon, of Gallatin, was born July 20, 1830, in Sumner County, a son of Rev. Lewis Miller and Lucinda (Hanna) Woodson. The father was of Welsh descent, born in 1806, in Montgomery County, Tenn. His father (grandfather of subject) was a native of Virginia, and immigrated to Montgomery County about 1790, being one of the Middle Tennessee pioneers. The Rev. Lewis M. Woodson lived in Sumner County at the time of his marriage, after which he settled in the Tenth District. He was a prominent minister of the Methodist Episcopal Church. For several years he was a traveling divine in Kentucky. He died December 2, 1862, and was buried at Bethpage. His wife was of Scotch-Irish descent, born in 1803 in Surry County, N. C., near Guilford C. H. When eleven years of age her parents came to Sumner County. April 17, 1816 the parents removed to Sumner County, Tenn., near Bethpage, the old homestead now owned by Dr. James B. Hanna. Mrs. Woodson departed this life May, 1872. Our subject received a fair academic education. In 1850 he graduated in medicine at the University of Louisville, Kentucky, medical department. In 1854 and 1855 he attended the Jefferson Medical College, Philadelphia; previous to this, in 1850, he began his practice at Hanna's postoffice, Sumner County, where he remained until 1874, when he moved to Gallatin. He is a member of the American Medical Association. He was vice-president of the Tennessee Medical Society in 1873, and the same year president of the Sumner County Medical Society. He has contributed extensively to professional periodicals, also to the transactions of the several societies of which he is a member. Among his most valuable contributions were "Pneumonia—its Treatment;" "Dysentery—its Treatment by Large Doses of Ipecacuanha" and "Cases of Disease of Cerebro Spinal Centers." July 18, 1855, he wedded Miss Amelia, daughter of Rev. Luke P. Allen. She was born in 1834, in Sumner County. To this union have been born Edwin A., a farmer; John C., a druggist at Bethpage; L. Miller, an M. D. in New Mexico; Bettie; Virginia and Tennessee are twins. The Doctor and entire family belong to the Methodist Episcopal Church South. The Doctor has an extensive and lucrative practice. He is president of the board of education at Gallatin, a member of the I. O. O. F., Mason, Council degree, and Knight of Honor. He is a Democrat, and gave his first presidential vote for Gen. Scott, in 1852.

Col. A. R. Wynne was born in Sumner County in 1800, and is now one of the leading farmers and stock raisers of the First District. His parents were Robert and Cynthia (Harrison) Wynne. The father was a native of North Carolina, and moved with his parents to Sumner County when a boy; he married in this county, and soon after moved to Wilson County where he died in the prime of life in 1802. The mother was born in South Carolina, and died in Jackson, Miss., a devout member of the Methodist Episcopal Church South. After the death of his father our subject lived with his grandfather Wynne until sixteen years of age in Wilson County, receiving most of his education at Hickory Ridge, in same county. Mr. Wynne then returned to Sumner County, and entered a mercantile house at Cairo, where he clerked for several years, then commenced business upon his own responsibility at the same place, but sold out three years later and went to Stampson's Mill, and engaged in the milling business. In 1834 he purchased the farm on which he now resides, and has since then made it his home, owning 432 acres of Sumner County's most valuable land, the home tract of 290 acres being at Castalian Springs. Mr. Wynne is one of the leading farmers of Sumner County, is widely known and respected by all. Under the old military rules he was colonel of the militia having command of 1,200 men between Gallatin and Hartsville. In 1866 he was elected to represent Sumner County in the upper branch of the State Legislature. March, 1825, he married Miss Elmira, daughter of Gen. James and Susan Winchester, of Sumner County. Fourteen children were born to this marriage, three sons and three daughters living: Joseph G., Andrew J. of Alabama, Winchester, Louisa, Susan and Mary M. Mrs. Wynne was born in Sumner County in 1804, and died in 1882, a member of the Methodist Episcopal Church South. Mr. Wynne has been a life-long

Democrat; his first presidential vote was cast for Gen. Jackson in 1828. He was a great admirer of Jackson, Polk and Johnson. He is an influential and consistent member of the Methodist Episcopal Church South, and has been postmaster at Castalian Springs for forty-seven years.

SMITH COUNTY.

G. D. Alexander, merchant, was born in Smith County, in June, 1849, and is one of nine children of J. L. and Sarah D. (Donaho) Alexander. The father, Scotch in origin, born in Smith County in 1818, has been a physician near Dixon Springs for forty-six years, and is also a farmer, possessing about 500 acres of the Cumberland River bottom lands, one of the finest farms in the county. The mother, French in ancestry, was born in Sumner (now Trousdale) County in 1829. Educated chiefly at Dixon Springs, our subject began merchandising at nineteen years of age in Smith County, continuing about three and a half years. For five years then he was employed by Jos. T. Thompkins & Co., dry goods, Louisville, Ky., and then before engaging in his present business at Dixon Springs, he spent four years on his father's farm. In December, 1885, he married Bettie, daughter of Jas. and Clarissa (Bravard) Crenshaw, and born in what is now Trousdale County, in 1863. Mr. Alexander is a Democrat, and his wife is a member of the Christian Church.

J. D. Allen, a prominent farmer and stock raiser, one-half mile east of Dixon Springs, was born in Sumner County in 1835, a son of George W. and Louise F. (Douglass) Allen. His father was of Irish descent, born in Gallatin, Sumner Co., Tenn., about 1810. He was a lawyer of great brilliancy and prominence. He was attorney-general of Davidson and Sumner Counties for seven years, about 1840. He was the first judge of the Sumner County Court, which position he retained a number of years. He died in May, 1880. His wife was of Scotch origin, also a native of Sumner County, born near Gallatin about 1817, and died in 1849. She was the mother of four children. Our subject was educated in his native place, and at the age of seventeen began merchandise business for himself, the firm being Allen & Cantrell, in which he continued until the war, when he was appointed by Gov. Isham G. Harris to the commissary department, and ordered to Camp Trousdale; afterward was assigned to Robert Hatton's regiment, Seventh Tennessee, and went to Virginia. He served as commissary all through the war. He was in the battles of Murfreesboro, Seven Pines, and all the engagements around Richmond and Bentonville. At the time of the surrender he was at Hillsboro, N. C. He was paroled and returned home, resuming his former business. Three years later he went to Brownsville; after one year in trade there he came to Smith County and purchased the farm upon which he now resides; it contains 250 acres, well cultivated, with a pleasant residence and all necessary outbuildings. He is a Democrat and respected, worthy citizen. In 1868 he married a daughter of Morgan David and Elizabeth Buford, Miss Clara V., born near Dixon Springs in 1846. To this union have been born Ella L., John H., George W. and Alice. Mrs. Allen is a member of the Christian Church.

Jackson C. Apple, a well known resident of the Eighth District of Smith County, was born at the place where he now resides, in 1825. That section was then called Jackson County, afterward Putnam. Jackson C. is one of eleven children born to David and Mary (Thackton) Apple. The father was of German descent, born about 1783 in North Carolina. He came to Tennessee when a young man, settling in the vicinity in which the son now lives. He owned considerable land and engaged in farming, tanning and shoemaking till the time of his death in 1855. The mother was of English descent, born in 1802 in Sumner County, Tenn., and died in 1882. The subject of this sketch received his education in the log-cabin schools of his neighborhood. He remained at home with his parents till after his majority. In 1848 he married Mary J., daughter of Jonathan and Elizabeth (Apple) Holford. Mrs. Apple was born in 1832 on Indian Creek, Jackson (now Smith) County. Their union resulted in the birth of three children, two of whom were raised: John H. and Tennie (the deceased wife of Prof. S. T. Clark). Immediately after marriage Mr. Apple moved to the farm on Indian Creek, which he had bought, but remained there only a few months. At the division of the homestead he removed to the portion allotted to him. The first official duties Mr. Apple performed was as justice of the peace of the Eighteenth District of Jackson County, at which time he was only twenty-two years of age. In 1852 he was elected sheriff of the county and moved to Gainesboro; at the expiration of his term he bought an interest in a mercantile house, where he was actively engaged for a year. In 1855 he purchased the entire homestead and moved his family there. During his absence Putnam County was re-established, which included his homestead. Until 1860 his attention was given exclusively to agriculture. He was made justice of the peace of the Twelfth District, serving a term of six years, and was also chairman of the county court in 1862–63. The war interrupted his official duties. April, 1866, he again became justice of the peace in same district. In

1868 the county line was changed, and he became a resident of Smith County. Soon afterward he was elected to same office (justice of the peace), but by presumption of State authority his commission was refused on account of supposed ineligibility, because of his sympathy for the Rebellion. After the amended constitution of 1870 he was called to the office of justice of the peace of the Eighth District of Smith County, and continued to hold the office. He was also county assessor in 1875, giving entire satisfaction. From 1877 to 1887 he was chairman of the county court. At the latter date failing health caused him to decline further service in that capacity. In 1872 he was the Democratic nominee for representative of his county, but was defeated by the Independent candidate, Samuel Allison. Mr. Apple is one of the most efficient and honored men in Smith County. Previous to the war he was a Whig, and is now a Democrat. His first presidential vote was cast for Zachary Taylor in 1848. He is a member of the Masonic fraternity, Granville Lodge, No. 342. Mr. Apple, wife and son, are consistent members of the Methodist Church, as was also the deceased daughter.

W. A. Baird is a farmer and stock raiser near Gordonsville, District No. 15. He was born in Smith County in 1845. He is the eldest of eight children of Jesse H. and Jane (Cochrum) Baird. Both parents are natives of Smith County, born in 1824 and 1829 respectively. The father was for several years justice of the peace; he is now living on his farm. Our subject was educated in the common schools of his native county. At the age of nineteen he began farming on his own responsibility. Ten years later he engaged in merchandising at Hickman Mills; he remained there four years, then sold out and came to Gordonsville. He entered into partnership with B. A. James, in the same line of business. After two years he sold his interest in the house to Mr. James, and purchased a farm, upon which he now resides. In 1864 he was married to Miss M. J., the daughter of Hon. J. R. and Martha James. Mrs. Baird was born in Smith County, in 1843. She was a consistent member of the Cumberland Presbyterian Church. Her death occurred in 1883, leaving two children: Callie C., wife of W. A. Davis and Robert J. In 1884 Mr. Baird was united to Miss Lucy, daughter of John and Martha Gwaltney, who was born in Smith County in 1855. Our subject is a stanch Democrat and an active member of the Cumberland Presbyterian Church. He owns 100 acres of valuable land on the Cumberland River, with a comfortable and commodious residence and all outbuildings. The farm is well stocked and improved. Mr. Baird is a highly respected and worthy citizen.

Hon. J. A. Barrett, farmer and miller, was born in 1838, in Smith County, Tenn., one of the children of James and Nancy (Ballenger) Barrett. The father, a farmer and minister, was born in North Carolina in 1812, and came to Smith County when a child. In 1837 he served in Col. Campbell's regiment, in the Florida war, under Gen. Jackson, and in 1847 was elected to the State Legislature. He was ordained as minister in the Missionary Baptist Church. He died in 1873, owning about 900 acres of land and other wealth. The mother was born in Culpepper County, Va., and is still living with her son, W. F. Barrett. Educated in a Sumner County college, our subject for three years was a teacher. In 1857 he bought his present 114 acres of land, in connection with which he is a large stock shipper. In 1861 he enlisted in Company F, Twenty-fourth Regiment Tennessee Volunteers, and was orderly sergeant at Shiloh. After the reorganization of the army in 1863 he became second lieutenant, and in August of that year was honorably discharged on account of disability. In 1856 he married Martha H., daughter of Judge W. B. and Elizabeth Whitley, and born in Smith County in 1844. She died in 1865. Their children are William A. and Edward E. In 1867 he married Emma C., daughter of Nicholas and Penelope Smith, and born in DeKalb County in 1848. Her death occurred in 1882. Their six children are Robert N., Alfred E., Charles S., Ocia E., Elmer G. and Ernest. He owns a two-thirds interest in a saw-mill. In 1871 he was elected justice of the peace; he was also member of the court. In 1874 he was elected to the State Legislature. He is a member of the Masonic order, being a F. & A. M. and R. A. C. and G. C., and is also a member of the Missionary Baptist Church.

Prof. S. T. Clark, of Dixon Academy, was born at Elmwood in 1845, one of five children of H. B. and Martha (Brown) Clark. The father, of Irish origin, born in Virginia in 1802, is a retired merchant and farmer, who lost much by the war. He was justice for several years, and is still living with his sons near Elmwood. The mother, born in Amherst County, Va., in 1806, died in 1866. Educated at Granville and Forest Home College, near Louisville, Ky., our subject began for himself when nineteen, in his chosen profession. In 1868 he married Tennie, daughter of J. C. and Mary J. (Holford) Apple, and born in 1852. Their three children are Compton, at Dixon Springs Academy; Wilbur A., with his grandfather Apple, and John B. (deceased). Mrs. Clark died in 1883. For four years from 1867 Mr. Clark taught at Granville, then for the same time had charge of Snow Creek Academy, when he built the Elmwood Institute in 1875. He was principal until 1878, when he associated with him Prof. J. H. Watts until 1883. Then after running it alone for fifteen months he took charge of Dixon Springs Academy, his present flourishing and promising institution. He is a Democrat, a Mason, and he, his wife and two children are members of the Methodist Episcopal Church South.

D. K. Conditt, teacher, was born in 1859 in Smith County, one of five children of J. M. and Mary A. (Trousdale) Conditt. The father, Welsh in ancestry, was born in 1819 five miles north of Elmwood. Leaving home at twenty-two he bought his farm near Elmwood where he remained until his death in 1880. The mother was born in 1818 at what is now Stonewall. Educated at Elmwood, our subject began teaching at twenty years of age. He owns eighty acres of the old homestead, and is at present entering on his second engagement as Professor at Elmwood. He is a Democrat, voting first for Cleveland. He is a professor of religion, though not yet a member of any church.

W. B. Cundall, one of the best known citizens and farmers of the Twelfth District, was born in Walpole County, Mass., in 1815. His parents were Edward T. and Patience (Bailey) Cundall. The father was of English descent, born in Rhode Island about 1798, a son of Abner Cundall, one of the famous Rhode Island Quakers. Edward T. was raised and married in his native State; afterward moved to Massachusetts, and about 1817 went to Washington County, Penn., where he died in 1866. He was a woolen manufacturer the greater portion of his life, but was a farmer a few years previous to his demise. His wife was also a native of Rhode Island. She died about 1880 at the age of eighty-four. Their family consisted of three sons and four daughters, four of whom are living. Both were members of the Old School Scotch Presbyterian Church. The subject of our sketch was educated in the common schools. March 5, 1839, he was married to Miss Emma C., daughter of John and Nancy Morgan, of Pennsylvania. Mrs. Cundall was born May 2, 1817, in Washington County, Penn., and died September 8, 1882. To their union nine children were born, of whom two sons and four daughters are living: Nancy (wife of Jones Racky, of North Nashville), John M., Harriet L. (wife of Augustus McEachern), Isaac B. (of Nashville), Anna M., and Clara S. (wife of D. W. McEachern). For several years in early life Mr. Cundall was a clothier, but farming and milling has been his chief occupation. He was coroner of Washington County, Penn., for three years. In 1870 he moved to Tennessee and located near where he now resides. In 1883 he settled on the farm. It contains 250 acres of land under good cultivation and well improved. He also owns a flouring and saw-mill at Flat Rock. He was school commissioner of the Twelfth District of Smith County from 1873 until 1885.

He is a member of the Cumberland Presbyterian Church, as was also his wife. For more than forty years he has been connected with the Masonic fraternity, and has always affiliated with the Democratic party, casting his first presidential vote for M. Van Buren, in 1840. He began life with nothing, but by industry and enterprise has accumulated sufficient to make him very comfortable. He is a man of fine business capacity, charitable and much esteemed.

Dr. L. H. Davis was born in 1813 in Surry County, N. C., one of ten children of Jacob and Winifred (Herring) Davis. The father was born in 1779 in Virginia; a farmer by occupation, and after 1783 lived in Surry County, N. C., until his death in 1838. The mother, born in Surry County, died in 1865. Our subject, educated in a Surry County academy, became one of the foremost teachers of the county. In 1840 he removed to Overton, Tenn., and the same year began studying medicine under Dr. W. R. Vawter of Salina, Tenn., and in three years began practice. In 1847 he took a course in the Botanical Medical Institute of Memphis, and in 1867 entered the Eclectic Medical Institute at Cincinnati. He has been a successful practitioner in the counties of Smith, Jackson, Putnam, Macon, Warren, DeKalb, Wilson, Overton, Clay, Sumner, Tenn., and Allen, Trousdale and Monroe, of Kentucky. Now about seventy-four, his work is chiefly office prescribing. He is a Democrat, and is a member of the F. & A. M. order, and of the Methodist Episcopal Church South.

Thomas Dies, a farmer and stock raiser of two miles east of Dixon Springs, was born in Smith (now Trousdale) County in 1817. He is of a family of ten children born to Thomas and Kizzy (Ventress) Dies. The father was of Irish descent, born in North Carolina in 1784. He came to Smith County when a boy. He was a prosperous farmer until the time of his death in 1847. His wife was a native of Smith County, and died in 1819, when our subject was two years old. Thomas Dies did not have many educational advantages. His instruction was received at Dixon Creek Church, which was the first organized in the county. At eighteen he began life as a farmer. In 1839 he married a daughter of John and Susan Merryman, Miss Mary, who was born near Lynchburg, Va., in 1821. To their union twelve children were born, only four of whom are living: Sarah, Francis, Virginia, and Alonzo, who is a farmer. Mr. Dies enlisted in the Confederate service, Capt. Bridgewater's company, Twenty-first Tennessee, and was elected orderly sergeant. On account of ill health he was discharged in 1862. He returned to his home and resumed farming, which occupation he has since continued with great success. He was a Whig previous to the war and is now a Democrat. He and the entire family belong to the Missionary Baptist Church. Mr. Dies is an honorable, industrious man, well and favorably known throughout the county where his life has been spent.

Dr. John Duncan Estes, a practicing physician and surgeon, of Elmwood, was born in 1841, in Wilson County, Tenn. He is the only surviving one of three children, born to Duncan N. and Fanny (Lawrence) Estes. The father was born in North Carolina about 1814, and came to Tennessee when a mere boy, locating in Wilson County, where he engaged in blacksmithing and farming. After his marriage with a native of the county (subject's mother), who was born in 1814, Mr. Estes and family moved to Texas. A few years later he went to Tennessee, where he remained until the late war, when he moved to Illinois, and from there to Kentucky where he died in 1864. He was a soldier in the Mexican war, and a stanch Union man during the late civil war. The mother died in 1846, in her native county. From five years of age our subject made his home with his grandmother, Mrs. Mary Lawrence, on a farm in Wilson County, where he was educated. At the outbreak of the war, in 1861, he enlisted in the Confederate Army, Company F, Twenty-fourth Tennessee Regiment, at Murfreesboro. He was discharged at Tripoli, Miss. He returned home, and one month later became one of Forrest's command, remaining as such until April, 1865. He took part in the battles of Shiloh, Murfreesboro, Bardstown, and was in numerous skirmishes. After the restoration of peace he attended the Three Forks Institute, in his native county. After two years' schooling he began farming on his grandmother's place and a smaller one adjoining his own; at the expiration of two years he embarked in the grocery business, and afterward general merchandise, at Commerce. The following six years he was thus engaged, and at the same time devoted every spare moment to the reading of medicine. In 1873 he attended a course of medical lectures at the Vanderbilt University, of Nashville. The next year he began to practice at Linnwood, Wilson County, and also at Commerce early in 1875. In November of the same year he located at Elmwood, where he has since had an extensive practice. His farm of forty-five acres is valuable and well cultivated. He is a member of the I. O. O. F., Saulsbury Lodge, No. 100, and a Democrat; his first presidential vote was cast for Horatio Seymour in 1868. In 1869 Dr. Estes married Mary, daughter of James and Nancy (Odom) Floyd. Mrs. Estes was born in Wilson County in 1850. Eight children have been born to this union: Howard W., Turner O., May Pearl, Herschel B. and Fanny Cora. Those deceased are John Clark, James Duncan and William Briggs. Mrs. Estes is a member of the Christian Church.

J. J. Eastes, a prominent farmer in the Fourteenth District, was born in Smith County, in 1848. He is one of a family of four children of J. W. and Mary (Walker) Eastes. The father was also a native of the county, born in 1811. He was a farmer by occupation and owned 200 acres of good soil, and was one of the best known and respected men in the Eighteenth District. About 1838 he moved to the Fourteenth District, where he died in 1850. His wife was born in 1814, in Virginia, and is still living on the homestead with her son, J. J., who was educated at the New Middleton Academy. He is one of the county's best teachers, being engaged in that capacity for a term of five months. He is also one of the most enterprising and prosperous farmers of the section. The farm consists of 200 acres, well cultivated, improved, and fenced. All the buildings are first-class. He is to a considerable extent interested in stock raising. He is a Democrat; cast his first presidential vote for Horace Greeley, in 1872. He is a Royal Arch Mason. In 1875 he wedded Tillitha, daughter of B. M. and Elizabeth F. Baines, who was born in 1854, in Smith County. Their union has been blessed with Wm. T., Lela, Alta D., Jonathan B. and Mary L. Mr. and Mrs. Eastes are consistent and highly esteemed members of the Missionary Baptist Church.

Wm. Farley, a well known farmer of Smith County, was born in 1818, in Goochland County, Va. He is one of a family of five children born to Roley and Mary (Radford) Farley. The father was born in Amhurst County, Va. about 1790, and came to Tennessee in 1835. He worked at his carpenter trade at Dixon Springs and Carthage. He died at Botten Bend of Caney Fork. The mother was also a native of Virginia. She died in 1837 near Dixon Springs, Smith County, Tenn. The subject of this sketch had but meager educational advantages. He attended school a short time at Chapel Hill. At the age of fourteen he was thrown upon his own resources. The following six years he was employed at various places in the neighborhood, going wherever he could get work of any kind. At twenty years of age he was elected constable of Carthage, District No. 1. He served in this capacity for six years, after which he purchased a farm on Bluff Creek, where he lived for several years. Later he bought the farm situated three miles northeast of Carthage, where he now resides. He married in 1844, Mary, daughter of Logan D. and Polly Key, who lived on Peyton Creek. This union resulted in the birth of four children: John E.; Mary, wife of William Bryant; Virginia, wife of John Ford, and William, deceased. Mrs. Farley died in 1850. Mr. Farley married the second time to Jane, daughter of Allen and Patsy (Stanford) Robinson, who was born in 1835. The fruits of this union were nine children, of whom but four are living: Andrew Johnson, Morris Brown, Alice (wife of Thomas J. Carter), and Leroy Cage. Our subject enlisted in the Confederate service, Company A, Forty-fourth Tennessee Regiment, at Carthage. At the battle of Shiloh he was wounded by a minie-ball, in the thigh. He received his discharge in 1862, in Tennessee, since which time he has been prosperously engaged in tilling the soil where he is at present living. He was cast off from home a penniless, mere boy, but by hard and diligent work, he has been able to accumulate considerable good property, although the war was the means of him losing about half of his possessions. His farm contains 400 acres, the bottom land of which is well cultivated. Mr. Farley is a Democrat, casting his first presidential vote for James K. Polk in 1844. He is a member of the Masonic fraternity, Car lodge, No. 14. Mrs. Farley and Morris B. are connected with the Methodist Episcopal Church, and A. J. is a Missionary Baptist.

Hon. T. J. Fisher, Sr., attorney at law, of Carthage, was born in De Kalb County, Tenn., February 22, 1847. He was a son of James and Rachel (Plunkett) Fisher. The father was born in Smith (now De Kalb) County in 1810. He was a prosperous farmer, owning 300 acres of land. He died in 1873 in the county where he was born and married. His parents were natives of North Carolina. His wife was also born in De Kalb County and died in 1864, at the age of forty-five. Their family consisted of seven sons and seven daughters, of whom twelve are living, our subject being the third child. He remained at home until his nineteenth year. His educational advantages had been meager and his desire to gain information great. He soon entered the New Middleton Institute, where, by application, his efforts were crowned with success. His means were limited, which occasioned him to leave school now and then to earn the necessary funds for the continuation of his education. For eighteen months he taught at Shop Springs, Wilson County, and then returned to his studies. During his last session he was assistant instructor. In 1871 he graduated with high honor, being the valedictorian and receiving the degree of A. M. He resumed teaching, but this time in the Geneva Academy at Carthage, and six months at Campbell's Institute, during which time he also studied law, his preceptor being Col. W. H. Dewitt, now of Chattanooga. He was admitted to the bar in 1873, and same year became superintendent of public instruction. He organized the schools under the present system and served a year and a half. In 1876 he was elected to the State Legislature, serving in the Ways and Means Committee, also taking an active part in passing the "four-mile law." In 1884 he was elected attorney-general of the Fifth

Judicial Circuit of Tennessee, to fill an unexpired term of H. C. Snodgrass, who resigned. In 1886 he was a candidate for chancellor; was defeated on account of there being six Democratic candidates, which so divided the vote that a Republican was elected. Our subject received more votes than any of his competitors in his party, 4,597 being the number, his next competitor receiving about 2,300 votes. September 2, 1875, he married Amelia, daughter of Nelson J. and Minerva Bryan, of Wilson County. Mrs. Fisher was born November 12, 1848, and educated at the Mary Sharpe College, graduating in 1875. To this union six children have been born: Albert Ernest, James Nelson, Minnie, Virgie, Alice and Thomas J. Our subject is one of the leading and most able lawyers in the county and has an extensive practice. In private life he is courteous and highly esteemed. He is a Council Mason. He and his wife are earnest members of the Baptist Church.

C. S. Fisher, the well known proprietor of a livery stable at Carthage, was born in that place in 1864, a son of Thomas and Mary Jane (Deadman) Fisher. The father was born April 24, 1817, in Smith County. He was a school-teacher, also deputy surveyor of the county. Afterward was elected to that office which he held six years. In 1856 he moved to Carthage and became clerk of the circuit court. He was re-elected in 1866, but counted out on account of being a Democrat. In 1870 he was elected, serving four years. He died in 1880. In 1838 he married Miss Deadman, who was born in 1822, same month and day of the month as her husband. Her death occurred in 1885. They had ten children, five of whom are living. At the age of thirteen our subject became an apprentice in a printing office, remaining there one year. In 1882 he obtained a position as traveling salesman for Hill, Woodcock & Co., of Nashville, a family grocery and confectionery house. In 1884 he established a grocery store in Carthage. In 1885 he embarked in his present business, in which he has been quite successful. He has some fine horses, buggies and all necessary vehicles, harnesses, etc., suitable for such trade. He is a young man of enterprise and determination, genial manners, and is a general favorite.

Col. John A. Fite, Judge of the Fifth Judicial Circuit, Tennessee, was born in 1832, in De Kalb County, a son of Jacob and Matilda (Baird) Fite. The father, of German origin, was born in North Carolina, and with his father came to Davidson County, then Smith County, and finally settled in De Kalb County, where he passed his days. Jacob married there, and was merchant at Alexandria as well as farmer. In 1846 he moved to near Lebanon, and died at the age of eighty-three. The mother, born in Hickman County, Tenn., died in 1876. Four of their eleven children are Dorcas R., widow of Leonard Scott; John A.; Dr. J. G. of Lebanon, and Edwin C. When fourteen years old our subject went to Wilson County and was educated in the university at Lebanon, and at Irving College. He began studying law at twenty-two, and in 1855 graduated from the law department of Cumberland University, and immediately began practice with his brother at Carthage. His brother being elected circuit judge in 1858, he formed partnership with Hon. W. D. De Witt, now at Chattanooga. In 1861 he enlisted in Company A, Seventh Tennessee Regiment, Moore's Guards, and was elected captain and fought in Seven Pines; promoted major in 1862; he was in Mechanicsville (where he had two ribs broken), Chancellorsville, Cedar Run (where he received a wound in the leg), Fredericksburg and Gettysburg (where he was captured and taken to Fort McHenry), thence to Fort Delaware, thence to Johnson's Island, where he was retained for nineteen months, and paroled in February, 1865, but remained in North Carolina. After the war he resumed practice with his brother, and in 1871 was also appointed clerk and master of chancery court holding it for over six years. In 1878 he and H. M. Hale became partners, and in 1882 he was elected to the State Legislature to fill an unexpired term, and elected to his present position in 1886. December 29, 1866, he married Mary M., daughter of Leroy H. and Eliza Mitchell, and born in Smith County in 1841. Their two children are Bettie and Mattie. He is a Master Mason and he and Mrs. Fite are members of the Methodist Episcopal Church South. For years he has been one of the leading lawyers of Smith County bar.

R. D. Flippen, farmer, was born in Smith County in 1827, the son of Roger D. and Elizabeth (Dyson) Flippen. The father, of English origin, was born in Virginia, and in his youth came to Tennessee with his father Armstead, who was one of the first settlers in the county. The father lived in Smith County at the time of his marriage and died in 1827. The mother, of Welsh descent, was born in Virginia and died here at the age of thirty years. Our subject, one of six children, two living, and left an orphan, lived with his grandfather, Mark Dyson, until about fifteen years old. He then attended school a few years at Rome, Tenn. He then began farming for himself. In 1847 he enlisted in Company D, Fourth Tennessee Regiment Infantry, Capt. Goodall; he was soon appointed orderly sergeant. April 18, 1850, he married Tennessee, daughter of Samuel and Sallie High, and born in Smith County in 1831. Their six children are Samuel H., Elizabeth, wife of S. F. Ward; Luther B.; Virginia, wife of W. E. Myer; Tabitha and Maud. After his marriage he began an overland journey to California, being ninety days on the road and sixty days' actual travel. He mined partly, and dealt in mine supplies by pack-mules, going out in the summer to buy stock, which trips were full of Indian adventure, and returning to camp in winter; but butchering occupied his attention the last four years. Returning in 1857 he soon settled on his present farm. Enlisting in Capt. Sander's Independent Company, and elected second lieutenant he fought the Northern forces at Fishing Creek and Shiloh, and at the reorganization of the army returned home. Mrs. Flippen died in 1873, and November 25, 1874, he married Mrs. Annie McFarland, born in Rutherford County in 1840. In 1865 he bought 383 acres, but as relief from growing cares he disposed of 230 in 1884. Formerly a Whig he has been a Democrat for years. He is a Mason. His wife and three daughters are members of the Baptist Church, and his son, Samuel H., a member of the Methodist Episcopal Church South.

G. C. Flippin, a prominent contractor and builder, was born in Smith County in 1822. He is a son of Abner A. and Eliza (Hobson) Flippin. The father was born in 1799 in Cumberland County, Va., where his wife was also born in 1806. After marriage in 1824 he came to Smith County where, in 1836, he was elected captain of State militia, serving in that capacity until 1845, when the law abolished the militia. He was an influential and highly respected man; his death occurred in 1860. His wife, who was the mother of thirteen children, died in 1877 in De Kalb County, Tenn. Our subject received a liberal education in the common schools of his native county. In 1849 he went to Nashville, where he was engaged as clerk in a city hotel, for about six years, after which he returned to Smith County, Seventeenth District, where he now resides and owns 50 acres of land. In 1856 he married Parthenia, daughter of Michael and Elizabeth Heelmantoller, who was born in the county in 1828. To this union have been born Robert H., Candace P., Tenn F., Bettie G., John A. and Joseph C. At the outbreak of the war in December, 1861, Mr. Flippin entered the Confederate Army. He enlisted in Company C, Fifty-fifth Tennessee Infantry Volunteers. On December 25 he was promoted to regimental commissary, acting at same time for the brigade. He took part in the battle of Shiloh; he was honorably discharged in May, 1862. He is connected with the K. of H., and is one of the most esteemed, honorable and worthy citizens of the county. Mr. Flippin and wife are active and earnest members of the Missionary Baptist Church.

W. W. Ford, clerk of circuit court, was born in 1854 in Smith County. He is the son of Christopher C. and Martha (Nichols) Ford. The father was born in Smith County, Tenn., about 1821, and the grandfather, Zach. Ford, was one of the earliest settlers of the county. The father married in Smith County and is the owner of 124 acres in the Sixteenth District. He has been magistrate for over thirty years. The mother was born in Smith County in 1827. One of ten children, our subject, lived at home until twenty years old, and was educated at Snow Creek Academy. In 1875 he and his brother established a general store at Snow Creek, now Elmwood, and after eighteen months began speculating. In 1880 he was elected as register to fill out an unexpired term of a deceased incumbent. In August, 1886, he was elected to his present office. He married, February 28, 1883, Gertrude, daughter of Hugh and Martha Bradley, and born at Dixon Springs, Smith County; their only child is Nannie L. In politics he is a Democrat, and he and his wife are both members of the Methodist Episcopal Church South.

Col. A. E. Garrett, attorney at law of Carthage, was born in 1830, in Overton (now Pickett) County, a son of Stephen and Sarah (Flowers) Garrett. The father was of English-French descent, born in Buckingham County, Va., in 1802. When ten years of age he immigrated with his father, Elijah Garrett, to what is now called Pickett County. He was one of the first white settlers of that portion of Tennessee. It was here that Stephen married, and died in 1860. His wife was of Irish-French descent, born in 1806 in Virginia, and died in 1882. The Flowers family is noted for longevity. Mrs. Garrett's parents lived to the age of eighty-three and ninety-six respectively. Her brother reached the unusual age of one hundred and six, and there are now five sisters living, the eldest one being ninety-four, the youngest seventy-two. Our subject is the only surviving child of his father's family. He remained on the farm until his majority, assisting his parents, who were in limited circumstances. He had inferior educational advantages, but was eager to gain information. He accumulated as much money as possible, and entered the Poplar Spring Academy in Kentucky, attending several sessions. About this time he also commenced the study of law, under guidance of W. W. Goodpasture. In March, 1852, he married Miss Louisa Greer, who was born in Barren County, Ky. Four children of this union are living: Clarence, Isaac, Belle (wife of Jas. Barkett) and Louisa. After marriage they located on the old home place, taking many of the cares and responsibilities of the farm. After the father's death the mother made her home with him until she, too, was called away. In 1853 our subject was admitted to the bar. He was a stanch Whig previous to the war and a Democrat afterward, yet a strong Union man. In May, 1861, he enlisted in Company C, First Kentucky Cavalry. At the expiration of eighteen months he was authorized to raise a regiment. It was the First Tennessee Mounted Infantry; he was lieutenant-colonel and commander. For fourteen months he remained in Tennessee. At Grandville, Jackson County, July 1, 1864, one of his men attempted assassination; Col. Garrett was shot through the bowels and right hip, the right limb being paralyzed below the knee. His family had located in Carthage in 1863, and in 1865 he was elected to the Legislature. In 1868 he became a candidate for Congress, his opponent being Wm. Stokes. Col. Garrett was elected by a complimentary and large majority, but Gov. Brownlow ruled that 2,700 votes should not be counted, consequently Mr. Stokes got the seat. In 1870 he became candidate, and our subject received a majority of 6,500. In 1876 the Colonel lost his wife, and the following year he married Mrs. Addie McDonald, *nee* Hayes, a daughter of Addison Hayes of Nashville, Tenn. Mrs. Garrett's brother, A. Hayes, Jr., married ex-President Jefferson Davis' daughter. Mrs. Garrett was born at Holly Springs, Miss. Her first husband was Col. McDonald, who was killed in Memphis during the war. To this union there was one child, Charles, who is head bookkeeper for the Standard Oil Company, Nashville. To Colonel and Mrs. Garrett have been born three children: Addison, Ellison and Addie. Mrs. Garrett is an elegant, accomplished woman, and member of the Episcopal Church. The Colonel belongs to the Missionary Baptist; he is also a Royal Arch Mason. He is a self-made man in the true sense of the word, an able and prominent lawyer, and one of the most worthy and respected citizens of the county.

G. H. Glass, a well known farmer and brick-mason, was born in 1822 in Nelson County, Va. He is one of nine children born to Thomas and Sophia (Dameron) Glass. The father was born in 1783, in Halifax County, Va. In 1827 he moved to Kanawha County, W. Va., where he remained until his death in 1863. He was a shoemaker by occupation. His wife was born in 1787, and departed this life in 1822, when G. H. was born. Our subject received a good practical education in the common schools of his native county, and located in Smith County in 1840. In 1844 he was wedded to Eliza A., daughter of Moses B. and Nancy Reeves, who was a native of the county, born in 1827. In 1880 Mr. Glass was census taker of the Fourteenth District, and in 1882 he was elected by a most complimentary majority as justice of the peace, for the same district, and has given perfect satisfaction. He was one of a committee of five on the new courthouse, and superintendent of the construction of the new county asylum. He is a Democrat, and cast his first presidential vote for Henry Clay, in 1844; is also a Knight Templar in the Masonic order. Mr. Glass has been very prosperous, and is a judicious manager, and honorable man. He owns 135 acres of good land, highly cultivated, well fenced, and with first-class buildings on the place. There still remains on the farm a house which was erected in 1822, and was at that time considered one of the finest places in the section.

W. D. Gold, clerk and master of chancery court, editor of *The Record*, and lawyer, was born in Smith County, in 1847. He is the son of Pleasant and Constance (Gwaltney) Gold. The father, of English origin, was born in 1806, in Culpeper County, Va., and when fourteen he came to Wilson County, Tenn., with a sickly brother and four or five small sisters to care for, orphans. Here he was largely engaged in sawing lumber by whip-saw, and rafting it down to Nashville. In 1844 he bought a farm near Gordonsville, and from 1856 to 1870 he with his brother was merchandising, and speculating in tobacco a few years after. He died in 1876. The mother, born in 1812 in Smith County, is still living with her two younger sons. Our subject, one of seven children, graduated at New Middleton College (co-educational) in 1870. He taught five months' school in his 1869 vacation, and after graduating was principal of Liberty Masonic Academy, Tennessee, for twenty-five months. In 1873 he began the study of law under Hon. W. S. De Witt, Carthage, now of Chattanooga. Admitted to the bar the same year, he acquired a reputation for accuracy in chancery court proceedings. He devoted his entire time to practice until appointed clerk and master of chancery by Judge Crowley in 1877, since which he has held the office. He began his editorship in 1883. *The Record* is now one of the newsiest local papers in the State, with a weekly issue of 1,344 copies, and constantly increasing subscriptions, was practically a dead paper when he took it, issuing 600 copies free with no subscription list. Printed entirely at home, it now receives outside news by telegraph, and in its politics conservative and Democratic. In April, 1876, he married Willie Cullom, daughter of Mrs. V. A. Cullom, and born in Wayne County, Ky., in 1852. They have four children: William I., Marie, Virginia N. and Leslie J. Mr. Gold is a member of the Missionary Baptist Church, while his wife is a member of the Methodist Episcopal Church South.

John Harrison Gordon, a prominent merchant of Stonewall, was born in 1852, one mile north of Gordonsville, in Smith County. He is one of six living children of a family of ten born to Matthew A. L. and Lucy Lee (Ward) Gordon. Both parents were natives of Smith County. The father was of Scotch-Irish descent, born in 1828. He was a prosperous farmer. The principal portion of his life was spent tilling the soil. In 1853 Matthew took his family to Mississippi, where he had purchased a farm in Leake County. He remained there until the close of the war, when he returned to Tennessee and bought a tract of land, a portion of his grandfather's estate, where he died in 1876. The mother was born in 1830, and departed this life in 1879. The subject of our sketch received his education in the common schools of his native county, remaining with his parents until his majority, when he went to California. For two and a half years he engaged in farming and trading in the San Joaquin Valley. At the expiration of that time he returned to his father's place and carried on the same business. In 1878 he and his uncle, F. M. Ward, bought the mercantile stock of Perkins, Durham & Co. The firm of Ward & Gordon continued about three years, when J. A. Ward, a son, bought Mr. Gordon's interest in the concern. During the following year he traded extensively, and made a prospecting tour to Arkansas. After his return he purchased some stock and F. M. Ward's farm, which included the ferry and blacksmith shop. He also handles a great deal of tobacco, and with more success than the majority of traders. He is an enterprising, genial and well respected young business man, who by shrewdness and judicious management has accumulated considerable means, all since his return from California and by his own efforts. He is a member of the Methodist Church and a Democrat; gave his first presidential vote for Samuel J. Tilden in 1876. In 1880 he wedded Julia Hatten, daughter of Squire Henry and Araminta Perkins. Mrs. Gordon was born about one mile north of Stonewall in 1862. Four children were born to this union, two of whom are living: Elsie Lee and Herschel P. Henry A., the second child, was born April 3, 1882; died May 2, same year. An infant, now deceased, was the last born. Mrs. Gordon is an estimable lady and consistent member of the Missionary Baptist Church.

A. B. Hall, a prosperous farmer of the Seventh District, was born in Smith County in 1833. He is third of a family of seven children born to James and Annie (Deadman) Hall. The father died when our subject was about five years old. The mother was born in Smith County about 1812, and is still living. Her father, John Deadman, was a native of North Carolina, and came to Tennessee at an early day. He was one of the first settlers of Smith County, where he died in 1860 at the age of eighty-two. His wife lived to the unusual age of one hundred years. The subject of this sketch received a rather limited education in his native county. Bereft of his father at a tender age, he had to work hard and support his mother. In 1864 he married Louisa, daughter of Dr. Washington and Sallie Irwin. Mrs. Hall was born in 1843. To this union nine children were born: Lassie D., now Mrs. Lawrence; Mrs. Sallie W. (Hall) Davis, M. Bettie, James W., Ophelia B., Mattie, William P., Thomas P. and Daisy May. For several years Mr. Hall rented and engaged in agriculture. Meeting with success, he was soon enabled to purchase ninety acres, to which he has since added 135 more acres, all of which are well cultivated and improved. The farm is situated on the Alexander road, five miles from the town. Mr. Hall is an honest, industrious and highly respected man, and has accumulated his property by his own labor and good management. He is a life-long and stanch Democrat. Mr. and Mrs. Hall and three children are earnest members of the Missionary Baptist Church.

Henry E. Hart, physician, was born at Carthage, Smith County, in 1852, one of four children of H. W. and Laura (Young) Hart. The father, of Scotch origin, was born in the same place in 1822, and graduated in Lebanon Law School in 1847; an influential farmer, owning 214 acres of land. He served in the Mexican war under Gen. Taylor; served two years in the Legislature from 1852, and as county clerk four years from 1854. In 1861 he enlisted in an independent Confederate company of Tennessee volunteers, and was a captain during his service. Since 1873 he has resided in Nashville. The mother, of Irish origin, was born in Smith County in 1831, and is still living. Educated in St. Mary's College, Kentucky, our subject, in 1878, entered the medical department of Vanderbilt University, and graduated in 1882, and has successfully practiced ever since. In 1874 he married Sally, daughter of Dr. J. G. and Kitty Goodpasture. They have two children: Lucy and Alexander S. In politics he is a Democrat, and is a member of the F. & A. M. fraternity; in belief, a Methodist, of which church his wife is a member.

B. A. James, a merchant, farmer and livery man, of Gordonsville, was born in Smith County in 1831. He is the son of J. R. and Martha (Allison) James. His father was born in 1810, in Montgomery County, N. C., and was one of eight children born to Bartlett and Sarah (Rollins) James. The father (grandfather of our subject) was born in Virginia in 1780; he was a farmer by occupation, and moved to Montgomery County, N. C., when a young man. In 1823 he came to the Fifteenth District of Smith County, Tenn., and purchased 640 acres of land. He died in 1845. His wife was born about 1778, in Virginia, and died in 1855. J. R. James was educated in the common schools of Smith County and the Shady Grove Academy, near Gordonsville, Dr. F. H. Gordon being the principal. In 1830 he wedded Martha, daughter of Joseph and Elizabeth Allison, who was born in 1815, in Jackson County, Tenn., and died in 1871. Their children are Bartlett A., Sarah E., William N., Robert A., Martha G., John F., Eliza, Callie C., Joseph H., Mary J. and Henry Clay. In 1843 Mr. James was elected justice of the peace of his district, and served in that capacity twenty-six years. In 1845 he became chairman of the county court, holding the office about twelve years. In 1868 he became tax collector; after two years he resigned and was elected to the State Legislature. He is a Democrat, and cast his first presidential vote for Andrew Jackson in 1832. He owns 330 acres of land, highly cultivated, and with all modern improvements, and raises all kinds of stock. He is a worthy, respected citizen. He and the family are members of the Cumberland Presbyterian Church. The subject of this sketch was educated in the common schools of his native county. At nineteen years of age he began his career as an agriculturist. Twenty-six years later he embarked in merchandising at Gordonsville, in which he is still engaged, his partners being the Gold Bros. They have a substantial and extensive trade, being among the leading merchants of the county. In 1850 Mr. James married Miss Elizabeth, daughter of W. and Martha Dowell, who was born in Smith County in 1830. In 1861 our subject organized Company G, Fifty-fifth Tennessee Volunteers. He was elected captain, and served in that capacity until after the battle of Shiloh, when he was discharged and returned home. He was elected justice of the peace in 1868, and has held the office continuously since that time, having made an efficient and satisfactory officer. He is a stanch Democrat; no man in the community is better or more favorably known.

Dr. J. L. Jones was born in De Kalb County, Tenn., in 1849, one of ten children of Fredrick and Maria (Squires) Jones. The father, of Scottish origin, and a tailor by occupation, was born in Surry County, Va., and came to Smith County in 1837. After working at his trade until 1855, he engaged in the hotel business at Nashville—the Rock City Sun. From 1859 to 1870 he lived on his farm, of 200 acres, in Bradford County, but returned to Nashville, where he died in 1881. The mother was born in Smith County in 1811, and died at Nashville in 1873. Our subject was educated at Elmwood Academy, Bedford County, and at Union University, of Murfreesboro; graduated from the medical department of Nashville University in 1872, since when he has had an extensive practice. In 1874 he married Mary W., daughter of Joel M. and Martha L. Nichols, and was born in Smith County in 1854. Their two children are Mattie I. and Pearl. In politics he is a Democrat, and his wife is a member of the Methodist Episcopal Church.

W. T. Jones, a prominent agriculturist of the Seventh District, was born February 24, 1843, in Smith County, the sixth of eight children born to Isaac and Elizabeth (Malone) Jones. The father was of English-German descent, born in North Carolina in 1813, and came to Smith County about 1820. He served as magistrate of his district for fourteen years; he was an efficient officer and highly respected. His death occurred about 1881. The mother was of Scotch-Irish ancestry. Our subject received a liberal education in the academy at Alexandria. He assisted his father on the farm until his seventeenth year. At the outbreak of the war he enlisted in Company F, of the Twenty-fourth Tennessee Infantry. He took active part in all engagements into which his regiment was drawn, and of which he was sergeant. He was captured at the battle of Missionary Ridge, and retained as prisoner at Rock Island sixteen months, regaining his liberty but a short while before the close of the war. November 1, 1866, he was united in marriage to Miss Catherine E. Patterson, who was born December 1, 1845. To this union nine children have been born: J. Sidney, Edgar D., Frederick W., Willard S., Shela Wilson, Kate and Ula; Ada and Ora, deceased. After the war Mr. Jones began life a poor man. He rented and farmed. In 1868 he bought seventy-six acres near Alexandria. After buying and selling several times, he finally purchased the place upon which he now lives. It consists of about 210 acres of valuable and productive soil, situated on Hickman Creek, about six miles north of Alexandria. Mr. Jones is an industrious, energetic, honest man, respected by all. He is a life-long Democrat; cast his first presidential vote for Horace Greeley. Mr. and Mrs. Jones are active and exemplary members of the Cumberland Presbyterian Church.

James B. Jones, one of the leading farmers and tobacco dealers of the Twelfth District, was born one mile from where he now resides, in 1833. He is the fourth of eight children born to Jefferson and Nancy (Haynes) Jones. The father was a native of Tennessee, born about 1804, a son of Banks Jones, an early pioneer of Smith County. Jefferson received a good common-school education, and spent nearly all of his life as a tiller of the soil. He was a man of ability and influence, and for several years a magistrate. He died in 1851. The mother was born in Sumner County, and departed this life June, 1884, at the age of about eighty-two. Both were members of the Missionary Baptist Church. Of their children, four are living. Our subject's educational advantages were limited, as his parents were poor. He remained on the farm with his mother until 1861, when he married Miss Susan, daughter of John and Virginia Hughes. Mrs. Jones was born in Smith County, in May, 1846. Nine children have been born to them; those living are James F., William W., Nevada Lou, Cornelia, Susan, Virginia, and Thurman. Mr. Jones remained on the old homestead until 1880, when he purchased the farm upon which he now lives. It consists of 202 acres of land, well cultivated, with a fine and commodious dwelling. The place lies two and a quarter miles southwest of Dixon Springs. Our subject started in life a poor man, and has accumulated his possessions by industry and judicious management. He gives his children the best educational advantages, is charitable and honest. He and his wife are active and esteemed members of the Missionary Baptist Church. Mr. Jones is a Democrat, and cast his first presidential vote for Millard Fillmore in 1856.

W. L. Kemp, Jr., was born in Smith County in 1842, and is of a family of thirteen children born to Asa and Mary (Williams) Kemp. The father was born in 1823, in West Virginia, of English descent. He moved to North Carolina with his parents in 1833, and in 1840 came to Smith County, where he now resides. He is a prosperous farmer owning 220 acres of fine land. He is an influential and respected citizen. The mother was born in Smith County in 1827, and died in 1882. Our subject received a fair education in the schools of his native county. In 1861 he entered the Confederate Army, in William H. Hart's independent company Tennessee Infantry Volunteers. Soon after the organization he was elected orderly sergeant, and served in that capacity until 1863, when he was transferred to the command of Gen. John H. Morgan, cavalry brigade, when he was again elected to the same rank. He took an active part in the battles of Farmington and Corinth, Miss.; LaVergne, Stone River, Snow Hill, Milton, Dixon Springs and Greasy Creek, Ky. December, 1863, he was made prisoner and taken to Carthage, where he took the oath of allegiance and returned home. In 1864 he married Sarah T., daughter of William D. and Lucy H. McCawley, who was born in 1848, and died in 1869. Two years later, in 1871, Mr. Kemp was united to Mary A., daughter of William and Jane Hockette, who was born in 1855. To this union there are seven children: Claude E., Maud L., Eva S., Eddie M., Asa E., Sallie J. and Hettie L. In 1870 our subject was chosen to fill the unexpired term of eighteen months, of C. W. West, justice of the peace, of the Fifth District. August, 1871, he was elected by a large majority to the same office, which he held for six years, being re-elected at the end of the term. He was again called to fill out the unexpired term of E. J. Yeaman, deceased. In 1886 he was commissioned by Gov. William B. Bate as notary public, for four years. For seventeen years he has been one of the leading commercial men of the county. He was a heavy lumber dealer, and built two saw mills. In February, 1882 he had the misfortune to lose heavily by the rising of the Cumberland River, a large quantity of lumber being carried away by the water. He is now a member of the firm of Witt & Kemp. They have an extensive mercantile trade, and are among the most enterprising and successful merchants in the section. Mr. Kemp is a Democrat, and gave his first presidential vote for Horatio Seymour in 1868, and is also a member of the Masonic order. He is an earnest and respected communicant of the Missionary Baptist Church.

Dr. Abram Hassell King, a practicing physician and surgeon of Chestnut Mound, was born in 1850, at Carthage, Smith County, Tenn. He is one of the two living children out of a family of eight, born to Abram H., Sr., and Mary T. King. The father was of Scotch-Irish descent, born in 1810, near Gallatin, Sumner Co., Tenn., where he was raised by his uncle, Jennet Hassel, as his parents both died when he was quite small. Until the age of twenty, he was employed in the laborious duties of farm life. He became dissatisfied in tilling the soil, and resolved to prepare himself for a physician. After hard study, and graduating at Cincinnati, he became the most popular, skillful, and financially successful practitioner in all of Smith County. After a long useful and prosperous life, he died in 1873, at Carthage. The mother was of French origin, born in 1818, near where Dixon Springs is now located. She is still living in Carthage, an esteemed Christian woman; her health is quite feeble. Our subject received his literary education at New Middleton. When twenty-three years of age, he went to Nashville, and attended Vanderbilt University one session. He then returned home and located at present place of residence. In 1881 he married Miss Sadie Duke (Rev. Green P. Jackson officiating), who was raised and educated by her grandfather, Blake Thackston. Mrs. King was born in 1858 in Sullivan Bend, of Cumberland River, Smith County. To this union three children came: John Howard, Joseph Robert and Brien Thackston. The late civil war having destroyed all his father's accumulation, Dr. King was compelled to borrow money to complete his medical education, consequently, in 1875, when he settled to begin the practice of his profession, he was deeply in debt. Since that time, so extensive and lucrative has been his practice, that he has cleared his debts, bought a fine farm of 120 acres at Chestnut Mound, another of 107 acres at Carthage, each well cultivated, and valuable. He has also built an elegant modern residence, with all necessary improvements and outside buildings, and an office at the Mound. He is one of the most prominent physicians and enterprising, worthy men in the section. He is a stanch Democrat, casting his first vote for Horace Greeley in 1872.

Dr. R. W. King, a leading practicing physician of Gordonsville, was born in Wilson County in 1849. He is one of the four living children of a family of eleven, born to Ira W. and Deborah (Brown) King. His father is of Scotch-Irish descent, born in North Carolina about 1819. When a boy he located in West Tennessee with his father. He is a

Cumberland Presbyterian minister. In 1852 he settled in Smith County, and was elected trustee, which office he held about six years. He is now in the drug business in Alexandria. The mother was born in Wilson County in 1818 and died in November, 1874. The subject of this sketch was educated at the New Middleton Academy. He began the study of medicine in 1873. He attended the Vanderbilt University at Nashville during 1876-77. After his return home and remaining a short length of time, he went to Silver Springs, Wilson County, where he practiced about two years, then came to Gordonsville, where he has since had an extensive and lucrative practice. In 1879 he married Miss Mary, the daughter of John and Lucy Simpson. Mrs. King was born in Smith County in 1854. She is a sincere and respected member of the Cumberland Presbyterian Church. Dr. King is a Republican. He is a skillful and popular physician and widely esteemed citizen.

Elijah Haynie Knight, a physician and surgeon of the Eighth District of Smith County, was born in 1841 in the Sixteenth District, and is a son of Robert G. and Susan (Haynie) Knight. The father is of Scotch-English descent, born in 1811 in North Carolina. His parents died in his early childhood. At the age of eight years he came to Tennessee with his uncle, James High, and settled where Wm. Derickson now lives. Mr. Knight became a farmer and was quite prosperous. For many years he was thus engaged on the farm in the Sixteenth District now owned by William Gibbs. In 1858 he sold out and moved to Chestnut Mound where he now resides with his son, in the enjoyment of good health and a pleasant old age. The mother is of English origin, born in 1818 on Peyton Creek in Smith County. Of her family of seven children, five are still living. Mrs. Knight is highly esteemed by all who know her. Our subject received his literary education in the common schools of his native county. In the summer of 1858 he began the study of medicine in the office of his cousin, Dr. John P. Haynie, which he prosecuted until the breaking out of the civil war, when, in April, 1861, he joined Company B, Seventh Tennessee Regiment, Confederate service. He took part in the famous battles of Seven Pines, Gaines Mills, Ox Hill, South Mountain and Fredericksburg. At the latter place he was shot in the lung with a rifle ball, in consequence of which he was indefinitely furloughed. About eight months after his return home he was captured by Federal troops and taken to the prison at Gallatin, Tenn., where he was retained three months, at the expiration of which time broken down in health he took the oath of allegiance to the Federal Government and went home. While in the hospital at Charlottesville, Va., he attended a course of medical lectures, afterward devoting some two years to the study of the profession. He began to practice in 1866, at Chestnut Mound, where he has had an extensive patronage. Physical disabilities have forced him to abandon active practice for the past two or three years. He engaged to a considerable extent in the raising of stock, and farming, in all of which he has been successful. He owns 350 acres of fine land on Caney Fork, and 110 acres of ridge soil. He is not only a skillful physician and surgeon, but also a first-class manager and financier. He is a Democrat and gave his first presidential vote for Horatio Seymour in 1868. He is Master of Pekin Lodge, No. 563, Masonic order, and a member of the Missionary Baptist Church. In 1870 he was elected trustee of the county, serving one term of two years with entire satisfaction, and would, no doubt, have been re-elected had he not changed his place of residence to Putnam County, where he practiced four years. In 1872 the Doctor married Eliza, daughter of Robert E. and Jane (McKinley) Fain. Mrs. Knight is a native of Putnam County and was born in 1852. The fruits of this union are six children: Jeanne, Robert, Sam, Mabel, Tom and Frank. Mrs. Knight is an exemplary Christian and devout member of the Methodist Church South.

Michael Lancaster, an old resident and well-known farmer of the Ninth District, was born in Smith County, November 25, 1815, within one and a half miles of his present place of residence. He was the youngest of seven children born to Thomas and Frances (Lancaster) Lancaster. Both parents were natives of Virginia. The father, Thomas, was born about six months after the death of his father, and fifteen days after he entered this world, the mother, too, passed away, and he was raised by his grandparents. In 1808 he moved to Kentucky. After participating in the war of 1812, under command of Col. Allen, he settled with his family in Smith County, where after many years of prosperity he died in 1855. Our subject received a fair education in the common schools of his native county. He was about ten years of age before he ever had a pair of boots or shoes, either in summer or winter. The first pair he had were made of cow's hide, and tanned in a trough. He inherited from his father a number of slaves and about $5,000 worth of property. The war, of course, liberated his negroes, and desolated most of his land. He now owns 2,000 acres, a part of which is located on Smith Fork, and Caney Fork. From 1851 to 1861 he served as postmaster, and gave great satisfaction. He was also justice of the peace for six years, and constable four years, and always made an efficient officer. He has never united with any denomination, but is a liberal contributor to all charitable, religious, or worthy purposes. He was a Whig previous to the war, and is now a Democrat. May 8, 1845, he wedded Miss Jane Kelly, with whom he had several children, only one living to maturity—Mary Frances, now Mrs. Kelly. Mrs. Lancaster died in 1855, and the following year he married Miss Rox Laney Cowen. Their union resulted in the birth of ten children: Michael, Thomas, James, and the deceased are William R., Sarah M., Ira C., J. W., Wade C., West and an infant. Mr. Lancaster is an industrious, honorable and esteemed man, and in comfortable circumstances; would have been in affluence had he not had the misfortune to have several security debts to settle.

John B. Luster, editor of the *Carthage Mirror*, and attorney at law, was born in Summer (now Trousdale) County, in 1837. He is one of the three surviving children of William and Virginia (Bressie) Luster. The father was of English descent, born in 1806 in Buckingham County, Va.; came to Tennessee when a young man and located at Hartsville, where he remained until after the late war, when he moved to Alabama, where he died in 1886. He was a trader during the greatest portion of his business career. The mother was a Tennessean of Scotch-English origin. She was born in 1810, and died in 1853 at Hartsville. Our subject received a good common-school education. He worked on the farm until his seventeenth year, when he went to Nashville, and obtained a situation as clerk in a wholesale grocery house. Two years later he began the study of law, completing his course at the law school in Lebanon, Tenn. He was licensed to practice in the State in 1859; soon afterward he went to New Orleans, where he studied civil law and received his license in 1860. In 1861 he entered the Confederate Army and became quartermaster of a battalion organized by Col. J. G. Bennett, also second command organized by the same officer, in 1862, which became attached to Morgan's forces. He was engaged in battles of Shiloh and Farmington as aid to Gen. Ruggles. He was also in the battle of Hartsville, and numerous skirmishes. After the close of the war he located at Carthage, where he gave his attention to his profession in partnership with his father-in-law, James B. Moores. May 24, 1883, he established the *Carthage Mirror* which he has since so ably edited. He is a stanch Democrat; cast his first presidential vote for John C. Breckinridge. He is a member of the Masonic order, Carthage Lodge, No. 14. In 1861 he married Miss Moores, who was born in 1843, in Carthage. To this union have been born Berry, who is a resident of Texas; Percy J., who, though only nineteen years of age, is a licensed minister in the Methodist Episcopal Church, and is now filling an appointment in Williamson County, Tenn. Moores is sixteen years of age; he is assistant editor and foreman of the *Carthage Mirror*. Mrs. Luster is an esteemed and consistent member of the Methodist Church.

Thomas J. Mabry, a prominent agriculturalist of the First District, was born in 1841, in Overton (now called Clay County), Tenn. He is one of a family of nine children born to Thomas and Minnie (Creed) Mabry, both parents of Irish descent and natives of North Carolina and brought when small to Tennessee by their families. The father was born in 1805, and the mother in 1810. After their marriage they went to Illinois; two years later they returned to Overton County, settling on a farm where the mother died in 1883, leaving three children. The father departed this life in 1884 at his son's home in Smith County. Our subject was educated partly in the common schools of his native county, and Tompkinsville, Ky. When eighteen years old, he entered the Confederate service, Company A, Eighth Tennessee Regiment, at Celina. At the reorganization of the company he became lieutenant, and served in that rank until the close of hostilities. He took an active and gallant part in the battles of Perryville, Murfreesboro and Chickamauga. He was with Johnson all the way to Atlanta, and in many skirmishes. At Perryville he received a rifle-ball shot in the arm, and at Peach Tree Creek, near Atlanta, June, 1864, he was wounded in the knee. He was honorably discharged in 1865 at Macon, Ga. He returned home and began farming on his father's place. In 1867 he married in Monroe County, Ky., Mary A. daughter of Hamilton and Freelove (Martin) Savage. Mrs. Mabry was born in Jackson (now Clay) County, Tenn., in 1843. The fruits of this union are ten children: Minnie Freelove.; Sarah Rebecca; Willie Jeff; Hamilton Savage; Martha Bell; Davis Winfield; Jay; Mary Beulah and Ginla Cathaline. For several years Mr. Mabry lived in Clay County and in 1883 he moved to the farm he had previously bought in Smith County, which is one of the finest places in the vicinity; it contains 427 acres, well cultivated and highly improved. He has obtained his property and means by continued industry and careful management. He is a demitted member of the Masonic order, Celina Lodge, No. 398, and a stanch Democrat; his first presidential vote was given for Horatio Seymour in 1868. Mrs. Mabry and eldest daughter are members of the Christian Church.

Thomas A. McCall, a prominent citizen and farmer of the Thirteenth District, was born four miles southeast of Rome, August 25, 1841. The youngest and only living of two children born to Dr. John and Mary T. (Allen) McCall. The father was of Irish descent; born in North Carolina on November 6, 1803, a son of Alex. McCall, who was a native of Ireland, and immigrated to America when a young man, soon locating in Stokes County, N. C. He was married to Mary Armstrong about 1803. He moved to Tennessee. After spending some time in Jackson, Sumner,

Davidson and Wilson Counties, he finally settled in Lincoln County, where he passed the remainder of his life, dying in 1833. Four of his sons were prosperous and able physicians. Dr. John was raised in Smith County; educated in the common achools. He graduated in medicine at the Transylvania University in 1829, at Lexington, Ky., and immediately began to practice in Rome and that vicinity. For thirty years he was one of the most successful practitioners of the county. He was a man of intellect, literary accomplishments and keen judgment. He was a close observer and accurate reader of human nature. He died in 1884, on his farm near Rome. His wife was born in Trousdale County near Dixon Springs, February 23, 1818, and died in 1842, a member of the Presbyterian Church, and her husband of the Christian. Our subject was raised by his grandmother McCall, receiving his literary education at Rome, Franklin College, and Lebanon, completing his course at Bethany College, Va. In 1868–69, he attended the law department of the Cumberland University at Lebanon, but did not enter upon the practice of his profession. In 1861 he enlisted in Company E, Forty-fourth Tennessee Infantry, Confederate Army. He took part in the battles of Chickamauga, Drewry's Bluff, Va., and numerous severe skirmishes. He was captured at Perryville and retained four months. He was exchanged and rejoined his command in September, 1864. His attention has been always given to agricultural pursuits on his present farm, which contains 474 acres of land; it is located two miles south of Rome. He also owns sixty acres in Obion County, and 100 in Trousdale. He is a man of high cultivation and literary attainments, and devotes a great deal of time to reading and study. He was formerly a Whig, but affiliates with the Democratic party, although he has never cast a vote at a general election. He has been a faithful and consistent member of the Christian Church for nearly a quarter of a century. October 20, 1875, he married Miss Tobitha B., daughter of the eminent Dr. F. H. and Catherine C. Gordon. Mrs. McCall was born at the Old Clinton College farm, and educated partly in Smith County, and finished at the Cumberland University.

Mrs. Maria McClellan, who is an esteemed resident of the Second District, was born in Wilson County, Tenn., in 1838. She is one of thirteen children born to Dr. Thomas and Elizabeth (Clay) Norman. The father was of Scotch descent, born in Davidson County, Tenn., in 1801. He was an able physician and surgeon. His residence was in Lebanon. For about forty years he was the leading practicing physician of Wilson County. He died in 1876. His wife was a native of Smith County, born in 1814, and departed this life in 1857. The subject of this sketch received a liberal education at the Abbey Institute, of Lebanon, and a college at McMinnville. February 22, 1865, she married D. S. McClellan, who was the son of Samson and Louisa (Cornwell) McClellan. He was born October 24, 1833, in Smith County, and educated at Erwing College, Warren County, and Cumberland University at Lebanon. At the outbreak of the late war he enlisted in Capt. Hart's company, Tennessee Volunteer Infantry. He took an active and gallant part in the battle of Shiloh. In 1864 he was honorably discharged on account of disability. After marriage he located in the Second District, where he was one of the most prosperous farmers in the section. He owned 500 acres of productive soil. He was by trade a mechanic, and in connection with his farm operated a saw-mill, and was an extensive lumber dealer, also dealt in grain, shipping immense quantities of it to Nashville. He was a stanch Democrat, and a highly esteemed, honorable man. He never united with any church, but was a Christian, and died in the belief of a reward hereafter. His death occurred May 7, 1882. Mrs. McClellan is an intelligent, estimable woman, and held in the highest respect by the community. She is an exemplary member of the Presbyterian Church.

S. S. McDonald, a prominent agriculturist of Smith County, was born in 1828 near C[illegible]nville, Jackson (now Putman) Co., Tenn. He is one of a family of eight children, born to James P. and Susan (Edleman) McDonald. The father is of Irish descent and was born in 1809 in Jackson County. He was raised in comfort and without any knowledge of work, despite which fact he was of an industrious, active temperament and labored most successfully in after years. He is now eighty years of age, an honorable and respected old gentleman. He lives on his own farm about ten miles east of Carthage. He married at the age of eighteen. Miss Edleman was of Dutch extraction, born in North Carolina about 1807 and died in 1875, leaving five children. Mr. McDonald was married the second time to Mrs. Evaline Bolton. The subject of this sketch received but a limited education in the common schools of Smith County. He remained with his parents until after his majority, when, with his father's assistance, he purchased the farm upon which he was born. In 1862 he sold the place. He enlisted in the Confederate Army, Capt. McDonald's company, Twenty-eighth Regiment. He was a first-class teamster and was appointed driver of a six-mule team, which capacity he served in for two years, when he became ill with typhoid fever while in Walker County, Ga., and was taken on to Cherokee County, Ala., and left five miles west of Alpine with a family, where he was sick for three months. He returned home and bought an interest in the farm with his father, upon which the latter is residing. Three years later S. S. sold his interest and invested in a place containing 297 acres, where he is now living. It is situated near sand shoals of Cumberland River, in Smith County. In 1870 he married Fanny, daughter of Robt. J. and Fanny (Cook) Glover, of same county. Mrs. McDonald was born in 1848 at place of marriage. This union resulted in the birth of five children: Alva Wright, Edna Winfried, Mattie Lelia, Willie Sydney, and Callie May, the first child died in infancy in 1872. Mr. McDonald returned from the war a poor man, but by continued industry and judicious management has succeeded in accumulating some very good property, and with his brother owns the ferry that crosses Caney Fork of Cumberland River. His farm is moderately well cultivated and improved. Previous to the war he was a Whig and is now a stanch Democrat. His first presidential vote was for Gen. Winfield Scott in 1852. He was at one time a member of the Grange as was also his wife. Mr. McDonald has not united with any denomination but favors the Cumberland Presbyterian Church; his wife is a member of the Missionary Baptist Church.

Ridley R. McDonald, a well known resident and native of Smith County (formerly Jackson County), was born in 1830 near the present line between the two above mentioned counties. He is a son of James Porter and Susan (Edleman) McDonald. The father was of Scotch-Irish descent, born in 1809 in Jackson County and is at present living at the head of Hurricane Creek. The mother was of Dutch origin, born in North Carolina in 1807 and departed this life in 1875. The subject of this sketch received a limited education in the common schools of his native county. In 1853 he began farming, renting land for that purpose; about 1857 he was enabled to purchase a farm in Putman (now Smith) County, and remained on same about twenty-five years. He then bought his present place of residence, which is a farm of about 220 acres, situated on the Cumberland River. In 1853 he married Ruth, daughter of Robt. and Charity (Knight) Warren. Mrs. McDonald was born in 1837 on Caney Fork in Hill Bend. To their union eleven children were born, of whom seven are living: Leonard H., Lou, Landen A., Alfred A., Minoa Bostick, Bebie and Sidney. In 1863 Mr. McDonald enlisted in the Confederate Army, at Chestnut Mound, in the Twenty-eighth Tennessee. He was in active service about ten months, when he was honorably discharged at Shelbyville, Tenn., at which time he was a cavalier. He never participated in an engagement. He is a Democrat, previous to the war was a Whig and voted first time for Gen. Winfield Scott. Mr. McDonald is a self-made and highly respected man. By hard work, both day and night, he has become the possessor of a 300-acre farm, which is well cultivated and productive. His wife and the eldest five children are members of the Cumberland Presbyterian Church.

John McDonald, a respected and well known farmer of the Eighth District of Smith County, was born in 1837, in Jackson (now Smith) County, Tenn. He is a son of James P. and Susan (Edleman) McDonald. The father, who is still living, is of Scotch-Irish extraction, born in 1809, in Jackson County, Tenn. He is a farmer by occupation; has been twice married; the last wife was Mrs. Evaline Bolton. The mother of our subject was of Dutch descent, born in North Carolina in 1807, and died in 1875, leaving five children. John McDonald received but a limited education in the common schools of his native county. He remained beneath the paternal roof until about twenty-seven years of age. In 1864 he married Martha Washington, daughter of Robert and Fanny Glover, who was born in 1839, at the place where their marriage occurred. This union resulted in the birth of seven children: Leona C., wife of G. D. Saddler; Ada, George A., Sion B., Lassie and Calvin P.; the fourth born, Fannie, deceased. Soon after marriage Mr. McDonald settled on a portion of the homestead, and since that time purchased the interests of the brothers and sisters, now owning the entire farm, which consists of 240 acres. He enlisted in the Confederate Army in 1862, in the Twenty-eighth Tennessee, Capt. Trousdale's company. By the discharge of a gun in the hands of a careless party Mr. McDonald had his right forefinger shot off while on his way to enter the army. He was delayed by the accident until the following year, when he was elected second lieutenant of Capt. McDonald's company, in which capacity he served till the fall of 1863, when he was sent home as a recruiting officer. He was cut off from the Southern Army by the Federal troops, whose headquarters were at McMinnville. He was not again able to join the Confederates. He became a loyal citizen in the latter part of the same year. He was a Whig previous to the war, casting his first presidential vote in 1860; he is now a Democrat. He is an honest, industrious and enterprising man. By his own efforts he has become possessed of the old homestead, which is in a good state of cultivation and improvement. He and the eldest two sons are members of the Cumberland Presbyterian Church, and George is only waiting for an opportunity to join. Mrs. McDonald is connected with the Methodist Church.

Mrs. Julia G. McDonald, who is managing one of the best private boarding-houses in Carthage, was born in Union County, Ky., in 1817. Her parents were Abner and Charlotte (James) Davis. The father was also a native of Union County, a merchant and a farmer by occupation, and a prominent politician. He represented his district in the State

Senate one term. He died in 1880, at nearly eighty years of age. His wife was born in Davidson County, Tenn., and died in Kentucky in 1817, when our subject was but eighteen days old. She was raised by her grandfather, Thomas James, with whom she remained until her marriage in 1835. She wedded Edmond L. Powell, a native of Smith County, born in 1811, by whom she had four children. The only surviving one is James L., who resides in Nashville. Mr. and Mrs. Powell settled in Davidson County, where he owned about 250 acres of fine land. He died in 1841, and in 1846 Mrs. Powell married Col. Henry B. McDonald, who was born in 1793, in Chester District, South Carolina. He was a soldier in the war of 1812; was also in the battle of New Orleans, with Gen. Jackson. He settled in Smith County on a farm; about 1850 moved to Carthage, where he engaged in the practice of his profession—law. By this union Mrs. McDonald became the mother of four children, three of whom are living: Mary, wife of Col. Thomas Waters; Julia D., wife of John B. Robinson, a lawyer of Smithville, and David N., a graduate of West Point and second lieutenant in the regular army. Previous to his marriage with our subject Col. McDonald was a widower. Of his first union there are five children: Darthula, widow of Matthew McKinley; Melvina, wife of Dr. Lemons, of Texas; James, a resident of Anderson, Tex.; Dr. Henry C., of Carthage, and William H. H., a lawyer and professor. The Colonel died in 1872. He was an honorable, respected man, and one of Smith County's most distinguished citizens. Mrs. McDonald, since the war, has been engaged in keeping a boarding house, one of the best and most extensively patronized in the section. She is a devout member of the Methodist Episcopal Church South, and one of the most estimable and best known ladies in the county.

James E. Newbell, a well known agriculturist of the Seventh District, was born September 23, 1849, in Smith County. He is the third of five children born to Edman and Louisa (Dougherty) Newbell. Both parents were natives of Smith County. The father was born in 1814, was of English descent and a son of William Newbell. Edman was a clerk of the Missionary Baptist Church for many years. He was a man of extensive knowledge and cultivation, and a prosperous farmer, one of the most substantial and respected citizens in that section. His death occurred in 1870. The mother was born about 1827, also of English origin, and is still living with her sons. Our subject was educated in the common schools of his native county. Since his father's decease he and his brothers have been farming on their mother's place, which consists of 300 acres of fertile and valuable land. Mr. Newbell receives one-fourth of the proceeds of the farm. He has been an exemplary member of the Missionary Baptist Church since early manhood. He is a stanch Democrat and one of the most enterprising and esteemed residents of the district.

Henry Petty, merchant, liveryman, undertaker and hotel proprietor, was born in 1841, four miles south of Chestnut Mound, and is one of ten children (five dead) of Stephen and Sarah (Carr) Petty. The father, Irish in origin, was born in 1811 in Smith County, and the mother, of the same descent, was born in 1815 in Putnam County. The father, a farmer and prominent justice of the peace, died in the fall of 1885. The mother died in 1865 at the place where our subject was born and reared. Leaving home at the age of twenty-eight years, he became a clerk for S. H. Smith of Laurel Hill, Tenn., in general merchandise, and sixteen months later they went into partnership at Chestnut Mound. After 1874 Mr. Petty managed the business himself until he added trading in tobacco in 1877, when he added livery and feed stables and hotel-keeping. The undertaker's department he added in 1883. Besides these, he rented out two farms of twenty-five and 250 acres. In 1874 he married Harriett, daughter of A. M. and Elizebeth (Farmer) Betty, born in 1840. Their three children are Stephen A., Martha E. and Isaac S. Mr. Petty's first salary was $12.50 per month, and now, besides his four branches of business, owns 275 acres (100 acres from his father). He is a Democrat, a demitted member of the F. & A. M. fraternity, and he and his wife are members of the Methodist Episcopal Church.

S. M. Phelps, superintendent of the county poor, is a native of Davidson County, Tenn., born in 1831. His parents were Silas and Margret (Rigely) Phelps. The father was born in North Carolina in 1794, and immigrated to Tennessee after marriage, locating three miles from Nashville. His death occurred in 1869. His wife was born in Virginia, and died in 1860 at the age of sixty-five. They had thirteen children, our subject being the tenth. He remained with his parents until his eighteenth year. In 1849 he married Miss Martha, daughter of William Downs, who was born in Davidson County in 1831. To this union there is one child—Margret Jane, wife of G. T. Henry. After marriage Mr. Phelps hired to drive a milk wagon near Nashville, and worked four years. In 1857 he moved to Smith County and became an overseer, also driving a milk wagon. When the war broke out in 1861 he enlisted in Company B, Seventh Tennessee Infantry. After twelve months of faithful service he was discharged on account of disability. He was taken with the measles, and has since had poor health. In 1866 he was employed by the poor house committee to oversee the county poor, receiving $175 per annum, and board for himself and family. A year later he became the superintendent, his salary being $250. Twenty-one years he has held this position, giving the utmost satisfaction. When he first took charge the institution was situated on Peyton's Creek. In 1871 the commissioners purchased a farm of 211 acres in the Twentieth District, and erected frame buildings at a cost of $3,500. In 1885 they built a large and commodious brick building with all modern improvements, heated by two hot air furnaces. The home is kept in first-class order, neat and comfortable. The inmates are treated with kindness and respect by our subject and his estimable Christian wife. The county has just cause for the pride she feels in possessing such an institution and superintendent for her homeless unfortunates. The largest number of inmates in twenty years, at one time in the home, was forty-seven. The average is seventeen. At present there are fourteen, only one male. Mr. Phelps has by industry and economy become the owner of 180 acres of valuable land two and a half miles from Carthage. He is a Royal Arch Mason, and his wife a member of the Missionary Baptist Church.

J. C. Prichard, a highly respectable farmer of the Ninth District, was born June 19, 1840, in Smith County, and the eldest of six children of William D. and Rebecca (Malone) Prichard. Both parents were natives of Smith County, born in 1819 and 1822, respectively. The mother died in May, 1865. The subject of this sketch received his education in his native county, and assisted his father on the farm until July, 1861, when he enlisted in Company F, Twenty-fourth Tennessee Infantry. He was sergeant of his company. He was wounded at the battle of Stone River, and captured at Missionary Ridge, taken to Rock Island and retained sixteen months; was then taken to Richmond, Va., and paroled. From there he went to South Carolina, and was with Gen. Johnston's army at the time of surrender in 1865. The two following years he remained at home on the farm. February 20, 1867, he was wedded to Melissa, daughter of William and Elizabeth Lancaster. Mrs. Prichard was born February 25, 1848. To this union seven children were born: Willie, John and James. Four died in infancy. Mrs. Prichard is an estimable, intelligent woman, but has not yet connected herself with any church. Mr. Prichard is a member of the Cumberland Presbyterian. He is a Democrat and gave his first presidential vote for Horace Greeley. August, 1876, he was elected justice of the peace, which office he still holds to the entire satisfaction of all. He owns 390 acres of highly cultivated and productive soil, situated on Smith's Fork, twelve miles from Alexandria, and thirteen miles southeast from Carthage; a portion of this property was inherited from his father-in-law.

Thomas Prowell, a prosperous farmer of the Seventh District and member of one of the oldest families in the section, was born in Smith

County in 1834. He was the third of a family of six children born to David and Hannah (Baird) Prowell. His father was also a native of Smith County and died about 1852. The mother departed this life in 1847. His grandfather Prowell was a valiant soldier of the war of 1812, and took part in the battle of New Orleans. The maternal grandfather (Baird) was a native of North Carolina. He entered the matrimonial state when only sixteen years of age, and entirely without capital. He immigrated to Smith County in 1803, when the country was almost a wilderness, and filled with wild animals. He and his wife made their own clothing. Their shoes were often made from the skins of the beasts with which the woods abounded. Mr. Baird was a shrewd, close manager and became very wealthy; a large portion of his money was made by ginning cotton. The subject of our sketch went to live with his uncle, as both his parents died. He wedded Miss Minerva Waters, by whom he had five children: Bettie K., Ira and Iva (twins), Thomas Waters and William (deceased). For several years after marriage Mr. Prowell rented land and farmed until he was enabled to purchase 160 acres, where he now resides, and to which he has since added thirty-seven acres. His farm lies five miles north of Alexander, on Brush Creek. It is in a good state of cultivation and well improved; all has been bought by his own industry, economy and judicious management, as he never inherited but $170 in his life. In 1862 he enlisted in Capt. James' company, and served faithfully for fifteen months. On account of sickness he was honorably discharged in 1863 at Rome, Ga. He is independent in politics and votes for the best man, regardless of party. Mr. and Mrs. Prowell and daughter are sincere and esteemed members of the Presbyterian Church.

J. S. Prowell, a well known farmer of the Seventh District, was born about 1830 in Smith County. He is the second of six children born to David and Hannah (Baird) Prowell. The mother was a native of the Seventh District. The father was born about 1784 in North Carolina. He was an extensive and successful tobacco dealer. He sent the tobacco to New Orleans by boat, thus made twenty trips; twice he returned on foot. His father (grandfather of subject), Thomas Prowell, was a shoemaker by trade, at Cowpens, N. C. He was burned to death while at work on his bench in the fort when it was fired by the British Army. The maternal grandfather served in the war of 1812 under Gen. Jackson, and took part in the battle at New Orleans in 1815. The subject of our sketch received a fair education in the common schools of his native county. After his father's death he made his home with his uncle until his twenty-second year, when he began to teach writing, and traveled for three years. March 7, 1855, he wedded Miss Louisa Waters.

To them were born five children: Martha J. (Mrs. Agee), William D., Dora J., Sarah C. and James W. (deceased). Mrs. Prowell died April 28, 1879. He was married the second time September 26, 1880, to Miss Sarah Sykes. After marriage Mr. Prowell moved to a farm in Crittenden County, Ky., which he had previously purchased, but only remained there a few months and returned to Smith County, where he bought fifty acres, which he sold afterward and then invested in 275 acres, where he now resides. It is in a fine state of cultivation and improvement, located six miles northeast of Alexandria, on Hickman's Creek. With the exception of $110 inherited from his first wife, he has accumulated his possessions and means by his own efforts. Mr. Prowell witnessed the cars running on the first fifteen miles of railroad west of the Mississippi River. He is independent in politics, voting without regard to party. He and his family are consistent and respected members of the Cumberland Presbyterian Church.

Wm. Robinson, a prosperous farmer and native of Smith County, was born about 1840 in Horse Shoe Bend, on the Cumberland River. He is one of two children born to John and Agnes (Olmstead) Robinson. The father is of English descent, born in the vicinity of where William first saw the light of day, in 1810. After his father's death and at the age of eighteen, John began farming with his brother Allen on the place which had been left to them. Fifteen years later he sold out to his brother and purchased a farm in the same neighborhood. He is now living with William. The mother was a native of Smith County and died when our subject was a small child, at the place where the grandfather departed this life. The subject of this sketch had no educational advantages, but though deficient in that respect he has, since the age of twenty-five, been successfully engaged in tilling the soil of the farm partially owned by his father. It is located about three and a half miles northeast of Carthage in the bend of the Cumberland River. William's marriage was a romantic affair. John and Lavinia Smith, of Chestnut Mound, had a fair daughter, Louise, with whom our subject was deeply in love. The parents objected to the suitor, so the young couple made their escape and were married in 1858. Mrs. Robinson was born in 1841 near Ancient Creek, in Putnam County, Tenn. Their union was blessed with two children, Agnes and John. Mr. Robinson enlisted in the Confederate service, Company H, and three months after reaching Camp Trousdale, was very ill, consequently was sent home. He began life with comparatively nothing and no education, but has managed, by industry, shrewdness and economy, to accumulate about 500 acres of good land. He is a stanch Democrat, cast his first presidential vote for James Buchanan in 1856. Mr. and Mrs. Robinson are respected and earnest members of the Methodist Episcopal Church.

Elijah Saulmon, a well known and respected farmer of the Seventeenth District, was born in Virginia in 1807. He was the second of nine children born to John and Martha (Kidd) Saulmon, both of whom were of English descent. The grandfather Saulmon was a soldier in the Revolutionary war. He was taken prisoner by the Indians, and held in captivity for seven years. The maternal great-grandmother (Miss Williamson) was kidnapped in England when ten years of age, and traded to the owner of a ship in lieu of passage to America. Our subject immigrated to East Tennessee in 1817, and in 1835 came to Smith County and settled on Mulherin Creek. Until his majority he was hired out by his father, consequently never had any educational advantages, but is possessed of a good practical mind and sufficient knowledge to transact all his business affairs. When he reached manhood's estate he began life for himself without a penny. For three or four years he worked here and there wherever he could find employment. In 1831 he married Miss Martha Morris, by whom he had these children: Those living are Martha J. now Mrs. Buchanan, N. Caroline (wife of Mr. Davis), John W., Elizabeth, Francis T. (wife of Mr. Turner), and Thomas S. The deceased are Nancy, Mary A., Sarah G. and Minerva A. After marriage Mr. Saulmon rented land and farmed until he was enabled to purchase 100 acres, where he has since resided. He has added to his place and it contains 320 acres of valuable land on the Carthage and Alexander road, five miles from the latter place. He has been an industrious and honorable man all his life, and has the good-will and esteem of the community. He had the sad misfortune to lose his wife September 15, 1886, since which time his daughters have been house-keeping for him. The entire family are members of the Missionary Baptist Church. Mr. Saulmon is a stanch Republican.

Robert L. Scruggs, a respected farmer of the Twenty-second District, was born in the Tenth District of Smith County in 1835. He was one of four children born to James A. and Leona (Dillard) Scruggs. The father was of Irish descent, born in Virginia in 1809. He came with his parents, when but a small child, to Tennessee. They located in Caney Fork, in the present Tenth District, where James was raised and educated. He was a farmer and mechanic; remained in the vicinity all his life. He married a native of Smith County (mother of subject) who was born in 1812 and died in 1838, leaving two children. The father then married Louisa Mitchum, by whom he had ten children, three of whom are dead. Mr. Scruggs died in 1882. The step-mother lives with her son, Rufus Lee. The subject of this sketch was educated in the common schools of his native county. When he attained his majority he left home, rented some land and entered upon his career as a farmer. At the outbreak of the late war he enlisted in the Confederate Army, Company C, Smith's Fourth Tennessee Cavalry at Carthage. He participated in the battles of Fishing Creek, Murfreesboro, Chickamauga, and many minor engagements. He was captured on Salt River, Kentucky, in 1862, and held prisoner about thirty days, when he was exchanged at Vicksburg, Miss. He was wounded in the right arm and left hand at Murfreesboro, May, 1864, at New Hope, Ga., while Johnston was falling back to Atlanta, he received a shot in the left arm, which resulted in that member becoming two inches shorter. He was so severely disabled that he was unfit for further duties. He remained in the hospital until the close of the war. After his return home he again resumed his agricultural employments. In 1872 he bought 220 acres in the Twenty-second District, on Caney Fork. In 1874 he wedded Delia A., daughter of William C. and Nancy (Williamson) Avant, in De Kalb County, Tenn. Their family consists of six children: Hattie, Orleana, William, Fanny, Pearl and John Fite. Mr. Scruggs started life with nothing, although he received $1,000 in Confederate money from his grandfather, at the beginning of the war. He has, by continued labor and enterprise, met with considerable success. He owns 250 acres in a good state of cultivation and well improved; also, in partnership with G. W. Cardwell, owns five miles of Lebanon Turnpike, and Trousdale Ferry. He is a stanch Democrat, first presidential vote being cast for James Buchanan in 1856. He is a member of Masonic order, Snow Creek Lodge, No. 346. Mr. and Mrs. Scruggs are earnest and respected members of the Methodist Episcopal Church.

Dr. D. V. Seay, physician and surgeon, was born in Smith County, in 1831, one of nine children of Maj. W. W. and Ann (Stanfield) Seay. The father, of Scotch ancestry, was born in Virginia, in 1801, and was son of John Seay, a native of Halifax County, Va. He was one of the earliest settlers of Smith County, on Round Lick Creek, where he owns a large tract of land. Here the father was born, and spent most of his time as a farmer, and as a tobacco dealer for nearly forty years, shipping to New Orleans on flatboats twice a year. He was one of the most extensive farmers of this part of the State; a Knight Templar, a major of militia. He died in 1874. The mother was born in Virginia, in 1807, and died in 1872; both were members of the Methodist Episcopal Church. Educated chiefly at Clinton College, in 1853 our subject began the study of medicine under Dr. F. H. Gordon, and in 1855 and 1856 attended at Nashville University; practicing in Salisbury, Wilson County, until 1869, he removed to Rome intending to enter the drug business. His practice has been most successful. He owns about 270 acres of improved land, and since a resident of Rome has engaged in the drug business, and since 1872 added dry goods, etc. The stock is now worth about $3,500, and the firm name, Seay & Cato. In March, 1875, he married Julia, daughter of Robert H. and Amanda Cato. Their only child is Neva I. Mrs. Seay was born in Smith County, in 1850, and is a member of the Methodist Episcopal Church. Formerly a Whig, he has since the war been a Democrat. He is a Mason.

Hon. W. R. Shaver was born in Sumner County, April 28, 1837. He was educated at the Three Forks Institute, Wilson County. He owns the celebrated Clinton College farm of 500 acres, which was in its day the *alma mater* of noted ststesmen, and the finest college in Tennessee. He is president of both Farmers' Association of Smith County, and the Agricultural Mechanical Association of De Kalb County. He is a stockholder and director of the Lebanon National Bank, and president and chief stockholder in the Lebanon and Trousdale Ferry Turnpike Company. His herd of thorough-bred registered shorthorn cattle, and other stock are of the best. February 3, 1861, he married Lou C. Newby of Smith County. Their three children were Lou D., Hettie L. and Annie L. The first two died in childhood, and the last in her sixteenth year, December 5, 1883, at Maple Hill Academy. In politics a Democrat, he was elected senator to the XLIV General Assembly, November, 1884. He has been Deputy Grand High Priest of the Grand Chapter of Royal Arch Masons, in Tennessee; Grand Lecturer of the same, and Grand Master of the Grand Council in Tennessee. At present he is Grand Representative of the Grand Lodge and Chapter of Virginia, and Tennessee, and of the General Grand Council of the State of Minnesota in Tennessee. Both he and his wife are members of the Methodist Episcopal Church. His father was born in 1813, in Sumner County, and was a farmer and carpenter. After his marriage, in 1839, and about two years in Missouri, he came back to Lebanon and bought 100 acres near there, and while carpentering died in 1846, from lockjaw caused by running a nail in his foot. Mrs. Shaver's mother, Susan Sangford Shaver, was born in 1815 in Sumner County, Tenn., and died in 1881 in Benton County, Mo.

J. F. Shaw, proprietor of a lumber and flouring-mill, was born in Wilson County, in 1842, and is one of ten children of Solomon R. and Elizabeth Shaw. The father, of Irish extraction, was born in North Carolina in 1803, and came at two years of age to Smith County. He was a farmer and miller, and in 1863 died in Wilson County, from a wound received in Vicksburg. The mother, French in origin, was born in Smith County, in 1810, and is living with her children in Texas. Our subject began in the saw-mill business at twenty-two years of age, and two years later spent a year in Rutherford County, in the same occupation. He then returned to Wilson County, and in 1868 to Smith County, and engaged in his present business. In 1866 he married Mary, daughter of B. and J. Bufford, and born in Smith County, in 1847. Their five children are J. L., Phillip D., James (deceased), Jerry F. (deceased), and B. A. In 1862 Mr. Shaw enlisted in Company G, Fourth Tennessee Cavalry, and was at Red Mound, Fort Donelson and Spring Hill, and near Sparta disabled for about a year by an arm broken in an engagement, after which he returned home and resumed lumbering. He is a Democrat, once a Good Templar, a member of A. O. U. W., and his wife is a member of the Christian Church. He has been in the saw and flouring-mill business successfully for seventeen years.

B. F. C. Smith, a lawyer of considerable prominence, was born in 1832 in Smith County, Tenn. He is one of a family of ten children born to Josiah R. and Barthena (Cloud) Smith. The father was born in 1797 in Davidson County, Tenn. He was by occupation a farmer. About 1823 he was ordained a minister in the Methodist Episcopal Church, and entered the Holsten Conference, Tennessee, remaining in the work four years. He then returned to the homestead, serving the church in capacity of local preacher until his death in 1882. His wife was born in Lee County, Va., and is still living. The subject of this sketch was educated at Irving College, Warren County. His legal knowledge was acquired by his own efforts. He began practicing about 1854 in the county and justice's courts. In 1870 he was admitted to the bar, receiving his license from Judges Goodpasture & Fite and has been quite successful. In 1855 he was elected county surveyor, and served four years. In 1869 he was appointed by Gov. Senter commissioner of registration of voters. In 1870 he became clerk of the county court, holding that position four years. In 1853 he wedded Rhoda M., daughter of Dr. F. H. and Rhoda Gordon, who was born in Smith County in 1835, and died April 30, 1864. She bore two children who died in infancy. In 1873 Mr. Smith married Maggie T., daughter of John and Allie Wilson who was born in March, 1845. To this union three children have been born: B. F. C., Earnest C. and Maggie W. Mr. Smith is a Democrat, cast his first vote for Millard Fillmore in 1856. He is a member of the Masonic fraternity, being a Knight Templar. In 1853 he was elected Secretary of his lodge, and five years later became the Master, which office he filled four years. He was one of the charter members of the New Middleton

Royal Arch Chapter. He was Recorder about six years, and High Priest four years. He was commissioned Deputy Grand Master to organize a Council of Royal and Select Masters at Gainesboro. He is also a member of the Baldwin Commandery of Knights Templar. He was appointed by the governor as delegate to the Western Water Ways Convention at New Orleans, in 1884; was also acting as deputy United States commissioner during the war about six months.

Dr. Frank Swope, an eminent physician and surgeon of Carthage, was born December 31, 1850, in Overton County, a son of Maj. A. A. and Elizabeth (McKinney) Swope. The father is of German descent, born in 1819 in Cumberland County, Ky. His parents died when in his seventh year, and he made his home with his grandfather, George Swope, until his majority. His educational advantages were very limited, and his first work was in a coal mine. He soon was given a place in the office, devoting every spare moment to learning, as he had an ambition to cultivate his mind. Later he attended school, and then began teaching. At the age of twenty-four he began studying law. October, 1847, he was examined by ex-Gen. Wm. Campbell, and admitted to the bar. The same year he married Miss McKinney, a native of Overton County, who died in 1861. In 1865 he wedded Bethenia Douglass, *nee* Crutcher. For several years he made Jamestown, Fentress County, his home; there he did his first practicing and became deputy clerk of the circuit court, and was afterward elected clerk but resigned to resume his professional practice. In 1850 he moved to Lingston, and the same year was appointed as major of the State militia, Overton County. In 1865 he came to Carthage, where he has since resided. He has always been a stanch Jeffersonian Democrat. In 1882 he was elected member of the State Legislature, and took an active part in settling the State debt. He is one of the oldest citizens, most able lawyers, and respected men in the county. He has always been of the highest moral standing, never using liquor, and has ever been a leader in the temperance work. He has never sworn an oath. In 1882 he had the misfortune to lose his wife. Dr. Swope was fourteen years of age when his parents came to Carthage, and in that place he received his literary education in the Geneva Male and Female College, also at the Knoxville University of Tennessee, where he remained two years. At the age of twenty he began the study of medicine under tuition of Dr. A. H. King of Carthage. In 1873 he entered the Louisville Medical College, attending two sessions. He located at Granville, Jackson County, November, 1874. Three years later, owing to ill health, he returned to Carthage, where he has since been actively engaged.

December 18, 1884, he married Miss Mary Fuller, daughter of J. B. Love, who was born in Edgefield, Davidson County, Tenn., in 1862. They have one child, James B. Dr. Swope is one of the leading and most popular physicians of the county, and has an extensive and lucrative practice. He is in both private and professional life, highly esteemed. He is a stanch Democrat, giving his first presidential vote for Horace Greeley.

J. P. Temple, a physician and surgeon of the Fifteenth District, was born in 1856, in Smith County, Tenn. He is one of three children born to Dr. W. P. and Elizabeth (Davis) Temple. The father, was a native of Bedford County, born in 1828, and a physician and surgeon. In 1845 he began reading medicine with Dr. Preston Frazier, in his native county, and later entered the medical college at Nashville. He was a successful practitioner, and became very popular. His death occurred in 1859. The mother was born in 1830, in Smith County. She makes her home with her son, W. D., in Bedford County. Our subject received his literary education in the New Middleton Academy. In 1875 he commenced studying medicine with Dr. Lem Robinson, and a year later with Dr. Bridges of New Middleton; after ten months he entered the medical department of the Vanderbilt University at Nashville, and graduated in the class of 1878, since which time he has had an extensive practice. He is recognized as one of the most able and esteemed physicians in the county. In 1878 he wedded Nannie P., daughter of John S. and Betty Gill, a native of Smith County, born in 1858. Three children have blessed the union: Willie P., John G. and Jimmie D. The Doctor and his estimable wife, are members of the Methodist Episcopal Church South. The Doctor is a Democrat, and cast his first presidential vote for Samuel J. Tilden in 1876. He is also prominently connected with the Masonic fraternity being a Royal Arch Mason.

George W. Thackston, a prosperous merchant of Chestnut Mound, was born in 1855 in Jackson County, Tenn. He is a son of Anthony W. and Elizabeth (Dillard) Thackston. Both parents were of English descent, and natives of Smith County. The father was born about 1830. He was a cabinet-maker and carpenter, at which trade he worked until the outbreak of the war, when he enlisted in the Confederate service. He was a brave and valiant soldier, and met his death in 1863, at Baton Rouge, where he was shot. The mother died when George was about six months old. He was raised and educated by his grandfather, Blake B. Thackston. When about fifteen years of age he began clerking in a store at Snow Creek. Eighteen months later he bought an interest, and entered into partnership with J. N. Ford, in a general merchandise business, in which he has since been engaged. The firm has once changed, Mr. Ford going out and Wm. C. Boye being admitted. By their fair dealing and courtesy to patrons, they have established a large and substantial trade, being among the leading merchants of the county. Mr. Thackston, who began life with the small amount of $2, now owns a two-thirds interest in a fine farm of 215 acres, on Snow Creek, and a half interest in a good stock of first-class merchandise. He is an energetic, industrious man, and greatly respected. He is a stanch Democrat, casting his first presidential vote for Samuel J. Tilden in 1876. He is Master Mason of Snow Creek Lodge, No. 346. In 1879 he was united in marriage to Fanny B., daughter of Jesse and Martha (Vaden) Nichols. The ceremony took place at the residence of the bride's grandfather, B. J. Vaden, on Snow Creek, where Mrs. Thackston was born in 1862. To this union three children have been born: Lela N., Earnest W. and Jesse V.

Capt. R. R. West was born in Smith County in 1826. He is by occupation a farmer, and one of seven children of Jesse and Elizabeth (Harper) West. The father was born in Halifax County, Va., in 1795. With his parents, he came to Tennessee when a small boy, and located in Smith County, where for many years he was a prosperous farmer, and an extensive tobacco freighter as they were called in that day. He died in 1835. The mother was born about 1803 in Smith County, and died in 1866. Our subject received his education in the common schools of his native county. In 1849 he married Miss Sarah, daughter of Drury and Jane Cornwell, who was born in 1832 in Smith County, and died in 1854, leaving two children: Isaac Newton and Julia. Mr. West's second union was with Narcissus, daughter of Isaiah and Jane Pyron, who was born in 1832 in Jackson County, Tenn. Two children have been born to this union: William L. and Luther B. In 1846 our subject enlisted in Capt. W. B. Walton's company, First Tennessee Regiment Infantry Volunteers; was in active service for twelve months, took part in the battles of Monterey, Vera Cruz and Cerro Gordo. He was discharged in 1847. In 1861, when hostilities broke out between the North and South, Mr. West became one of the boys in gray. He organized Company H, Twenty-eighth Tennessee Regiment. He was elected captain, and did brave and gallant service at the battle of Fishing Creek, Ky., Shiloh and Chickamauga. Since the war he has been farming at his present place of residence, owning 414 acres of good land. He is also a tobacco dealer, shipping his produce to Nashville. He is highly respected for his honor and integrity. He is a Democrat, and cast his first vote for Zachary Taylor in 1848.

D. H. Witt, merchant, was born in 1849 in Smith County, Tenn., one of six children of D. A. and Elizabeth (Williams) Witt. The father was born in West Virginia and is a farmer and lawyer. Spending a short time in Macon County when a boy he came to Smith County, Tenn. Besides practicing law considerably he was justice of the peace and a heavy dealer in horses. The mother was born in Smith County and died in 1849. With a common-school education our subject in 1876 began mercantile life, and now has a stock worth about $3,000. He married Fanny Kemp, daughter of B. and L. Kemp, and born in Smith County in 1848. Their four children are Valeria E., Robert A., Howard S. and Geo. W. He and his wife are members of the Methodist Episcopal Church, and in his political faith he is Democratic.

W. C. Wright, merchant, was born in 1849 in Smith County. He is one of thirteen children of Stephen and Francis E. (Deadman) Wright. The father was born in 1826 in Illinois and came to Smith County when a boy. He is a farmer and stock dealer, owning 375 acres of improved land. He served in the Mexican war under Gen. Taylor. The mother, born in 1828 in Smith County, died in 1853. With ordinary school advantages our subject and his brother began two years of merchandising, after which he sold out and became a farmer. In 1877 he again became a merchant, and now successfully carries a stock of $4,500. In 1870 he married Callie, daughter of Joe and Elizabeth Moss, and born in 1850 in Smith County. She died in 1873. Their one child is Francis E.; in 1874 he married Nancy J., daughter of F. M. and Mary J. Ward, and born in 1856 in Smith County. Their six children are Cora A., Willie A., Surrepta I., Dealar L., Grace C. and Robert T. He is a Democrat politically and his wife is a member of the Missionary Baptist Church.

Hon. J. H. Young, farmer and stock raiser, of the Fourth District, two miles northeast of Dixon Springs, was born in Jackson County in 1828. He is of a family of fourteen children, born to James and Elizabeth (Draper) Young. The father was of English origin, born in South Carolina in 1788; he came to Tennessee when a small boy. He was a farmer and merchant of Jackson County. In 1814 the militia of Tennessee was ordered to New Orleans. He went under Maj. William Carroll, of Nashville, and served as adjutant of a regiment in the battle of New Orleans on the 8th of January, 1815, acquitting himself with high honor. He served his county in the capacity of sheriff and justice of the peace for many years. He represented Jackson County in the State Legislature of 1837-38; his death occurred in 1860; the mother was born in South Carolina in 1788 and departed this life in 1871. The subject of this sketch received his early education in the common schools of Jackson and Smith

Counties, and later attended Burritt College, at Spencer, Van Buren Co., Tenn. He began business for himself at the age of seventeen years. In 1849 he engaged in merchandising in Smith County, and continued until the outbreak of the war. In 1859 he married the only child of Wilson Y. and Mary B. (Bridgwater) Martin, Miss Nannie E. She was born in Smith County in 1834 and became the mother of three children: Sam M., who is justice of the peace in Smith County and a successful stock raiser; Mary M. (deceased), and Fannie M. Young, who is now a student in the Nashville College for young ladies. Mr. Young previous to the war was a Whig and is now a stanch and influential Democrat. He represented Sumner and Smith Counties in the State Senate in 1871, the first session of that body after the adoption of the new constitution. He served as justice of the peace in the Fifth District of Smith County from 1853 to 1857, resigning on account of other business duties. He has been unusually successful in life and now owns about 1,400 acres of valuable land. He is living now on the farm upon which the father of Judge Peter Turney was raised. Mr., Mrs. and Fannie Young are devoted members of the Christian Church. The grandfather of Mr. Young, whose name was William, was of English descent and was born in Virginia. When a lad he was taken prisoner by the Cherokee Indians and held by them eight years, and was exchanged by treaty. He married a Miss Holland and moved to South Carolina. Later, he moved to Simpson County, Ky., and about 1791 to Peyton Creek, now in Smith County, Tenn. He died on his farm there about 1799.

MACON COUNTY.

Nathaniel M. Adams, a farmer of the Twelfth District, was born in Clark County, Ky., in 1834. He is the son of Nathaniel M. and Nancy (Holiday) Adams, and the third of four living children. The father was of Scotch-English descent, and a native of Pittsylvania County, Va., born in 1795. He was the son of Harrison Adams, also a native of Virginia. Nathaniel M., Sr., was reared in his native State, and moved to Kentucky at the age of twenty, where he was married, and in 1836 moved to what is now Trousdale County, Tenn., locating on Goose Creek, and continuing his farming until his death in 1872. He served in the war of 1812, in the cavalry with Capt. Carter. He was afterward for many years magistrate of his district. The mother was born in Clark County, Ky., about 1798, and died in 1867, a member of the Missionary

Baptist Church. Our subject received his education at the common schools, and in February, 1863, enlisted in the civil war as one of the boys in gray, in Company E, Ward's regiment of cavalry, under Gen. Morgan. He was captured at Sulphur Trestle Works, Alabama, and taken a prisoner to Rock Island, Ill., where he remained until March 13, 1865, when he was taken to Richmond, Va., where he was soon paroled. He afterward joined the Twenty-second Tennessee Regiment of Forrest's cavalry, and remained until the final surrender at Gainesville, Ala., returning home after two years' gallant service and resuming his farming. In 1867 he settled on the farm he now owns of 165 acres. In January, 1874, he married Miss Isabella E., daughter of James and Mary Cage, of Smith County. She was born in Macon County, in 1850, and died September 8, 1877. Mr. and Mrs. Adams had two children, Llewella and James Nathaniel. Mr. Adams is a Democrat, but formerly a Whig, casting his first presidential vote for Fillmore in 1856. He is a member of the K. of H. and of the Christian Church.

Hon. M. N. Alexander, attorney at law and farmer near La Fayette, was born in Allen County, Ky., April 11, 1819. He is the son of Mayben and Margaret (Wygal) Alexander. His father was a native of Mecklenburg County, N. C., and was born in 1788. The grandfather was Andrew Alexander. He served in the war of the Revolution under Col. Mayben, in Gen. Lincoln's command, and was captured at the surrender of Charleston, S. C. He removed to Allen County, Ky., in 1801, where he died a few years after. Mayben (who was named for the Colonel mentioned above) was married in Allen County, Ky., in 1811, and made that his future home as a tiller of the soil. He died in 1848. The mother was a native of Virginia, born in 1788, and died about 1856, a member of the Methodist Church. Her husband was also a member and a class-leader. Hon. M. N. Alexander received his early education at the common schools. In 1840 he went to Watertown, Wilson Co., Tenn., and attended school about two years. He then went to Milton, Rutherford County, and studied medicine two years, but abandoned that and went to Nashville, Tenn., in 1847, and began the study of law. In 1848 he moved to Macon County, where he continued his study, and was licensed to practice in 1849, but did not begin until 1852. He entered as a partner with Hon. S. M. Fite, of Carthage, with whom he remained three years, since which time he has practiced alone. He is the oldest practitioner in Macon County, having practiced for over thirty-four years. In 1870 he was elected circuit court clerk of Macon County, and held the office four years. In 1881 he was commissioned by Gov. Hawkins to hold a special term of the chancery court at Smithville, DeKalb County.

He was also county superintendent of Macon County schools between 1879 and 1883, which position he held with distinction and credit. In 1842 he married Miss Minerva C., daughter of Rev. and Lurana Pickett, of Wilson County. By this union eight children were born, Matthew N. being the only one living. Mrs. Alexander died in 1880, a member of the Christian Church. In 1883 Mr. Alexander married Miss Sallie, daughter of Dr. David and Margerie (Hemphill) Graham. She was born in 1840, and a native of Carroll County, Ohio. Her father was a native of Ireland and her mother of Pennsylvania. Mr. and Mrs. Alexander are faithful members of the Christian Church, of which he has been an elder for some years. He was formerly a Whig, casting his first presidential vote for W. H. Harrison, in 1840. Since the war he has been a strong Republican, and a long standing and active member of the Masonic fraternity. Mr. Alexander owns a farm of 160 acres under a good state of cultivation and improvement.

E. H. Bratton, M. D., a prominent citizen of La Fayette, was born in Macon County in 1840. He is the son of Anderson and Theresa (Adams) Bratton, and the seventh of ten children. The father was a native of Kentucky, born in 1806, and was a son of William Bratton, who was a son of Charles Bratton, a native of South Carolina, who settled in Sumner County near White's Station at a very early day, where he was killed by the Indians. Dr. Bratton's mother was born in what is now Macon County in 1806, and died in 1855. In 1856 Anderson Bratton married Mrs. Rachel Flippen. By this union six children were born. Mr. Bratton was a farmer and a man of considerable means and ability, having held the office of magistrate for many years. In 1851 he was elected to represent Macon and Smith Counties in the State Legislature as floater. He died April 25, 1868. He and his wife were members of the Primitive Baptist Church and esteemed by the community. Dr. E. H. Bratton was educated at the common schools. In 1860 he began the study of medicine under Dr. W. G. Key. In 1860–61 he attended the medical department of the University of Nashville and immediately began to practice in his neighborhood where he soon established an extensive and lucrative business, being one of the leading physicians of the county. January 23, 1866, he married Miss Camille J., daughter of Dr. Hugh B. and Frances W. Flippen of this place. By this union six children have been born: Fannie (wife of Dr. E. K. Lamb, druggist at Alton Hill), Hugh A., Robert E., Edgar H., Martha J. and Roscoe A. In politics he is a Democrat, his first vote being cast for Seymour in 1868. Dr. Bratton is an earnest advocate of education and of charitable and religious enterprises, in which he is a generous supporter, and is giving his children excellent advantages. He is a Royal Arch Mason.

Pryor W. Carter, a farmer in the Twelfth District, and postmaster at Hillsdale, is the eldest child of William S. and Nancy Carter, and was born April 24, 1823, in the house where he now resides. He was educated in Smith now Macon County, and helped clear the farm where he now lives from the woods. He served about one and a half years in the last war, at the end of which time, under the conscription act, he was discharged on account of being over age. When twenty-five years of age he began working for himself. He went to West Fork, Goose Creek, and purchased the first land he owned, the money being earned by trading, hard work and flatboating to New Orleans. He made thirteen trips to New Orleans and the dangers and adventures he encountered would alone make a book. By his energy and activity he has succeeded in making himself quite comfortable, owning 450 acres of land on Carter Branch, seven and a half miles southwest of La Fayette. On December 13, 1865, he married Miss Mary A. Pursley, by which union three children were born: Margaret H. (deceased), William S. and James D. Mrs. Carter died July 24, 1884. Mr. Carter has filled several positions of note. He was appointed by Gov. Marks as commissioner to the Yorktown Centennial celebration, and was also appointed assistant commissioner of Macon County to the World's Industrial and Cotton Centennial Exposition at New Orleans, and besides has served his people of the Twelfth District for many years as magistrate and postmaster. In 1886 he was urged by a delegation of the most prominent citizens of Clay and Macon Counties to contest for the nomination as representative. He entered the race and the result was an active and exciting contest. He was only beaten for the nomination one vote, by the present member-elect. Mr. Carter measures six feet, eight inches in hight "with his boots on," possesses a rugged constitution, has an excellent command of language and a very retentive memory.

Samuel W. Carter, a farmer of the Twelfth District, P. O. Hillsdale, was born June 22, 1844, in Macon County, Tenn. He is the son of William S. and Nancy (Rickman) Carter, and the youngest of six children. William Carter was born in North Carolina in 1791, and came to what is now Macon County about the year 1804, and died in 1860. He served in Martin's company in the war of 1812, also under Gen. Jackson in the Indian war. Mrs. Nancy Carter was born in what is now known as Edgefield, a surburb of Nashville, in 1797. In 1822 she came to what is now Macon County, and is still living, and walks about as easily as most people twenty or thirty years her junior. Possessing a remarkable.

memory, it is a pleasure to hear her relate historical events. She is the mother of six children, the oldest being about sixty-four and the youngest forty-two years of age: Pryor W., Mary Elizabeth (now Mrs. Browning), Patsy (now Mrs. Carr), Sarah (now Mrs. Marshall), Mark R. and Samuel W. The latter was educated in the schools of Macon County. His father, dying when he was hardly of age, left him the care of a widowed mother. Mr. Carter is a Democrat, and served fifteen months in the last war in Capt. Duffy's company. He fought with his company in the battles of Shiloh, at which place he was wounded, and at Fishing Creek. He was discharged in July, 1862, because he was too young. In 1881 he married Miss Sallie J. Thompson, by which union was born one child, Robert Arnet. Mrs. Carter died in 1884. From his father Mr. Carter inherited some land and negroes, and by good management and industry he has added to his inherited property, until now he owns a fine farm of 150 acres on Carter Branch, seven and one-half miles from La Fayette. Mr. Carter is a worthy man, and is respected by all.

Dr. Benton Cothron, farmer, was born on January 10, 1826, in what is now Macon County. He is one of eleven children of Robert E. and Winifred (Brinkley) Cothron. The father was born in 1790 in North Carolina, and moved to Sumner now Trousdale County, about 1816, and came to Macon County (then Smith) about the year 1823. His memory and constitution were remarkable. He died in 1873. The mother was born in North Carolina, and came to this county with her husband. They were of Irish and English descent. She died about 1859, nearly seventy years of age; an excellent woman. Our subject, educated in Macon County, when of age began for himself, the first year working for $40, but by persistent effort and management he has become owner of a fine home of 160 acres. February 11, 1855, he married Nancy S. Burrow. Their five children are Samuel A., Letha E. (deceased), Louisa A. and Leona, now Mrs. McDuffy. Mrs. Cothron died in April, 1863. He was afterward married twice: first to Miss J. M. Anderson, and after her death, to Miss Susan Carter. Formerly a Whig, he has been a Democrat since the war. He and his children are members of the Baptist Church, and his wife of the Methodist Episcopal Church. He is a substantial and experienced pioneer.

Jacob Eller, a millwright and farmer in the Fourth District, P. O. Hillsdale, is the son of Joseph and Sarah (Stephens) Eller, the fourth of thirteen children, and was born in North Carolina in 1822. Joseph Eller and wife were born in North Carolina and were of Dutch and Irish descent. Joseph Eller died in September, 1863. Mrs. Eller died September 25, 1846. Mrs. Eller's father was with Gen. Jackson in the Indian war and participated in the famous fight at Horse Shoe Bend on the Tennessee River, where he was killed. Jacob Eller is a self-made man, getting his education while at his work without outside assistance. He has an excellent memory and is well posted on the history of the country. He is also a born mechanic, early adopting the millwright business as his chosen vocation. As a millwright he is sought far and wide to construct mills, even going outside the State in many instances. He is also quite an inventor, having invented some very useful articles. He was reared a Whig, and since the dissolution of that party he has voted the Democratic ticket. He cast his first presidential vote for Gen. Harrison when only sixteen years old, which was allowable in North Carolina to young or old if they could pay the poll tax. Mr. Eller began life with horse, saddle and bridle; and by his industry, foresight and good management has accumulated quite a handsome competency. He first bought near Heartsville, sold out there and purchased a farm of 165 acres, beautifully situated and nicely improved, near the Heartsville and La Fayette road, six miles from the latter place. January 17, 1844, he married Miss Nancy M. Wood, by which union nine children were born: Susan F., now Mrs. Meador; Joseph A.; James J.; Jno. S. W. (deceased); Sarah P. (deceased); Wm. J.; Nancy M. (deceased); Lillian C. (deceased) and Marian M., now Mrs. Adams. Mrs. Eller died August 30, 1880, and he married Miss Eleanor Royster June 23, 1881. Himself and family, excepting one child, are members of the Missionary Baptist Church. For many years Mr. Eller ably served his friends and neighbors as magistrate. He has been a very energetic and active man. He is now sixty-five years old and has still a good share of the fire and vim of his younger days. At his advanced age he can do more work and display more mechanical skill than many young men in the county, His ancestors are noted for their long life, his grandfather reaching the age of one hundred and eight years, and being actively engaged in the work of his trade until death. Jacob Eller bids fair to rival his ancestors for longevity and is still using his first pair of glasses, showing how little his eyes have failed.

J. H. Forgason, tobacco merchant, was born November 11, 1829. He is one of thirteen children of Dixon and Hannah (Towson) Forgason. The father, born in Virginia about 1795, came with his father to Tennessee about 1810 and settled in Smith County, now Macon County. He was for many years a respected class-leader in the Methodist Episcopal Church. He died in 1861. The mother was born near where her son now resides and died in September, 1876. Educated in Macon County, our subject married, December 14, 1856, Amanda Rison. Their ten children are Edgar B., Lula M. (deceased), Mary H. (now Mrs. Wakefield), Jno. H., Cora M. (deceased), William J., Herbert, Myrtle A., Jas. A. (deceased) and Ernest L. Reared on a farm and thrown on his own resources at twenty-one, he followed various occupations until the breaking out of the civil war, when he, in the fall of 1862, enlisted in Company D, Fifteenth Tennessee Cavalry, and served until he was captured near Pomeroy, Ohio, taken to Camp Chase, then to Camp Douglass, Chicago, where he remained until the close of the war. He has been an able magistrate for many years. He owns a farm of about seventy-five acres, six miles south of La Fayette. He, his wife and eldest daughter are members of the Missionary Baptist Church. His grandfather Towson was a soldier of the Revolution and came from Wales to Smith County about 1790.

W. J. Gray, clerk of the circuit court of Macon County, and son of William and Minerva T. (White) Gray, was born in Jackson County in 1844, and is the fifth of seven children, only two of whom are living. The father was born in Jackson County in 1808, and was of Irish extraction. He was married about 1829, and in 1851 removed to Macon County, and settled three miles northwest of La Fayette, where he resumed his farming. He died in 1867. He was one of the county's most thrifty and well-to-do farmers. The mother was also a native of Jackson County; born in 1809 and died in 1862. She was a member of the Christian Church. Our subject's grandfather, William Gray, was a native of Ireland, and after reaching manhood, and being married, immigrated to the United States, and located in Jackson County, Tenn., where he remained until his death. He was a farmer. Our subject was educated in La Fayette, and in the common schools. At the of age seventeen he entered the service in Company I, Ninth Kentucky Infantry (Union Army), and was engaged in the principal battles of the war. He was discharged in January, 1865, and returned home after nearly four years of gallant service. In 1869 he married Miss Prudie A., born in 1851, and the daughter of John W. and Polly Atkerson. To them were born two children: Marietta and Joseph G. Soon after his marriage Mr. Gray removed to the Cherokee Nation, but a few months after went to Illinois, and from there to Arkansas, and then to Macon County, Tenn., where he was soon after elected constable. He served two terms, and in 1880 was elected sheriff of Macon County, and re-elected in 1882. He then removed to his farm, and in 1886 was elected to the office of circuit court clerk. He has filled that office in a highly creditable manner up to the present. He has a good farm of 160 acres, well cultivated, and also has a house and lot in town; besides this he has over 240 acres in two other tracts. He is an ardent and active Republican in politics, and cast his first vote for Gen. Grant in 1868. He and wife are members of the General Baptist Church.

T. J. Gregory, county clerk of Macon County, and of the firm—the La Fayette Handle Company—was born in Jackson County in 1851, the fourth of seven children, our subject and a younger sister only, living. His parents were W. T. and Sabrina (McDuffy) Gregory, the former born about 1820 in Smith County, the son of Pitts Gregory. The father, W. T., chiefly self-educated, enabled himself to become a teacher for several years. When about twenty-one he married, and soon removed to Jackson County, and in 1851 removed to Macon County, and was engaged in farming, and afterward at La Fayette in merchandising. For several years constable, he was elected as sheriff, serving six years, after which he was elected magistrate, and also engaged as a merchant. He died in 1871, an able and well-informed man. The mother, born in Smith County about 1825, died in 1876, and was a member of the Christian Church. Educated at La Fayette, our subject began for himself when nineteen years of age, as a teacher, after which he was clerk for Marshall & Tuck, La Fayette, and soon after began merchandising for himself until 1874. He was then elected to his present office at the age of twenty-three, serving ever since, being re-elected against a usual 200 majority in favor of his political opponents. The war and his father's death left his mother and four sisters mainly dependent on our subject's own efforts; but besides caring for them until their death, he has become a financial success. In October, 1875, he married Letha, daughter of W. H. and Angeline Wright, of Macon County. Their three children are Maude Almer, William Taylor and Verner Odell. Mrs. Gregory was born in 1854 in Macon County. Besides his fine home, he owns 100 acres near town. Politically, an ardent Democrat, his first vote was for Greeley. He is a member of the F. & A. M., I. O. O. F., K. of H. and I. O. G. T. orders. He and his wife are members of the Christian Church.

S. C. Harlin, a farmer in the Ninth District, postoffice Salt Lick, was born in Macon County, November 25, 1843. He is the son of Isaac and Nancy (Comer) Harlin, and the third of five children. Isaac Harlin was born in Monroe County, Ky., and came to Smith (now Macon) County in 1842, and died in Macon County in 1851. He died when quite a young man, leaving a family to be cared for by his wife. When S. C. Harlin grew to manhood, he provided for his mother until his marriage in March, 1869, to Miss Phebe Depp, of Barren County, Ky. By this union seven children have been born: Depp Lola, Isaac Clay, Sarah Lela, William Robert, John B., Phebe and Edward. Mr. Harlin began life with $300 or $400, and is now worth about $5,000, accumulating the most of it in the last twenty years. He owns a well improved farm of 260 acres. He is a Master Mason. He was school commissioner for several years, taking quite an interest in education. In politics he is a Democrat, casting his first presidential ballot for Horatio Seymour. He and wife are loyal members of the Missionary Baptist Church.

William C. Johnson, farmer and merchant, whose postoffice is Hillsdale, Macon Co., Tenn., was born December 22, 1819, in Goose Creek, Smith Co., Tenn., what is now Macon County. He is the eighth of a family of nine children, born to John and Gracy Johnson; his mother's maiden name was Ellis; she was born in South Carolina during the Revolutionary war and was thirty-one years of age when married. The father was twenty-five years of age at that time. He was a farmer and he and wife came to what is now Macon County about the year 1800. They were of English descent. William C. Johnson was educated in the common schools of Macon County, and from the time of his father's death, which occurred when he was only fifteen years of age, he lived with and helped to support his mother until he was twenty-three years of age. At that time he married Miss Adaline Wright, December 22, 1842. To them thirteen children were born: Leatha S. (deceased), Sarah E., now Mrs. Johnston; John B.; Hannah J., now Mrs. Sullivan; Andrew G., William E., Alexander N., Theodocia A., Mary H. and Martha A. (twins, deceased), and twins who died in infancy, and Joseph J. Mrs. Johnson died July 5, 1863; for the four succeeding years his daughters kept house for him. He then married his second wife, Nancy A. Sears, May 14, 1867, by which union three children have been born: Paul, Lucy and Gracy. He has been very successful in the management of his affairs. He inherited a small tract of land, some money and a negro boy, and by his perseverance and energy has accumulated quite a handsome competency. He owns where he resides, 800 acres of fine broken land, located on the Hartsville and Lafayette road, seven miles from Lafayette. He was reared a Whig, but since the dissolution of that party has cast his lot with the Democrats. He held the office of justice of the peace for six years; has been a member of the Missionary Baptist Church forty-seven years; is deacon and has been for many years; four of his children (three daughters and one son) belong to the same church; one daughter is now in Kansas, the son in Texas. He is a thorough and consistent Christian, and an earnest advocate of prohibition.

William G. Key, M. D., a farmer and prominent citizen of the Eleventh District, was born in Sumner County, Tenn., in 1834. He is the son of James and Lucinda (Thurman) Key, and the second of eight children, only two of whom are now living. His father was of Scotch-English descent, and born in Sumner County about 1810. He was a son of William Key, a native of North Carolina and an early settler of Sumner County. James was a successful farmer and useful citizen, and died in 1863. The mother was also a native of Sumner County, dying at about the age of fifty-four years, in about 1878. Dr. Key was principally educated at Rural Academy. In 1854 he began the study of medicine with Dr. James M. Head. In 1855 he entered the medical department of Nashville University and took one course of lectures. In 1856 he came to Macon County, locating on Long Creek, three miles north of where he now resides, and began the practice of his chosen profession. In 1857 he moved to his present home, and has since practiced here with much success, being one of the most successful physicians of Macon County. He is the owner of 247 acres of land under a good state of improvement, besides 50 acres in another tract, all of which he has accumulated by his own management. He served his friends and neighbors six years as magistrate, to the satisfaction of all. In October, 1856, he married Miss Mahala M., daughter of Henderson and Mary Holland, of Simpson County, Ky. By this union four children were born, three now living, as follows: Martha D., wife of John H. Rickman; James H. and Talmage. Dr. Key is a Democrat, casting his first presidential vote for James Buchanan in 1856. He and his wife are members of the Methodist Episcopal Church South, while he has been a member of the Masonic fraternity for twenty-nine years. Mrs. Key was born in Macon County in 1836.

M. L. Kirby, M. D., and druggist, was born in Macon County in 1844, one of ten children, seven living, of Jessie B. and Elizabeth S. (Young) Kirby. The father, born in Jackson County, Tenn., in 1799, was a son of Pleasant Kirby, a native of England, and who came to America when a boy, and served in the war of 1812. He was a merchant. Jesse, the father, was married in 1820, and soon removed to Macon County, where he spent his life as a farmer, and died in 1850. The mother was born in Virginia in 1802, and died in 1872. She was a member of the Methodist Episcopal Church. Our subject is a self-educated man, and in 1863 enlisted in Company A, Eighth Tennessee Mounted Infantry, Federal Army, and remained in active service until the close of hostilities. He then returned home, and in 1870 studied medicine under Dr. E. H. Bratton, of La Fayette. In 1875 he graduated from the medical department of Nashville University, since which he has built his extensive practice in La Fayette, and is now one of the county's most popular physicians.

Since 1881 he has been examining surgeon for Tennessee and Kentucky. He also has the only drug business in town. In November, 1885, his entire business property, stock and building, were destroyed by fire, with a loss of about $10,000. A successful financier, he at once erected a new block and residence combined, and is now established on a more extensive scale. He owns also about $12,000 worth of Lane County (Kas.) real estate. In January, 1867, he married Martha D., daughter of T. J. and Eliza A. Wakefield. Four of their five children are living: Alice, Miriam, Alvis, Merlin and Anna Manson. In 1882 and 1883 Dr. Kirby represented Macon and Clay Counties in the Legislature, and in 1886 refused the nomination. A Democrat in politics, his first vote was for Gen. McClellan. He is a member of the High Priesthood of the Masonic order, and of the I. O. O. F. Lodge. Mrs. Kirby was born in Macon County in 1847; is a member of the Christian Church.

George McKinnis, a farmer and lumber merchant in the Seventh District, is the son of Neal and Elizabeth (Anderson) McKinnis, and the sixth of a family of seven children, and was born July 29, 1843. Neal McKinnis was born April 1, 1803, in North Carolina. He came with his father in company with Gen. Jackson, and settled first at Fort Blount. His father, James McKinnis, was born in Edinburg, Scotland, and when six years old came to North Carolina. He, with five brothers, served in the war of 1812. He was also in the Indian war under Gen. Jackson in 1813–14, and in the war of 1836 in Florida. He died April 24, 1868. Mrs. McKinnis was born about 1816, and died October 18, 1877. George McKinnis received most of his education while lying wounded in the hospital during the late war. He served in Company D, Ninth Kentucky Infantry. He was elected first corporal, then first sergeant. After he joined the Eighth Tennessee Regiment he was appointed adjutant, which promotion was given him unsolicited—most excellent testimony as to his efficiency as a soldier. He served in all the principal engagements in which his regiment took part, except when wounded and in the hospital. Mr. McKinnis began life with only $250, but by good management and industry has made himself and family quite comfortable. Through the solicitation and influence of the leading men of Jackson County, he was appointed sheriff by Gov. Brownlow at the organization of said county. Among the officers of the newly organized county after the war he was very influential. He was several years United States storekeeper and gauger in the Fifth Revenue District. His principal business successes have been in the lumber business and in farming, paying the most attention to the former. In politics he is a Republican. August 7, 1865, he married Miss Amanda J. Holland, by which union one child was born,

Mary (deceased). He served as magistrate with much success in the district where he then resided. He has been delegate four times to the State convention, and was alternate to the Republican National Convention at Chicago in 1884. Mr. McKinnis has two adopted children: Lena Josephine and Oliver Futt. Himself and wife are worthy members of the Baptist Church.

William B. Mooningham, a farmer and prominent citizen of the First District, was born in Smith County in 1844, and is the only child of John and Sarah W. (Rose) Mooningham. His father was of English descent and born in Smith County. He was a farmer and son of Matthew Mooningham. In 1843 John was married and in 1844 died, in the prime of life. W. B. Mooningham's mother was born in Smith County in 1821. She is still living and a member of the Methodist Church, of which her husband was also a member. W. B. Mooningham was raised by his mother, his father dying when he was an infant. He received his education at common schools and at La Fayette. At the age of fifteen he moved to Macon County, but in five years returned to his native county, and in nine years he again moved to Macon County and located on the farm he now owns of 200 acres. December 23, 1869, he married Mary B., daughter of William and Martha Payne of Smith County. By this union three children have been born: John W., George W. and Louisa J. Mrs. Mooningham is a native of Smith County and is a devoted member of the Missionary Baptist Church. In politics Mr. Mooningham is an uncompromising Democrat; his first presidential vote was cast for Horatio Seymour. He is also a prominent member of La Fayette Lodge, No. 149, of the Masonic fraternity.

Dr. F. M. Puttie was born in Madison County, Tenn., September 26, 1853. He is the son of George M. and Nannie (Loveall) Puttie, and the third of seven children. George Puttie was born December 24, 1819. He is of Dutch descent and a farmer by occupation. His father came from North Carolina to Madison County, Tenn., in 1806. Mrs. Puttie was born in 1822. Dr. F. M. Puttie passed his youth without prominent event and attended the medical department of the University of Tennessee, and graduated at the Ohio Medical College, Cincinnati, in 1881. Since that time he has been practicing his chosen profession. He first practiced at Gainesboro, Tenn., but in 1882 he moved to his present location. Although a young man and a perfect stranger when he first came to this locality, he has built up a large practice, which is the best testimony possible of his skill and of the confidence reposed in him by the public.

I. L. Roark, attorney at law and a citizen of La Fayette, was born in

Smith (now Macon) County in 1830. His parents were William and Elizabeth Roark; his mother was Elizabeth Meador, a native of Virginia; his father was a North Carolinian. His grandfather, John Roark, emigrated from North Carolina to Smith County. William Roark served as magistrate a long time, and made farming his life-long pursuit, and died May 2, 1882. Elizabeth Roark was born in Virginia in 1801, and died in 1855. I. L. Roark was educated at the common country schools, and at the La Fayette Academy and by close study and observation, not having any schooling until he attained the age of nineteen years. He is, truly, what is known as a self-made man. In 1851 he began the study of law under Col. W. H. DeWitt. He was licensed in 1853 and immediately began the practice of law at La Fayette, where he has actively engaged in the practice ever since, competing with some of the ablest lawyers of the State. In 1860 he was placed upon the presidential electoral ticket for the Fourth Congressional District, as elector for Stephen A. Douglas. At his country's call in 1861 he enlisted as a private in the Confederate Army, Thirtieth Tennessee Volunteers, and was appointed sergeant-major, and served with the regiment until the fall of Fort Donelson, when the regiment was captured; but making his escape he went with the retreating Confederate Army south, where he did active service as a skirmisher and sharpshooter, under detail by the Confederate officers. When Gen. George H. Morgan, in 1863, made a raid into the State of Kentucky Mr. Roark was with him, and while on detail with a scouting party was captured near Elizabethtown by the Federal soldiers, and was charged of being a spy and tried, but was acquitted and held as a prisoner of war. He was taken to Camp Chase, Ohio, and afterward to Rock Island, Ill., where he underwent all the privations and hardships of a military prison life, until the winter of 1864, when he was paroled—as he says, turned out to die—his health having failed and his physical system broken down; he returned home to find himself reduced to abject poverty, his country devasted and property squandered. He resumed his practice at the bar, and has thus continued since. November 28, 1855, he married Miss Mary E., daughter of M. B. and Laurinda Johnson. By this union three daughters were born: Mary L., Meredith J. (wife of Jas. Key) and Sallie E. Mr. Roark is an active Democrat, casting his first presidential vote for Franklin Pierce in 1852; he is also a member of the Masonic fraternity; he is next to the oldest practicing lawyer in Macon County. He has been a close student since he commenced the study of law. Mrs. Roark was born in Macon County in 1840 and is a member of the Methodist Episcopal Church South. She contributed largely, by instructing her husband, in his struggles for an education. He served as a member of the State Legislature in 1879.

H. C. Smith, physician and merchant in the Tenth District, was born March 10, 1845, in Smith County, Tenn. He is the son of William and Mary Smith, and the second of seven children. William Smith was born in Virginia and came to Tennessee and settled in Smith County in 1820. Mrs. Smith was born in Tennessee. Dr. Smith was educated mostly in Macon County, and received his medical education at Bellevue Medical College, Nashville, and began the practice of medicine where he is now located. In 1873 he married Miss Eliza Morris, by which union two children have been born: Minnie Leota and Frank Oscar. Dr. Smith began life with $43 and a horse. Since his marriage he has accumulated quite a fortune. His prosperous business and extensive practice are the best testimony possible as to the respect and confidence the people have for him. In politics he is conservative, although throwing his support mostly to the Republican party. Mrs. Smith is a member of the Missionary Baptist Church. The grandfather of Dr. Smith came to Smith (now Trousdale) County in 1820.

Rev. J. L. Talman, a minister of the gospel, farmer and magistrate in the Ninth District, was born October 29, 1840, in Warren County, Tenn. He is the only son of Jno. Armstrong and Lidy V. Talman. His parents were married ten years and were then divorced, and Mr. Talman took his mother's maiden name. His mother was born in Virginia in 1825, and came to Warren County, Tenn., in 1828. Mr. Talman was educated in Monroe County, Ky. He enlisted at the breaking out of the civil war in Company H, Fifth Indiana Infantry, of which company he was second lieutenant. He served during the entire war, his regiment operating mostly in Virginia. He was mustered out September, 1865. The severest engagement in which he took part was the battle of Gettysburg, Penn., where he was wounded. He was also at the first battle of Bull Run. Mr. Talman began life with nothing, and what he has now he accumulated by his own tact and good management. He owns a fine farm of 126 acres, on Long Fork Creek of Baron River. He was elected magistrate three times, but accepting it only the last time, which was August, 1886. Mr. Talman's grandmother was Gen. Harrison's youngest half-sister. There has not been a war since the establishment of the Government, but that some of Mr. Talman's ancestors took part. He had two uncles who died in the Mexican war. His oldest uncle was in the war of 1812, under Gen. Jackson. Mr. Talman has all his life been a Republican, though reared a Democrat. His first presidential vote was cast for Abraham Lincoln in 1864. January 9, 1866, he married Elizabeth E. Morgan. She was born October 16, 1848, and is a descendant of Col. Morgan of Revolutionary war fame, he being her great-uncle. Gen. Morgan, of the late war, was also a descendant of the same family. To Mr. and Mrs. Talman two children were born: Fennettia (now Mrs. East) and Nancy E. (deceased). Mr. Talman and family are members of the Missionary Baptist Church, in which he is a minister.

Geo. L. Walton, of Walton & Haley, merchants, was born near La Fayette in 1822, and is one of nine children of Edward M. and Agnes (Turner) Walton. The father, of English origin, was born in Virginia in 1797, a son of T. Walton, native of England, who came when a boy to Virginia, and in 1807 located in Smith County, Tenn., and in 1814 finally settled four miles northwest of La Fayette, the birthplace of our subject. In 1818 the father, Edward, was married and spent the remainder of his life on the above mentioned farm, and died in 1869. The mother, born in Bedford County, Va., in 1795, died in 1874, a member of the Christian Church. Our subject remained at home until twenty-six years of age, received the most of his education from his father, an intelligent and well informed man. June 2, 1850, he married Maria, daughter of Jonas Griffith. Their three children are Maria, wife of W. H. Carter; Rebecca M., wife of Hon. J. S. Wootten and Laura, wife of Hon. A. R. Harlin. Beginning life as clerk at La Fayette when twenty-six, two years later he entered partnership with M. B. Johnson and J. C. Marshall with whom he remained until 1859. An able man, he has served as register of Macon County for eight years from 1850, after which he was county clerk until 1874. After a year as county assessor, he was elected county trustee in 1876, serving four years. In 1884 he resumed mercantile life, abandoned at the beginning of his county clerkship, with his present partner, Capt. William Haley. Their stock of about $4,500 is the most complete in La Fayette. In politics he was a Whig, voting for Gen. Taylor, but since the war has been a Republican. He is a prominent Mason, and was formerly an Odd Fellow. He and his wife are members of the Christian Church.

Hon. Jesse West, farmer and prominent citizen of La Fayette, Tenn. and son of Miles F. and Susan (Payne) West, was born in Smith County in 1844, and is the second of three children, all of whom are living. The father is also a native of Smith County, born in 1819, and a son of Jesse West, of Tennessee, who was a son of Miles West, a native of Virginia. Miles F. West, our subject's father, was twice married, his first wife being the mother of our subject. She was born in Smith County about 1817, and was married in 1841. She died in 1856. In 1859 Miles F. married Miss Mary Denton, who bore him three children. He is still living in the Sixth District of Macon County, and is a farmer and Baptist minister by profession. He removed to Macon County in 1855, and resumed his ministerial duties, which he has followed for twenty-five years. Our subject was reared at home and educated in the common schools. At the early age of seventeen he enlisted in Company C, Twenty-eighth Tennessee Infantry (Confederate Army), and took part in all the battles in which his command engaged. He was wounded at the battle of Peach Tree Creek, which rendered him ineffective for duty several months. He returned home and resumed his labors on the farm after four years of gallant service. In April, 1868, he married Miss Sarah F., daughter of Robert and Mary Hudleston of Smith County, and by her became the father of nine children—six sons and three daughters: Mary Susan, Selden Lee, Perry Bunyan, Miles Robert, Felix Jesse, Henry Ora, Merlin Aolis, Veva May and Verdie Clyde (twins). After marriage Mr. West located in the Sixth District, where he remained until 1873 as a tiller of the soil. He then sold out and removed to Fayette, where he has since resided, being the owner of 200 acres of good, productive land, on which is a valuable and productive sulphur spring that is destined to make the place a famous health resort. He was magistrate of the Sixth District, but resigned to accept the position of trustee, to which he was elected in 1880. He was twice re-elected, serving six years to the general satisfaction af all. In 1886 he was elected to represent Macon and Clay Counties in the State Legislature. He is a lifelong Democrat, and cast his first presidential vote for Horatio Seymour in 1868. He and wife are faithful and consistent members of the Primitive Baptist Church.

V. M. Whitley, attorney at law at La Fayette, was born in Macon County in 1855, and is a son of Wiley A. Whitley and a grandson of Taylor Whitley, who was born May 8, 1796, in Nash County, N. C. The father of our subject was of Anglo-Irish extraction, born February 2, 1829, in Smith County, Tenn., and married Lucinda Chitwood, November 16, 1854. She was of Anglo-German descent, born December 16, 1835, in Macon County, and was a daughter of Charles Chitwood, who was born in what is now Macon County, Tenn., March 10, 1806. When Wyley was a young man he went to Macon County and settled in the Sixth District, where he has since remained on a good farm. He is a man of considerable influence and ability and is now serving his second term as magistrate of his district. During the late war he enlisted in Company D, Ninth Kentucky Infantry, as first lieutenant, serving in that capacity until after the battle of Shiloh, when he returned home on account of ill health. Some time after he joined the Eighth Tennessee as wagon master and remained in service until the cessation of hostilities. Both he and wife are respected and esteemed members of the Missionary Baptist Church. Our subject was raised under the parental roof and educated in Concord Academy, Clay County; Red Springs, Bellwood Academy, and finished at Clementsville, in Clay County. He spent several years of his earlier life as a teacher in Macon and Smith Counties, where he gained considerable note as an educator. In August, 1882, he was elected to the office of clerk of the circuit court of Macon County, and held the position for a term of four years to the general satisfaction of the public. He refused to be re-elected, choosing rather to enter upon the duties of his chosen profession, having received his license to practice law in 1886. Judging from his past life he has a brilliant and prosperous future before him. He is one of the county's promising young men, possessing rare abilities, keen judgment, temperate habits and a genial social disposition. Politically he has cast his lot with the Republican party and his first presidential vote was for R. B. Hayes in 1876.

Hon. J. T. Wootten, lawyer, was born in Macon County in 1848, one of two children of Sarah A. Wootten, born in Claiborne County, Tenn., in 1823. She came to Macon County in 1843, where she has since resided. She is a member of the Christian Church. Her parents were Edward and Rosanna (Dean) Wootten, natives of North Carolina, where they were reared and married in 1814. They removed to East Tennessee, where the father died about 1833. Removing to Illinois about 1851, the mother remained there until her death. Edward's (the grandfather's) parents, were William and Sallie (Lloyd) Wootten, natives of Wales and early settlers of Halifax County, N. C. From five to fourteen years of age, our subject was apprenticed to H. S. Young, of Lafayette, and then was dependent on his own resources. He, at the early age of fifteen, enlisted in Company K, Thirty-seventh Kentucky Mounted Infantry for one year, and served for eighteen months in Virginia in active service and in many severe engagements. He then re-enlisted in Company D, Eighth Tennessee Mounted Infantry, and continued until the close of the war. After finishing his education in Spencer County he taught two years in Indiana and then in Macon County, Tenn. For four years after 1868 he was deputy county clerk. January 1, 1871, he married Rebecca M., daughter of George L. and Mary G. Walton. Their five children are George Irvine, Gerda A., John E., Effie G. and an infant. Mrs. Wootten was born in Macon County, in 1853, and is a member of the Christian Church. From 1872 to 1876 Mr. Wootten served as county superintendent of public schools. After several years in general trading, in 1880 he began the practice of law, and is now one of the most promising and popular members of the Macon County bar. In 1884 he was elected to represent Macon and Clay Counties in the State Legislature, and in 1886 was a candidate for the office of attorney-general, but his party was defeated, although he received the largest Republican vote ever given in the district. He is a progressive man, and has always been Republican in politics, first voting for Gen. Grant. He is a member of the I. O. O. F.

TROUSDALE COUNTY.

J. A. Andrews, of J. A. Andrews & Co., dry goods, groceries, boots and shoes, was born in Rockingham County, Va., March 15, 1812. He is one of thirteen children of Samuel and Jane (Wells) Andrews. The father was born March 22, 1774, in Virginia. His father, William, a merchant, came from Scotland at an early day, being born there in 1737. Samuel came to Sumner County in 1818, and was an old Jackson Democrat. He died August 24, 1857. The mother, born in September, 1789, in Virginia, came to Wilson County, Tenn., in 1818, and died in 1834. Our subject, a self-made and educated man, began, when twenty-two, in his present business, with a small stock at first, but now carries an average year's stock of about $10,000. He has been a subscriber to *The Nashville American* ever since it was first established. In 1844 he married Lumiza Sewell. They had one child who died in infancy. Mrs. Andrews died in 1846. In 1852 he married Georgetta Smith, who died the same year. His first wife was a member of the Cumberland Presbyterian Church, and his last wife belonged to the Christian Church. Mr. Andrews has always been a Democrat in politics.

Col. D. L. Goodall, present clerk of the county court of Trousdale County, and a son of David and Tobitha (Clark) Goodall, was born in Smith County, now Trousdale, in 1823. He was the sixth of ten children who lived to be grown, only two of whom are now living. The father was a native of Virginia, born about 1781 and grew to manhood in his native State. He was twice married, his first wife being a Miss Davis. He removed to Smith County at a very early day and resumed his agricultural pursuits which he followed up to the time of his death in 1856. The mother was also a native of Virginia. She was a worthy member of the Christian Church, as was also her husband, and died in 1851. Our subject was reared at home on the farm, and received his education in the common schools of the county. Upon reaching his majority he came to

Hartsville and acted as a clerk in a dry goods store at that place until the war with Mexico when he enlisted in Company F, First Tennessee, of the Polk Guards, commanded by ex-Gov. W. B. Campbell. He took part in the battles of Monterey, siege of Vera Cruz, Cerro Gordo, and several sharp skirmishes. At the end of his enlistment (one year) he returned to Hartsville and engaged in the mercantile business which he continued up to the civil war. He then organized Company F, Second Confederate Tennessee Regiment, of which he was made captain and at the organization of the regiment at Nashville he was elected lieutenant-colonel and acted in that capacity until the battle of Shiloh when he took command of the regiment after Col. Bate (Maj. Doak was killed) was wounded. After that battle he was discharged on account of ill health. He then returned home and again engaged in mercantile pursuits, which he followed for several years, after which he returned to his earlier employment of farming and continued until 1878, when he was elected to the office of county clerk. He has held this position to the general satisfaction of the people ever since, having been twice re-elected. In politics he has been a life-long Democrat and cast his first presidential voted for James K. Polk in 1844. He is an active member of the Masonic fraternity.

Hon. W. M. Hammock, lawyer, is the son of Capt. L. and M. J. (Gammon) Hammock; was born in Texas in 1856. Of the three children, he and a sister are now living. The father was of Scotch-Irish extraction, and born in Virginia, about 1812; removed to Smith County, Tenn., with his parents when a child; reared there, when thirty-seven years of age he married, and in 1855 resumed farming until 1858; he then returned to Smith County, where he died in 1859. In early life he spent several years as captain on a river steamer. He was a stalwart Whig. The mother was born in Smith County in 1823 and died in 1858, a member of the Baptist Church. Left an orphan, our subject was cared for by W. Martin, of Smith County, until twelve years of age, when he had to do for himself. Attending the common schools, and a session in the Tennessee University, Knoxville, in 1871–72, he finished by attending in 1876–77 the law department of Cumberland University at Lebanon. Since then he has practiced at Hartsville, and has become one of the best attorneys in this section, and a self-made man. When twenty-one he was elected mayor of Hartsville, serving two years, and in 1886 elected to represent Trousdale and Sumner Counties in the Legislature. He has served as special judge on several occasions in these two counties. He also owns considerable real estate in Hartsville. In April, 1877, he married Bettie, daughter of Arch and Francis Allen, of Hartsville. In politics an active and uncompromising Democrat, his first vote was for Gen. Hancock. He is a member of the Cumberland Presbyterian Church. Mrs. Hammock was born in Trousdale County in 1858; is a member of the Missionary Baptist Church.

W. W. Jenkins, farmer and trader, was born January 24, 1849, one of eight children of John T. and Fannie (Williams) Jenkins. The father was a merchant and farmer. Our subject left home when sixteen and engaged in farming and trading for two years. Until his marriage, in 1873, he traveled in Texas, Arkansas, Mississippi, Louisiana, and West Tennessee, for trading purposes. He then returned to the community where he now resides and married Mrs. Elizabeth Ward, May 15, 1873. They have three children: Fannie, Mary Elizabeth, and John T. Mr. Jenkins has been a life-long Democrat, voting his first presidential ticket for Seymour. In 1873 he purchased a fine farm of 276 acres, seven miles from Hartsville, and besides this owns two other farms, which aggregate 379 acres, in Smith County, on the Hartsville and Carthage pike.

E. P. Lowe, Jr., of the firm of Neely & Lowe, freight agents at Hartsville Landing, was born in Wilson, now Trousdale County, in March, 1855. He is one of four children of E. P. and Nancy B. (Ward) Lowe. The father, of Irish origin, was born in Smith County in 1813, and as a farmer and trader has become an extensive land owner with about 400 acres, and lives near Hartsville. He was justice for about twelve years and chairman of Wilson County Court about ten years. When cut off from Wilson into Trousdale County, he still held his office of justice and was soon elected chairman of Trousdale County Court, which he held five years, refusing re-election on account of old age; an able and respected officer. His wife was born in Smith, now Trousdale County, in 1813 and died in 1869. She was Irish in origin. Our subject, educated at Hartsville and East Tennessee University, Knoxville, the latter in 1873 and 1874, was dependent on himself at twenty, and began farming, his present business, together with his freight agency. In October, 1884, he married Lucy, daughter of Henry and Lucy Neely, and born in Sumner, now Trousdale County in April, 1859. In politics he is a Democrat, and he and his wife are members of the Missionary Baptist Church. He is one of the leading farmers, owning 200 acres of improved land near Hartsville.

J. H. Neely, farmer and freight agent at Hartsville, was born in Sumner, now Trousdale, County in 1854, and is one of six children of Henry M. and Lucy A. (Paisley) Neely. The father, of Irish origin, was born in Sumner County in 1820, and was a dentist, but in his old age retired to farming and trading and was a universally successful man. He was a Jackson Democrat in politics and died in 1878. His wife was born in Logan County in 1829 and died in Sumner County in 1863. Educated in Hartsville Academy, our subject began for himself when nineteen years of age as freight agent in his present position, of the firm of Neely & Lowe. At present Dictator of K. of H. Lodge at Hartsville, he has held every office in the organization there. He votes the straight Democratic ticket, first voting for Tilden. Their landing is a shipping point for over ten surrounding counties, shipping in 1886 over 1,000,000 feet of lumber and about 1,000 hogsheads of tobacco. Mr. Neely owns about 235 acres improved, and three-fifths of the Hart Ferry tract on which he lives, about 173 acres, all on the Cumberland River.

J. W. Rankin, farmer, was born July 12, 1841, on his present farm, one of four children of John and Mary C. (Forgason) Rankin. The father, born in 1775, came to Tennessee at an early day and settled near where his son resides. He died in 1847. The mother was born in what is now Trousdale County, January 8, 1818, and died July 2, 1854. Our subject was educated at Irving College, Tenn., and October 25, 1860, married Sarah Wilson, who was born December 6, 1842, in what is now Trousdale County. Their two children are John, born February 8, 1862, and Lee Madden, born April 30, 1867. Leaving home at twenty, our subject rented the first ten years of his married life, and then bought his present farm five and one-half miles from Hartsville, on the Hartsville and La Fayette road. He is a Master Mason, and he and his wife are members of the Christian Church. Mr. Rankin has succeeded in accumulating about 450 acres of land by his own efforts.

INDEX
Prepared By
Lallah Wright, Ft. Worth,
Texas